CBT for Psychosis

"This exceptional book contains state of the art theory, research, and therapeutics of CBT for psychosis. The editors have assembled a superb set of authors who are amongst the leaders in the field. Bedrock chapters feature an innovative symptom-based cognitive-behavioral approach to hallucinations, delusions, and negative symptoms. In addition, outstanding supporting chapters cover assessment, the therapeutic alliance, relapse prevention, trauma, substance abuse, and vocational rehabilitation. Clinicians and researchers interested in developing an up-to-date understanding of CBT for schizophrenia will find this book indispensable."

Aaron T. Beck, University Professor Emeritus of Psychiatry, School of Medicine, University of Pennsylvania

"This book provides an excellent overview of current developments in the field of CBT for psychosis, with innovative contributions from numerous international experts. It will be of value to both clinicians and researchers and will promote the psychological understanding and treatment of psychosis"

Tony Morrison, Professor of Clinical Psychology, University of Manchester, UK

This book offers a new approach to understanding and treating psychotic symptoms using cognitive behavioural therapy (CBT). *CBT for Psychosis* shows how this approach clears the way for a shift away from a biological understanding and towards a psychological understanding of psychosis. Stressing the important connection between mental illness and mental health, further topics of discussion include:

- the assessment and formulation of psychotic symptoms
- how to treat psychotic symptoms using CBT
- CBT for specific and co-morbid conditions
- CBT of bipolar disorders.

This book brings together international experts from different aspects of this fast developing field and will be of great interest to all mental health professionals working with people suffering from psychotic symptoms.

Roger Hagen, PhD, PsyD, Associate Professor, Department of Psychology, Norwegian University of Science and Technology, Trondheim, Norway.

Douglas Turkington, MD, Professor of Psychosocial Psychiatry, Newcastle University, Newcastle-upon-Tyne, United Kingdom.

Torkil Berge, PsyD, Psychologist, Vinderen Community Mental Health Centre, Diakonhjemmet Sykehus, Oslo, Norway.

Rolf W. Gråwe, PhD, PsyD, Head of R & D Unit, Drug and Alcohol Treatment in Central Norway, Norway.

The International Society for the Psychological Treatments of Schizophrenias and other Psychoses book series

Series editor: Brian Martindale

The ISPS (the International Society for the Psychological Treatments of the Schizophrenias and other Psychoses) has a history stretching back more than fifty years during which it has witnessed the relentless pursuit of biological explanations for psychosis. The tide is now turning again. There is a welcome international resurgence of interest in a range of psychological factors in psychosis that have considerable explanatory power and also distinct therapeutic possibilities. Governments, professional groups, users and carers are increasingly expecting interventions that involve more talking and listening. Many now regard skilled practitioners in the main psychotherapeutic modalities as important components of the care of the seriously mentally ill.

The ISPS is a global society. It is composed of an increasing number of groups of professionals, family members, those with vulnerability to psychosis and others, who are organised at national, regional and more local levels around the world. Such persons recognise the potential humanitarian and therapeutic potential of skilled psychological understanding and therapy in the field of psychosis. Our members cover a wide spectrum of approaches from psychodynamic, systemic, cognitive, and arts therapies to the need-adaptive approaches, group therapies and therapeutic institutions. We are most interested in establishing meaningful dialogue with those practitioners and researchers who are more familiar with biological based approaches. Our activities include regular international and national conferences, newsletters and email discussion groups in many countries across the world.

One of our activities is in the field of publication. Routledge has recognised the importance of our field, publishing the ISPS journal, *Psychosis: Psychological, Social and Integrative Approaches* (www.isps.org/journal. shtml). The journal complements Routledge's publishing of the ISPS book series, which started in 2004. The books aim to cover many topics within the spectrum of the psychological therapies of psychosis and their application in a variety of settings. The series is intended to inform and further educate a wide range of mental health professionals as well as those developing and implementing policy.

Some of the books will also promote the ideas of clinicians and researchers well known in some countries but not familiar in others. Our overall intention is to encourage the dissemination of existing knowledge and ideas, promote healthy debate, and encourage more research in a most important field whose secrets almost certainly do not all reside in the neurosciences.

For more information about the ISPS, email isps@isps.org or visit our website, www.isps.org

Other titles in the series

Models of Madness: Psychological, Social and Biological Approaches to Schizophrenia
Edited by John Read, Loren R. Mosher & Richard P. Bentall

Psychoses: An Integrative Perspective
Johan Cullberg

Evolving Psychosis: Different Stages, Different Treatments
Edited by Jan Olav Johanessen, Brian V. Martindale & Johan Cullberg

Family and Multi-Family work with Psychosis
Gerd-Ragna Bloch Thorsen, Trond Gronnestad & Anne Lise Oxenvad

Experiences of Mental Health In-Patient Care: Narratives from Service Users, Carers and Professionals
Edited by Mark Hardcastle, David Kennard, Sheila Grandison & Leonard Fagin

Psychotherapies for Psychoses: Theoretical, Cultural, and Clinical Integration
Edited by John Gleeson, Eión Killackey & Helen Krstev

Therapeutic Communities for Psychosis: Philosophy, History and Clinical Practice
Edited by John Gale, Alba Realpe & Enrico Pedriali

Beyond Medication: Therapeutic Engagement and the Recovery from Psychosis
Edited by David Garfield and Daniel Mackler

Making Sense of Madness: Contesting the Meaning of Schizophrenia
Jim Geekie and John Read

Psychotherapeutic Approaches to Schizophrenic Psychosis
Edited by Yrjö O. Alanen, Manuel González de Chávez, Ann-Louise S. Silver & Brian Martindale

CBT for Psychosis

A Symptom-Based Approach

Edited by Roger Hagen,
Douglas Turkington, Torkil Berge
and Rolf W. Gråwe

Routledge
Taylor & Francis Group

LONDON AND NEW YORK

First published 2011 by Routledge
27 Church Road, Hove, East Sussex BN3 2FA

Simultaneously published in the USA and Canada
by Routledge
711 Third Avenue, New York NY 10017 (8th Floor)

Routledge is an imprint of the Taylor & Francis Group, an Informa business

Typeset in Times by Garfield Morgan, Swansea, West Glamorgan
Printed and bound in Great Britain by TJ International Ltd, Padstow, Cornwall
Paperback cover design by Hybert Design

This publication has been produced with paper manufactured to strict
environmental standards and with pulp derived from sustainable forests.

British Library Cataloguing in Publication Data
A catalogue record for this book is available from the British Library

Library of Congress Cataloging-in-Publication Data
CBT for psychosis : a symptom-based approach / edited by Roger Hagen . . .
[et al.].
        p. ; cm.
    Includes bibliographical references.
    ISBN 978-0-415-54946-2 (hardback) – ISBN 978-0-415-54947-9 (pbk.) 1.
Psychoses–Treatment. 2. Cognitive therapy. I. Hagen, Roger, 1968-
    [DNLM: 1. Psychotic Disorders–therapy. 2. Bipolar Disorder–therapy. 3.
Cognitive Therapy–methods. 4. Hallucinations–therapy. WM 200 C386
2010]
    RC512.C39 2010
    616.89–dc22
                                                        2010014886

ISBN: 978-0-415-54946-2 (hbk)
ISBN: 978-0-415-54947-9 (pbk)

Contents

PART IV
CBT and bipolar disorders

Figures and tables

Figures

Tables

Contributors

Jean Addington is Professor of Psychiatry at the University of Toronto, Research Scientist at the Centre of Addiction and Mental Health, Toronto, and Director of Prime Research and of Psychosocial Treatments in the First Episode Psychosis Program, CAMH, Canada.

Morris Bell, PhD, is a Professor at the Department of Psychiatry, Yale University School of Medicine, and a Research Career Scientist at the Rehabilitation Research and Development Service, VA Connecticut Healthcare System, USA.

Torkil Berge, PsyD, is a Psychologist at the Vinderen Community Mental Health Centre, Diakonhjemmet Sykehus, Oslo, Norway.

Max Birchwood, PhD, DSc, is Professor of Mental Health at the School of Psychology, University of Birmingham, and Director of the Early Intervention Service, Birmingham and Solihull Mental Health Foundation NHS Trust, United Kingdom.

Caroline Bryant, BSc, is Research Assistant at Newcastle University, United Kingdom.

Pauline Callcott is a Registered Mental Nurse at Newcastle Cognitive Therapy Centre, Newcastle-upon-Tyne, United Kingdom.

Jimmy Choi is Associate Professor at the Department of Psychiatry, Yale University School of Medicine, and was a Research Psychologist at the VA Connecticut Healthcare System, USA.

Robert Dudley, PhD, is Consultant Clinical Psychologist at South of Tyne Early Intervention in Psychosis Service, Northumberland Tyne and Wear Mental Health NHS Trust, and Research Tutor at the Institute of Neuroscience, Newcastle University, United Kingdom.

Mark Freeston, PhD, is Director of Research and Training at Newcastle Cognitive Therapy Centre, Newcastle-upon-Tyne, United Kingdom.

Paul Grant, PhD, is Assistant Professor of Psychology in Psychiatry at the Psychopathology Research Unit, Department of Psychiatry, University of Pennsylvania, USA.

Rolf W. Gråwe, PhD, PsyD, is Head of the R & D Unit at the Drug and Alcohol Treatment Centre in Central Norway.

Andrew Gumley, PhD, is Senior Lecturer at the Section of Psychological Medicine, University of Glasgow, and Consultant Clinical Psychologist at ESTEEM, North Glasgow First Episode Psychosis Service, United Kingdom.

Maria Haarmans, MA, MED, is a Therapist at the Prime Clinic and the First Episode Psychosis Program (FEPP) at the Centre of Addiction and Mental Health, Toronto, Canada.

Roger Hagen, PhD, PsyD, is Associate Professor at the Department of Psychology, Norwegian University of Science and Technology, Trondheim, Norway.

Live E. C. Hoaas, PsyD, is a Psychologist at the Norwegian Centre for Violence and Traumatic Stress Studies, Oslo, Norway.

David Kavanagh, PhD, is a Professor at the School of Medicine, University of Queensland, Australia.

Peter Kinderman, MA, MSc, PhD, is Professor of Clinical Psychology, University of Liverpool, and Honorary Consultant Clinical Psychologist, Merseycare NHS Trust, United Kingdom.

Claude Leclerc, PhD, is Professor of Mental Health Nursing, University of Quebec, and Director of the Caring Laboratory, University of Quebec, Canada.

Tania Lecomte, PhD, is Assistant Professor at the Department of Psychology, University of Montreal, and Adjunct Professor at the Department of Psychiatry, University of British Columbia, Canada.

Sara Eidsbø Lindholm, PsyD, is a Psychologist at the Josefinesgate Community Mental Health Centre, Oslo University Hospital, Norway.

Victoria Lumley, RMN, is a Cognitive Therapist at the Tees, Esk and Wear Valleys NHS Foundation Trust, United Kingdom.

Paul Lysaker, PhD, is Associate Clinical Professor at the Department of Psychiatry, Indiana University School of Medicine, and was a Clinical Psychologist at the Roudebush VA Medical Center, Indiana, USA.

William R. McFarlane, MD, is Professor of Psychiatry at the University of Vermont, and Director of The Center for Psychiatric Research at the Maine Medical Center, USA.

Dr Maria Michail, BSc, MSc, PhD, is a Research Fellow at the School of Psychology, University of Birmingham, United Kingdom.

Kim Mueser, PhD, is a Professor at the Department of Psychiatry, Dartmouth Medical School, Hanover, New Hampshire, USA.

Enza Munusco, MED, is a Therapist at the Prime Clinic and the First Episode Psychosis Program (FEPP) at the Centre of Addiction and Mental Health, Toronto, Canada.

Emmanuelle R. Peters, BSc, MSc, PhD, is Senior Lecturer in Clinical Psychology at King's College London, Institute of Psychiatry, United Kingdom.

Jan Scott is Professor of Psychological Medicine at the University of Newcastle-upon-Tyne, and Honorary Professor of Psychological Treatments Research at the Institute of Psychiatry, London, United Kingdom.

Sally Standart, MR, CPsych, is a Consultant Psychiatrist and Cognitive Therapist at the Newcastle Cognitive Therapy Centre, Newcastle-upon-Tyne, United Kingdom.

Neal Stolar, MD-PhD, is Clinical Associate Professor at the Department of Psychiatry, University of Pennsylvania, USA.

Sara Tai, BA (Hons), MSc, DclinPsy, is a Lecturer in Clinical Psychology at the School of Psychological Sciences, University of Manchester, United Kingdom.

Douglas Turkington, MD, is Professor of Psychosocial Psychiatry, Newcastle University, Newcastle-upon-Tyne, United Kingdom.

Acknowledgements

We are most grateful to the *Journal of the Norwegian Psychological Association*, which in 2007 published a volume entitled *Towards a new understanding of psychosis*. The journal has given permission to use many of the chapters from this volume as a basis for this book and those chapters have been updated, with new chapters added in this process.

We are also thankful for all the valuable help we have received from the editor of the ISPS series, Brian Martindale. In the editorial process he has given us valuable comments and feedback, which have been extremely helpful for us in making this book. The editors are indebted to Brian, who is a very skilful editor for the ISPS series at Routledge.

Preface

The understanding of psychotic disorders is undergoing a very considerable transformation. One aspect of this is a serious questioning in recent decades as to the utility and validity of the discrete diagnostic classificatory systems for psychosis (Bentall, 2003; van Os & Kapur, 2009). It is increasingly recognised from population and clinical studies that a dimensional approach based on more discrete symptoms better reflects the evidence of a continuity between mental illness and mental health and between the "psychotic" and the "normal".

This book is compiled with the intention of elaborating this approach and in particular to demonstrate how a cognitive behavioural framework is well suited to offering clinical treatment and therapy to the new symptomatic approach within psychosis. The book brings together international experts in the different aspects of this fast developing field, and should be of great interest to all mental health professionals working with people suffering from psychotic symptoms.

References

Bentall, R. P. (2003). *Madness Explained. Psychosis and Human Nature*. London: Penguin Books.
van Os, J. & Kapur, S. (2009). Schizophrenia. *The Lancet, 374*, 635–645.

Part I

Cognitive models of psychosis and their assessment

Chapter 1

Introduction

CBT for psychosis: A symptom-based approach

Roger Hagen and Douglas Turkington

This chapter will start with a brief outline of cognitive behavioural therapy (CBT). This outline will be followed by an introduction to the use of CBT for psychotic problems. The final part of the chapter serves as an introduction to the rest of the book and how the book is organized.

What is cognitive behavioural therapy?

Cognitive behavioural therapy emphasizes the importance of the role of cognitions and behaviour in the formation and maintenance of psychiatric disorders and emotional problems. Even if there could be said to be various alternative versions of delivering cognitive behavioural therapies, there are some common factors related to treatment principles and cognitive behavioural techniques which integrate these different approaches. We will shortly try to describe some of these common treatment principles and cognitive behavioural techniques, but for a further in-depth description for those who are not familiar with CBT, see Beck (1995) or Wright *et al.* (2006) which serve as excellent introductory textbooks to cognitive behavioural therapy.

CBT interventions are designed to treat specific disorders or problems. The patient and the therapist try to set explicit goals to overcome these specific problems in the beginning of therapy, and the cognitive and behavioural interventions are tailored to treat these problems based on the patient's problem list. The patient's difficulties and goals for therapy are then operationalized in what is called a cognitive case formulation, which could be described as a hypothesis about the nature of psychological difficulties underlying the patient's symptoms. The cognitive case formulation is derived theoretically from existing models of human learning and cognition. The cognitive behavioural therapies emphasize a collaborative relationship between the patient and the therapist, and require that both the patient and the therapist take an active role in the treatment process and progress.

Based on the notion that cognitions and behaviour play an important role in both the formation and the maintenance of most psychiatric disorders, cognitive behavioural interventions seek to reduce distress and enhance adaptive coping by changing maladaptive beliefs and providing new skills (Grant *et al.*, 2005). The various approaches differ somewhat in the extent that they emphasize cognitive mechanisms or more behavioural ones (Hollon and Beck, 2004). The goal of cognitive behavioural interventions is to change maladaptive beliefs and behaviours using a wide range of techniques. These techniques include elements of self-monitoring; identifying and challenging negative thoughts and assumptions that maintain problematic behaviour and experiences; de-catastrophization; scheduling activities; and behavioural experiments that in turn aid further self-monitoring and challenge dysfunctional beliefs (Wright *et al.*, 2006). CBT appears to be effective for a broad range of clinical and medical disorders. Moreover, there are numerous indications that cognitive and cognitive behavioural interventions may produce more lasting changes than other psychotherapeutic interventions to both Axis I and Axis II disorders (Butler *et al.*, 2006).

What is CBT for psychosis?

Historically, we distinguish between three paradigms in our understanding of psychosis (Morrison *et al.*, 2004). *The illness paradigm* was introduced by Kraepelin (1899/1990) at the beginning of the twentieth century. A clear distinction was drawn between normality and abnormality, and the causes of a certain number of diagnosable mental illnesses were understood as inherited brain disorders or infections, e.g. syphilitic mental disorders. The second paradigm is called the *stress vulnerability model*, where biologically and psychologically predisposed individuals may become psychotic if they are exposed to stressing life experiences (Zubin and Spring, 1977). The various disorders, for example schizophrenia, are thought to lie along a continuum with normal behaviour and experiences, and there is a possibility that one can make therapeutic change by influencing the environment and strengthening the person's ability to cope with the psychotic disorder. The third paradigm is the *symptom-focused paradigm* (Bentall, 2003). Here each single symptom is emphasized, for example voice hearing, delusions/unusual assumptions, thought disorder or negative symptoms, rather than using broad diagnostic categories. One is concerned with the possibility of coping with and understanding the symptoms and the ability to be able to function socially and professionally, more than curing the disorder as such. Cognitive behavioural therapy for psychosis has come to recognize the importance of focusing on each single symptom, as this seems to create a foundation for better results for treatment. Psychotic experiences are, from a cognitive behavioural view, seen as experiences and not just as symptoms of an underlying disorder. The exploration of the individual's experiences and beliefs related to their symptoms is therefore essential.

Bentall (2003) further suggested that there is a need for a radically new way of thinking about psychotic symptoms, mostly related to the fact that the boundary that has been set between bipolar disorders and schizophrenia has been disputed in relation to new research in this field. Psychotic symptoms such as mania, delusions and voice-hearing are actually difficult to sort into neat categories as diagnoses, and are best understood on a continuum of symptoms. Kingdon *et al.* (2008) have taken this approach further and suggest that there might be five distinct subgroups of schizophrenia based on symptoms and causation. These are: sensitivity disorder (high vulnerability, negative symptoms and cognitive deficits); traumatic psychosis (trauma contributing to causation, critical hallucinations and depression); drug-induced psychosis (hallucinogen use, paranoid delusions and negative symptoms); anxiety psychosis (schema vulnerability and systematized delusions); and catatonia. In line with this approach CBT plays an important role in both the understanding and the treatment of symptoms.

Since the first description of cognitive therapy for paranoid delusions (Beck, 1952), the empirical support for using CBT to treat psychotic symptoms has been widely established (Dickerson, 2004; Gaudiano, 2005; Gould *et al.*, 2001; Rathod and Turkington, 2005; Rector and Beck, 2001; Turkington *et al.*, 2006; Tarrier and Wykes, 2004). For many decades the dominant view was that psychosis was considered a biological condition insusceptible to psychological interventions; however, more recent research has shown that positive symptoms are on a continuum with normality and therefore may be treatable with the same CBT techniques used to treat anxiety and depression (Bentall, 2007; Kuipers *et al.*, 2006). The cognitive model of psychosis conceptualizes a combination of factors that shape and maintain positive symptoms such as delusions and auditory hallucinations (Garety *et al.*, 2001), where reasoning and attributional biases may play a particular role in symptom formation and the maintenance of these symptoms (Bentall, 2003; Freeman and Garety, 2004).

In this introduction we will try to sketch out a brief synopsis of the most essential therapeutic processes and interventions in CBT for psychosis. To therapists who are not familiar with this approach to treating psychotic symptoms, we recommend Kingdon and Turkington (2005) and Wright *et al.* (2008), which will serve as introductory books for novices carrying out CBT for psychosis. Some of the chapters in Part II of this book could also serve as good examples explaining the essential aspects of CBT for psychosis.

The primary goals in CBT for psychosis are to teach the patient to identify and monitor their thoughts and assumptions in specific situations, and to evaluate and correct these thoughts and assumptions against objective external evidence and actual circumstances. Delusional beliefs and auditory hallucinations are based upon thoughts and assumptions that the patient believes to be true and real, and they are held with great intensity and often preoccupy the person. These beliefs cause distortions in the processing of new information, which also maintain the patient's delusional beliefs and auditory hallucinations (Hagen and Nordahl, 2008).

The CBT of psychosis can be divided into different phases related to therapeutic processes taking place between the patient and the therapist. In the beginning of therapy, the focus is set on engaging the patient in therapy and trying to create a therapeutic alliance. Non-specific therapeutic factors such as empathy and warmth are of great importance in the process of building a collaborative relationship between patient and therapist. A style of active listening, trying to have a common language for the patient's symptoms, having an openness to their experiences and avoiding using a confrontational style are all factors which could enhance engagement in therapy (Chadwick, 2006; Kingdon and Turkington, 2005).

The next phase is related to the process of education and normalization of the patient's psychotic symptoms. The aim of this is to promote an understanding of other psychological phenomena that resemble symptoms of psychosis. Research shows that normalizing is a main factor predicting a good clinical outcome when it is linked to other formulation techniques, such as tracing the antecedents of breakdown, de-catastrophizing psychosis and education about the psychotic illness (Dudley et al., 2007). Normalization is closely related to the assumption already described in this chapter that psychotic experiences are continuous with ordinary human experiences, and that normalization could be used as a therapeutic tool towards forming a strong therapeutic alliance. Integrated in the normalization process is also psychoeducation. This seems crucial for people suffering from psychotic disorders because of the myths surrounding these illnesses. Psychoeducation and information about the illness must be adapted to the individual psychotic symptoms. Given in an appropriate manner, this can help people feel listened to and understood. Education that normalizes is highly valued (Kingdon and Turkington, 2005).

Embedded in the process described above are assessment and information gathering, related to the process of developing and sharing a case formulation with the patient. The ultimate goal of the therapist is for both parties to try to understand the patient's psychotic symptoms. The two most important areas to identify when working from a cognitive behavioural viewpoint with psychotic patients are how the psychotic symptoms appear, and what sense the patient makes of them. Case formulation develops out of the assessment process, and will sometimes guide it, and provides a framework for developing therapeutic interventions (Kingdon and Turkington, 2005), which is the next phase when carrying out CBT for psychosis.

Based on the formulation, a treatment plan is made in which the patient and the therapist are working with the individual's beliefs and thoughts related to their understanding of their symptoms, and trying to build new alternative explanations and coping strategies. The aim is not to make the psychotic symptoms go away, but to restructure old appraisals of voices and delusions, and to generate new alternatives which are not as distressing as the original ones. Instead of just focusing on a decline in symptoms, the treatment should be seen as effective if there is a decline in emotional distress in the patient as a result of therapy (Birchwood and Trower, 2006) and an improved social outcome (Turkington et al., 2007). The use of cognitive and behavioural techniques is implemented in a non-confrontational and collaborative manner in this working phase.

The closing phase of CBT for psychosis is the process of relapse prevention and recovery. Feelings of fear, depression, helplessness, hopelessness, embarrassment and shame seem to be common factors prior to relapse in psychosis (Gumley and Schwannauer, 2006). Relapse prevention is an essential aspect in CBT for psychosis, and it is of great importance that psychotic relapse is avoided, related to the personal costs and suffering to the patient. Avoiding relapses is important, but must not overshadow the road to emotional recovery and an improvement in quality of life. Research related to recovery from psychosis suggests that there are both personal and environmental factors which both therapist and patient could build on to make a recovery fully possible (Wilken, 2007). Generating hope and belief that recovery is possible and giving the patient a high quality of professional services are criteria which we can say are already implemented in cognitive behavioural therapy for psychosis.

The content of this book

The content of this book follows a logical progression in learning about CBT for psychosis, and is divided into four parts, each focusing on different aspects. Part I focuses on the cognitive models of psychotic symptoms and their assessment. Chapter 2 (Kinderman) presents an update on the cognitive models of auditory hallucinations and the general consensus in the CBT field that auditory hallucinations arise from misattributed cognitions, but less consensus from research as to the specific nature of these cognitions. This chapter reviews these different theories and also gives examples on how auditory hallucinations can best be understood from within a cognitive behavioural framework. Chapter 3 (Turkington et al.) explores the cognitive models pertinent to delusion formation and maintenance. Case vignettes are used to illustrate the key CBT techniques pertinent to engaging, formulation and the reality testing of delusions. The pertinence of schemas to delusional content is described. Chapter 4 (Peters) is about assessment in psychosis. As already described, in recent years there has been a growing and fruitful debate on the merits of using a symptom-based approach to psychosis instead of traditional, diagnostic categories. Assessment tools reflect these developments and in this chapter, the benefits and disadvantages of traditional psychiatric measures and symptom-based measures are discussed.

Part II focuses on how to treat psychotic symptoms using cognitive behavioural therapy. Hoaas *et al.* (Chapter 5) start this section by describing the importance of having a good therapeutic alliance when doing cognitive behavioural therapy with psychotic patients. A variety of important factors in the building of a therapeutic alliance are reviewed, and this leads to advice on how to go on to build a good rapport between patient and CBT therapist. Dudley and Turkington (Chapter 6) write about the role of normalizing in cognitive therapy, and also how this process can be adapted when working with psychotic symptoms. Normalization is a key aspect when delivering CBT for psychosis.

Early intervention is of great importance in the treatment of psychotic disorders. Addington *et al.* (Chapter 7) review the role of cognitive behaviour therapy for first-episode individuals as a part of comprehensive treatment and also for those at clinical high risk of psychosis. Command hallucinations are a particularly distressing and sometimes dangerous type of hallucination about which relatively little is known and there is a need for evidence-based treatments. Michail and Birchwood (Chapter 8) present a treatment approach giving clear steps from formulation to intervention, which will serve as a valuable tool for clinicians working with patients suffering from these types of hallucinations. Negative symptoms and formal thought disorders are common symptoms in schizophrenia, but little emphasis has been placed on treatment of these symptoms in CBT. New research seems to suggest that dysfunctional negative beliefs and attitudes may play a role in negative symptoms and formal thought disorder. Grant and Stolar (Chapter 9) show us how cognitive behavioural therapy can be used to uncover such beliefs and to determine alternative viewpoints.

As has already been mentioned earlier in this introduction, relapse prevention is an important phase in the therapy process. Gumley (Chapter 10) presents a cognitive behavioural therapy framework for targeting emotional recovery and relapse prevention. This approach considers the cognitive, interpersonal and developmental aspects involved in recovery and vulnerability to the recurrence of psychosis. Finally in this treatment part of the book, Lecomte and Leclerc (Chapter 11) write about the paradox that even if there are multiple studies giving evidence of the effectiveness of CBT for psychosis and clinical guides recommending its implementation, there are problems in achieving this. Lecomte and Leclerc define the barriers and make suggestions as to how these might best be overcome.

Part III of the book focuses on cognitive behavioural therapy for co-morbid conditions and also how CBT can be tailored to work with families and employment. Co-morbid conditions such as substance abuse and trauma are rather common in people suffering from psychotic symptoms. Kavanagh and Mueser (Chapter 12) show how substance misuse in people with serious mental disorders has a wide-ranging negative impact. The best approach to these problems is an integrative treatment of both the substance misuse and the psychotic symptoms, and this chapter gives an update of the current evidence for this treatment approach for patients suffering from dual disorders. The relation between trauma and psychosis has lately attracted a lot of research in trying to understand the possible relationships between these psychological conditions. Callcott *et al.* (Chapter 13) write about research and theoretical perspectives about the possible connections, but also draw together how current knowledge could be used in treatment to benefit people suffering from both traumatic experiences and psychotic symptoms. McFarlane (Chapter 14) focuses on how we can best integrate the family in the treatment of psychotic disorders. Family psychoeducation has been shown to be remarkably effective in breaking through problems that limit options of living and quality of life. In this chapter McFarlane describes the theoretical background for the multifamily group approach, the major components of how it is implemented and evidence for its effectiveness. This part of the book ends with ways in which cognitive behavioural therapy can improve employment outcomes for people with psychiatric disabilities. Bell *et al.* (Chapter 15) examine in depth how psychological interventions can be used to augment work programs in key areas such as finding and keeping employment.

The final part of the book, Part IV, concentrates on cognitive behaviour therapy for bipolar disorders. As suggested by Bentall (2003), the classification of psychotic symptoms in schizophrenia and bipolar disorders may represent an artefact grounded in a neo-Kraepelinian approach to categorizing psychiatric problems – i.e. it may be that these presentations are best understood as part of a continuum of psychotic disorders. Tai (Chapter 16) focuses on the growing recognition of the importance of understanding bipolar symptoms and their underlying mechanisms in psychological terms, and also discusses the emerging empirical evidence for the development and maintenance for the disorder. Scott (Chapter 17) develops this topic further when she looks at the key aspects of the cognitive models of bipolar disorders. She also comments on the clinical applicability of cognitive therapy and reviews the outcome studies available.

Cognitive behavioural therapy is a promising intervention for psychotic problems, but is not just a matter of technique. It is also an attitude in how to relate to people. A man who was diagnosed with schizophrenia was asked what was needed in order for him to have a life outside the hospital. His answer was thought-provoking: what he needed was a place to live, something to make a living from, something to live for and someone to live with. Let us all make this wish our first priority. We hope this book, along with patient and carer CBT of psychosis guides (Turkington *et al.*, 2009), are examples that assist in pointing people in the direction of social recovery.

References

Beck, A. T. (1952). Successful outpatient psychotherapy with a schizophrenic with a delusion based on borrowed guilt. *Psychiatry*, *15*, 305–312.

Beck, J. S. (1995). *Cognitive Therapy. Basics and Beyond*. New York: Guilford.

Bentall, R. P. (2003). *Madness Explained. Psychosis and Human Nature*. London: Penguin Books.

Bentall, R. (2007). The new psychology and treatment of psychosis. *Journal of the Norwegian Psychological Association*, *44*, 524–526.

Birchwood, M. and Trower, P. (2006). The future of cognitive behavioural therapy for psychosis: Not a quasi-neuroleptic. *British Journal of Psychiatry*, *188*, 107–108.

Butler, A. C., Chapman, J. E., Forman, E. M. and Beck, A. T. (2006). The empirical status of cognitive behavioural therapy: A review of meta-analyses. *Clinical Psychology Review*, *26*, 17–31.

Chadwick, P. (2006). *Person-based Cognitive Therapy for Distressing Psychosis*. London: John Wiley.

Dickerson, F. (2004). Update on cognitive behavioural psychotherapy for schizophrenia. *Journal of Cognitive Psychotherapy*, *18*, 189–205.

Dudley, R., Bryant, C., Hammond, K., Siddle, R., Kingdon, D. and Turkington, D. (2007). Techniques in cognitive behavioural therapy: Using normalizing in schizophrenia. *Journal of the Norwegian Psychological Association*, *44*, 562–572.

Freeman, D. and Garety, P. (Eds.). (2004). *Paranoia: The Psychology of Persecutory Delusions*. Hove, UK: Psychology Press (Maudsley Monograph No 45).

Garety, P., Kuipers, E., Fowler, D., Freeman, D. and Bebbington, P. E. (2001). A cognitive model of the positive symptoms of psychosis. *Psychological Medicine*, *31*, 189–195.

Gaudiano, B. A. (2005). Cognitive behaviour therapies for psychotic disorders: Current empirical status and future directions. *Clinical Psychology: Science and Practice*, *12*, 33–50.

Gould, R. A., Mueser, K. T., Bolton, E., Mays, V. and Goff, D. (2001). Cognitive therapy for psychosis in schizophrenia. An effect size analysis. *Schizophrenia Research*, *48*, 335–342.

Grant, P., Young, P. R., DeRubeis, R. J. (2005). Cognitive and behavioural therapies. In Glen O. Garbbard, Judith S. Beck and Jeremy Holmes (Eds.), *Oxford Textbook of Psychotherapy*. Oxford: Oxford University Press.

Gumley, A. and Schwannauer, M. (2006). *Staying Well After Psychosis. A Cognitive Interpersonal Approach to Recovery and Relapse Prevention*. London: Wiley & Sons.

Hagen, R. and Nordahl, H. M. (2008). Behavioural experiments in the treatment of paranoid schizophrenia: A single case study. *Cognitive and Behavioral Practice*, *15*, 296–305.

Hollon, S. D. and Beck, A. T. (2004). Cognitive and cognitive behavioural therapies. In M. J. Lambert, *Bergin and Garfield's Handbook of Psychotherapy and Behaviour Change* (5th edition) (pp. 447–492). New York: John Wiley.

Kingdon, D. G. and Turkington, D. (2005). *Cognitive Therapy of Schizophrenia*. New York: Guilford Press.

Kingdon, D. G., Vincent, S., Kinoshita, Y. and Turkington, D. (2008).

Destigmatizing schizophrenia: Does changing terminology reduce negative attitudes? *Psychiatric Bulletin, 32*(11), 419–422.

Kraepelin, E. (1899/1990). *Psychiatry: A Textbook for Students and Physicans. Vol. 1. General Psychiatry.* Canton, MA: Watson Publishing International.

Kuipers, E., Garety, P., Fowler, D., Freeman, D., Dunn, G. and Bebbington, P. (2006). Cognitive, emotional and social processes in psychosis: Refining cognitive behavioural therapy for persistent positive symptoms. *Schizophrenia Bulletin, 32,* 24–31.

Morrison, A. P., Renton, J. C., Dunn, H., Williams., S. and Bentall, R. P. (2004). *Cognitive Therapy for Psychosis. A Formulation Based Approach.* Hove: Brunner-Routledge.

Rathod, S. and Turkington, D. (2005). Cognitive behaviour therapy for schizophrenia. A review. *Current Opinion in Psychiatry, 18,* 159–163.

Rector, N. A. and Beck, A. T. (2001). Cognitive behavioural therapy for schizophrenia: An empirical review. *Journal of Nervous and Mental Disease, 189,* 278–287.

Tarrier, N. and Wykes, T. (2004). Is there evidence that cognitive behaviour therapy is an effective treatment for schizophrenia? A cautious or cautionary tale? *Behaviour Research and Therapy, 42,* 1377–1401.

Turkington, D., Kingdon, D. and Weiden, P. J. (2006). Cognitive behaviour therapy for schizophrenia. *American Journal of Psychiatry, 163,* 365–373.

Turkington, D., Bryant, C. and Kingdon, D. (2007). Optimising functional outcome in schizophrenia: Combining cognitive behavioural therapy with antipsychotic therapy. *Progress in Neurology and Psychiatry* (suppl), 10–13.

Turkington, D., Kingdon, D., Rathod, S., Wilcock, S. K. J., Brabban, A., Cromarty, P. *et al.* (2009). *Back to Life, Back to Normality: Recovery, Cognitive Therapy and Psychosis.* Cambridge: Cambridge University Press.

Wilken, J. P. (2007). Understanding recovery from psychosis: A growing body of knowledge. *Journal of the Norwegian Psychological Association, 44,* 658–665.

Wright, J. H., Basco, M. R. and Thase, M. E. (2006). *Learning Cognitive Behaviour Therapy. An Illustrative Guide.* Washington: APPI.

Wright, J. H., Kingdon, D., Turkington, D. and Basco, M. R. (2008). *CBT for Severe Mental Disorders. An Illustrative Guide.* Washington: APPI.

Zubin, J. and Spring, B. (1977). Vulnerability: A new view on schizophrenia. *Journal of Abnormal Psychology, 86,* 103–126.

Chapter 2

Cognitive models of auditory hallucinations

Peter Kinderman

Introduction

There is widespread consensus that auditory hallucinations arise from misattributed cognitions – cognitive events that are not recognised by the individual as being generated internally, and instead are attributed to external sources. There is less consensus as to the specific nature of these cognitions, with subvocal speech, disconnected memories or traumatic flashbacks, and intentions all cited as candidates. In addition, a wide range of personal, physical, environmental, psychological and situational factors have been found to impact on the central source-monitoring or reality-monitoring processes involved. A theoretical model of auditory hallucinations must therefore allow for individual variation within this general framework. Formulations developed with individuals in therapy, equally, will be highly individual. While some people experience few difficulties when they have these experiences, for other people they can be highly distressing. Psychological therapies, based on the analysis outlined here, can be effective for helping people experiencing hallucinations. Such therapies are, however, highly individualised, relying on complex and sophisticated individual case formulations bringing together many of the issues discussed here.

It is usual for people – psychologists as well as others – to comment that auditory hallucinations are "common and distressing psychotic phenomena" (Csipke and Kinderman, 2006, p. 365). And in some senses that is true. Hallucinations are indeed very common experiences in people with mental health problems and they can be highly distressing for many people. Auditory hallucinations are closely associated with the diagnosis of schizophrenia, with up to 75 per cent of individuals receiving a diagnosis of schizophrenia reporting auditory hallucinations. Indeed, in the ICD-10 diagnostic system, it is possible to receive a diagnosis of schizophrenia (in certain specific circumstances) with auditory hallucinations as the only observed phenomenon.

But it is also clear that auditory hallucinations are a much more common, and more 'normal', phenomenon than this account would suggest. First, people with other conditions or diagnoses not typically associated with psychosis, such as depression or post-traumatic stress disorder, also experience similar phenomena (Bentall, 1990). Hallucinations are common features of bereavement, with people frequently hearing or even seeing recently deceased loved ones. Hallucinations are also relatively common following traumatic experiences. Second, large numbers of the general population experience such phenomena quite commonly. Estimates for the lifetime incidence of auditory hallucinations in the general population range from a conservative 1 to 2 per cent to 10–15 per cent (Tien, 1991). Up to 30–40 per cent of a student population have experienced occasional, brief hallucination-like events, such as hearing one's own thoughts. Many commentators therefore conclude that hallucinations exist on continua with other 'normal' experiences experienced by many individuals.

Romme *et al.* (1992) found that 44 per cent of individuals who reported hearing voices were not receiving any psychiatric care. In some cases, although certainly not all, hallucinations can be regarded as neutral, entirely normal or even positive parts of human experience. What seems to characterise the differences between people who experience few problems while hearing voices and those that end up having difficulties is that people in the former group report having control over their voices, and are consequently significantly less distressed.

There are at least two important psychological consequences of these observations. First, we should be cautious about what is inferred from the use of the term 'hallucination'. Most studies of 'hallucinations' refer to studies of highly distressed individuals struggling to cope with hallucinations in the context of significant and evident psychological disorder. But these experiences clearly commonly occur outside of that context. Essentially, the term 'hallucinations' has come to mean hallucinations which cause distress. This means, as Bentall (2003) points out, that decisions to intervene to help people experiencing phenomena such as hallucinations should be predicated not on notions of illness, or even in terms of 'symptoms', but on the basis of personal distress.

Brain disease

Clearly, a wide range of injuries, insults to the brain and chemical intoxications can induce hallucinations. Indeed, many people in Western Europe apparently enjoy ingesting a range of street drugs, a principal effect of which is often to induce hallucinations. The power of LSD, and other dopaminergic drugs, in particular, to induce hallucinations has been a driver behind the so-called dopamine hypothesis of schizophrenia (see Bentall, 2003).

In fact, brain dysfunction as a biological illness appears to be a relatively unimportant causal factor. Not only does the very widespread incidence of hallucinatory or hallucination-like experiences in the normal population indicate that brain illness is not necessary, but medical investigations of hallucinating people indicate that biological causes are very rarely found and mainly relate to visual hallucinations of a characteristic type. This is not to say that physical or biological agents are not important – a simple consideration of the effects of LSD proves this to be false. But it does mean that brain 'disease' is rarely a cause of hallucinations.

Hallucinations are misattributed cognitions

The dominant psychological formulations of auditory hallucinations are based on the hypothesis that individuals are mistaking their own internal, private cognitions for external events (see Morrison and Haddock, 1997). More precisely, there is compelling evidence that hallucinations stem from misattributed inner speech. In the development of the modern science of psychology, the role of inner speech has had a chequered history, and it would be unwise to reprise that history here. But it is fair to conclude that inner speech or sub-vocalisation is extremely common, accompanying nearly all mental activities involving thought or autobiographical memory, and is, as Richard Bentall claims (Bentall, 2003, p. 197) "an important vehicle of self-awareness". People use both inner and overt speech while engaged in activities, although they may not always be aware that they are doing so.

For relatively obvious reasons, sub-vocalisations have been studied extensively in the area of hallucinations. All studies point to the conclusion that hallucinations are misattributed sub-vocal speech. As early as 1948, muscular activity of the lips and tongue was discovered to be associated with hallucinations (Gould, 1948). Oddly, a number of researchers have reported that these sub-vocalisations are associated with audible speech. Researchers have also been able to detect audible speech sounds (whispers) – which the person was unaware of – during hallucinations. These findings have been paralleled by a series of studies investigating the functional neuroanatomy of hallucinations. Using EEG, SPET and PET technologies, researchers have found that auditory hallucinations are reliably associated with activity in those areas of the brain (for instance Broca's and Wernicke's areas) associated with language production and comprehension. Taken together, these findings are usually taken (see Bentall, 2003) as clear evidence that hallucinations are misattributed inner speech.

Why? In what circumstances?

A simplistic response to this analysis might be to suggest that the origins of auditory hallucinations have been established: hallucinations are misattributed inner speech. But it is important to establish why, and in what circumstances, sub-vocalised speech is misinterpreted as external, why this is (or is not) distressing, and what can be done to help people who are distressed. In this issue, as in all instances of mental disorder (Kinderman, 2005), psychological processes are involved in determining the source of perceptual experiences. In the case of hallucinations, there is evidence that people who hear voices have difficulties with 'reality discrimination', i.e. the ability correctly to identify events as internal or external (Bentall, 1990).

Researchers have employed many different, closely related, techniques to investigate source or reality monitoring. Perhaps the clearest example would be a methodology in which a participant might be presented with a list of words read out by an experimenter (that is, words clearly external to the participant) to which they may be asked to generate a response – often this is presented as a simple word-association exercise. Clearly, the participant's response is self-generated. At a later time, the participant may then be presented with a mixed list of initial stimulus items (experimenter-generated) and their own responses (participant-generated), and asked to determine whether these words were, indeed, self-generated or experimenter-generated. Source monitoring or reality monitoring are measured, in part, by the proportion of participant-generated items that are incorrectly judged to have been experimenter-generated. The fact that these items are logically related in a word-association exercise means that this discrimination is not as simple as it might appear.

Bentall and Slade (1985) found that hallucinating individuals were more likely to fail in correctly identifying the source of a signal than those not hallucinating. Not surprisingly, the people hearing voices believed internally generated signals were external more frequently than did people not hearing voices. In a similar study, non-patient research participants disposed to hallucinations (as measured by the Launay-Slade Hallucination Scale) were more likely to attribute their thoughts to an external source than were research participants without a proneness to hallucinate. Source monitoring or reality discrimination difficulties appear to relate to material other than the specific content of hallucinations, and often relate to material supplied by researchers, rather than the individuals' own cognitions. In this paradigm, our understanding of hallucinations now relates to the issue of why such source monitoring or reality discrimination processes could fail.

Cognitive disruption

Without necessarily accepting the idea of illness or disease, a number of researchers have suggested that hallucinations result from a cognitive deficit – a problem with cognitive processes related to source monitoring. In this context, researchers have implicated memory impairments and language planning disruptions as well as fundamental problems with 'theory-of-mind'. These findings are supported by a wide range of psychological and neuropsychological evidence indicating a range of cognitive problems in people experiencing hallucinations (Brunelin *et al.*, 2006).

It seems likely that such cognitive deficits are indeed associated with hallucinations. It is also relatively easy to understand how such difficulties might contribute to misattribution of cognitions to external sources. At the same time, the distribution of hallucinations in everyday life and in otherwise 'normal' members of the community (Tien, 1991) equally suggests that these difficulties do not constitute a 'cause' of hallucinations, but rather are part of a complex pattern of vulnerabilities. That means a wide range of cognitive abnormalities such as those outlined here could impact on source discrimination processes. More pertinently, it suggests a possible circular relationship. Since hallucinations can be distressing, and since stress can impact negatively on a wide range of mental processes (see Bentall, 2003), it is not unreasonable to suppose that people distressed by hallucinations might experience increasing difficulties with reality discrimination. It is hardly surprising that the auditory hallucinations of persons with schizophrenia worsen in a negative mood (Haddock *et al.*, 1993).

This discussion serves to illustrate an important psychological point. Biological factors can be expected to have their effects on mental disorder through the disruption of psychological processes (Kinderman, 2005). In the case of hallucinations, it appears that these processes form part of the normal architecture of cognition. That is, all people can be expected to use source discrimination mechanisms to attribute cognitions and experience appropriately – but not flawlessly. And, for all of us, circumstantial and biological factors that impact on these processes will, quite naturally, affect source discrimination. It is worth stressing that errors in source monitoring are common and can often be influenced by straightforward factors such as environmental noise, demand characteristics and expectations (Johnson *et al.*, 1993). But there may also be rather more specific factors in the case of hallucinations that cause distress and lead people to seek help.

Traumatic events

There are clear relationships between one broad class of circumstantial factors – traumatic experiences – and hallucinations. The relationship between trauma and psychosis more generally will be addressed in Chapter 13, and it is clear that reports of traumatic experiences such as warfare, assaults (including sexual assaults) in adulthood, and childhood sexual assault are very common among users of psychiatric services generally, people with psychotic experiences in particular, and specifically people hearing voices (Read *et al.*, 2005).

Some of the possible links between trauma and psychosis will be discussed in Chapter 13, but it is clear that a potent combination of highly intrusive, very distressing thoughts, with clear schematic implications for the individual, is 'normal' following traumatic events. In addition, many people report dissociative experiences following trauma, and it is easy to see how this may contribute to the likelihood of source misattribution.

Traumatic memories, or intrusive thoughts, following traumatic events may be examples of how a particular type of cognitive event could be misinterpreted as coming from an external source. It does not necessarily mean that all hallucinations are indicative of childhood sexual abuse, but it does illustrate some of the elements that contribute to misattribution.

Characteristics of intrusive thoughts

Intrusive thoughts can be defined as unwanted, unacceptable or uncontrollable, unrealistic or ego-dystonic thoughts which arise unbidden in the mind. Intrusive thoughts are often accompanied by distress and they interrupt ongoing mental activity. Such intrusions are very common.

People experiencing auditory hallucinations have reported high levels of negative intrusive thoughts (Csipke and Kinderman, 2006). This is entirely consistent with the idea that hallucinations are misattributed sub-vocalisations, because of the close relationship between the two. Anxious states are typically associated with increased ruminations. In particular, anxiety can be defined as a mood state in which an individual becomes ready or prepared to attempt to cope with upcoming negative events. This preparation may be done by mentally rehearsing possible events and actions that may occur in the future. Self-talk is very often used to guide such behaviour and prepare for future action.

There are several characteristics of intrusive thoughts that may make source discrimination difficult. First, cognitions that emerge as a result of effortful processes tend to be correctly recognised as self-generated, whereas effort-free cognitions (thoughts that just 'pop into your mind') tend to be more likely to be misattributed (Johnson et al., 1993). As outlined above, stress impacts negatively on source monitoring, and many negative intrusive thoughts are very distressing. Clearly, anxious ruminations and by definition 'intrusive thoughts' can be both highly distressing and effort-free. Intriguingly, Morrison and Baker (2000) proposed that thoughts which are in the second person perspective (i.e. 'You are a fool') may sound more like a second party is speaking to the voice hearer than thoughts that are in the first perspective (e.g. I am a fool), and hence may be more likely to be misattributed.

Interpretative biases and metacognitive beliefs

Certain metacognitive beliefs – beliefs people hold about the acceptability of certain thoughts and thought processes – may also be associated with hallucinations (Morrison et al., 1995). First, some metacognitive beliefs may contribute to the distress experienced with intrusive thoughts. Thus beliefs about the importance of being in control of one's thoughts and being responsible for one's thoughts may lead to distress if one has unwanted thoughts (Lobban *et al.*, 2002), whereas people prone to hallucinations are more self-conscious about their thoughts, more likely to believe thoughts should be controllable and more likely to believe that certain types of thoughts are dangerous. Rachman (1997) pointed out that a sense of mental pollution, or cognitive dissonance, occurs when individuals involuntarily think repugnant thoughts – unacceptable violent, sexual or blasphemous thoughts.

Treatment

Psychological and psychosocial treatments for psychotic phenomena are now clearly rooted in evidence and have considerable organisational support – as discussed in Chapter 1. Psychological approaches to hallucinations more specifically have been shown to be effective (Haddock *et al.*, 1998). Haddock *et al.* (ibid.) suggest a number of different elements or techniques that have been developed specifically for hallucinations. Distraction techniques have been employed, with mixed results. Researchers have investigated a range of different environmental manipulations on the severity of auditory hallucinations. Essentially, it appears that the effectiveness of different interventions in impacting upon (although not necessarily treating) hallucinations appears to depend on the degree to which the interventions involve verbalisation. When people experiencing hallucinations are asked to engage in an activity (for instance reading meaningful material out loud), a positive impact is seen on hallucinations. This, of course, is consistent with, and support for, the misattributed inner speech model of hallucinations.

Haddock *et al.* (ibid.) report most positive effects for therapeutic approaches that attempt to address some of the underlying psychological issues. This is likely to be because such approaches address some of the issues – outlined above – that contribute to distressing misattribution of intrusive thoughts or sub-vocalisations to external sources. In particular, Haddock *et al.* commented on the positive effects of interventions that included the modification of beliefs surrounding hallucinations. In these approaches (see Morrison, 2004), therapists use the conventional techniques of cognitive behavioural therapy to elicit individuals' key beliefs concerning the hallucinations themselves, the meaning of the hallucinations to the individual, the content of the hallucinations, metacognitive beliefs etc. These are then modified, again using very conventional cognitive behavioural approaches, in order to address the distress cause by the voices as experiences, and to address the distress induced by their content. Thus, a therapist is likely to explore an individual's beliefs about mental disorder generally, mental illness more specifically and indeed the experience of hallucinations themselves.

People's beliefs concerning such matters vary widely from person to person (Kinderman *et al.*, 2006) and can be important. These beliefs may, if appropriate, be addressed in therapy to lead to a more normalised attitude to the problems. Similarly, metacognitive beliefs (as discussed above) may be elicited and, as before, modified. The rationale here is that such beliefs (whether about mental disorder, the hallucinations, or thoughts in general) may contribute to both distress and misattribution. If one believes such events are both impossible and highly negatively significant (i.e. "this can only mean I'm mad"), both misattributions and distress are likely. Clearly such an approach should be combined with psychoeducation, explaining the evidence for, and significance of, a psychological account of hallucinations. In addition, therapists are likely to focus more on the personal significance of the hallucinations. Thus, therapists are likely to explore the nature of any relationship between the individual and the voices (or more properly, perhaps, the entities believed to be responsible for the voices). Thus issues of power relationships and the benevolence or malevolence of the voices may be explored (Chadwick and Birchwood, 1994). These schema may well be of considerable significance, in that there appears to be a significant relationship between issues of social status, dominance and subjugation and the experience of malevolent hallucinations (ibid.). For more details on treatment methods for auditory hallucinations see Chapter 8.

Conclusions

Clearly, there is much still to be learned about hallucinations. As with many other psychotic phenomena, there are many issues of both causation and treatment that require extensive research. Nevertheless, the experience of auditory hallucinations does appear to be amenable to both understanding and care. Auditory hallucinations appear to be misattributed cognitions – most commonly misattributed inner speech. Research (much of it in 'normal' psychology) has offered considerable understanding of the characteristics of cognitions which are likely to be misattributed; principally more automatic, unwilled and emotionally challenging cognitions. There is also now considerable evidence as to the kinds of experiences and events that lead to misattributed cognitions – and therefore auditory hallucinations. Not surprisingly, these events are those which are likely to give rise to traumatic, emotionally challenging, intrusive and unwanted thoughts, such as trauma and abuse. Because of this understanding, we are now closer to therapeutic techniques. By helping people understand these processes of intrusion and misattribution, relatively straightforward psychological techniques offer considerable optimism for people troubled by auditory hallucinations.

References

Bentall, R. P. (1990). The illusion of reality: A review and integration of psychological research on hallucinations. *Psychological Bulletin*, *107*, 82–95.

Bentall, R. P. (2003). *Madness Explained: Psychosis and Human Nature*. London: Penguin Press.

Bentall, R. P. and Slade, P. D. (1985). Reality testing and auditory hallucinations: A signal detection analysis. *British Journal of Clinical Psychology*, *24*, 159–169.

Brunelin, J., Combris, M., Poulet, E., Kallel, L., D'Amato, T., Dalery, J. and Saoud, M. (2006). Source monitoring deficits in hallucinating compared to non-hallucinating patients with schizophrenia. *European Psychiatry*, *21*, 259–261.

Chadwick, P. D. J. and Birchwood, M. (1994). The omnipotence of voices: A cognitive approach to auditory hallucinations. *British Journal of Psychiatry*, *164*, 190–201.

Csipke, E. and Kinderman, P. (2006). A longitudinal investigation of beliefs about voices. *Behavioural and Cognitive Psychotherapy*, *34*, 365–369.

Gould, L. N. (1948). Verbal hallucinations and activity of vocal musculature. *American Journal of Psychiatry*, *105*, 367–372.

Haddock, G., Bentall, R. P. and Slade, P. D. (1993). Psychological treatment of auditory hallucinations: Two case studies. *Behavioural and Cognitive Psychotherapy*, *21*, 335–346.

Haddock, G., Tarrier, N., Spaulding, W., Yusupoff, L., Kinney, C. and McCarthy, E. (1998). Individual cognitive behavior therapy in the treatment of hallucinations and delusions: A review. *Clinical Psychology Review*, *18*, 821–838.

Johnson, M. K., Hashtroudi, S. and Lindsay, D. S. (1993). Source monitoring. *Psychological Bulletin*, *114*, 3–28.

Kinderman, P. (2005). A psychological model of mental disorder. *Harvard Review of Psychiatry*, *13*, 206–217.

Kinderman, P., Setzu, E., Lobban, F. and Salmon, P. (2006). Illness beliefs in schizophrenia. *Social Science and Medicine*, *63*, 1900–1911.

Lobban, F., Haddock, G., Kinderman, P. and Wells, A. (2002). The role of meta-cognitive beliefs in auditory hallucinations. *Personality and Individual Differences*, *32*, 1351–1363.

Morrison, A. (2004). *Cognitive Therapy for Psychosis: A Formulation-Based Approach*. Hove, UK: Brunner-Routledge.

Morrison, A. P. and Haddock, G. (1997). Cognitive Factors in source monitoring and auditory hallucinations. *Psychological Medicine*, *27*, 669–679.

Morrison, A. P. and Baker, C. A. (2000). Intrusive thoughts and auditory hallucinations: A comparative study of intrusions in psychosis. *Behaviour Research and Therapy*, *38*, 1097–1106.

Morrison, A. P., Haddock, G. and Tarrier, N. (1995). Intrusive thoughts and auditory hallucinations: A cognitive approach. *Behavioural and Cognitive Psychotherapy*, *23*, 265–280.

Rachman, S. J. (1997). A cognitive theory of obsessions. *Behaviour Research and Therapy*, *35*, 793–802.

Read, J., van Os, J., Morrison, A. P. and Ross, C. A. (2005). Childhood trauma, psychosis and schizophrenia: A literature review with theoretical and clinical implications. *Acta Psychiatrica Scandinavica*, *112*, 330–350.

Romme, M. A. J., Honig, A., Noorthorn, E. O. and Escher, S. (1992). Coping with hearing voices: An emancipatory approach. *British Journal of Psychiatry, 161,* 99–103.

Tien, A. Y. (1991). Distribution of hallucinations in the population. *Social Psychiatry and Psychiatric Epidemiology, 26,* 287–292.

Chapter 3

Cognitive models for delusions

Douglas Turkington, Caroline Bryant and Victoria Lumley

Introduction

Cognitive theories of delusions can be used to provide a link between the biological and phenomenological explanations of schizophrenia and its symptomatology. Historically, delusions are considered to be:

> False beliefs held with absolute certainty despite evidence to the contrary and out of keeping with the patient's social, educational, cultural and religious background.
>
> (Hamilton, 1984)

There are many ideas about delusions that contradict this definiton such as:

> Delusions often contain a core of truth and relate to premorbid interests and ideas.
>
> (Kingdon and Turkington, 1994)

There are also many bizarre, unscientific beliefs held by a large proportion of the population, e.g. beliefs in telepathy, poltergeists, alien abduction, horoscopes, etc. (Kingdon *et al.*, 1994). If presented with the right circumstances anybody from the general population can develop delusional beliefs. Paranoid ideation and transient delusional beliefs are much commoner in the general population than had been expected (Freeman *et al.*, 2005). However, research over the years has promoted many different conceptualisations of delusions and has indicated that delusions are multifaceted, with many different elements and subgroups.

Roberts (1991) described how delusions could be understandable in relation to a patient's life history and could even make sense in relation to such a narrative. In relation to this work it has become apparent that delusions form in a number of different ways for different patients. Some seemed to jump into delusional certainty early in the prodrome often with linked negative symptoms. For others the emergence of a delusion seemed to occur only after a prolonged period of increasing anxiety and appeared to act to reduce the escalating anxiety and protect against underlying depression (Kingdon and Turkington, 1998). Some believe that delusions may act as a psychological defence. Attributional style may be used to identify underlying styles of thinking related to depression in order to explain possible causes and maintaining influences in some delusional beliefs.

Turkington and Kingdon (1996) provided a clear process of CBT for delusions, working from superficial interventions (engaging, building trust, developing a range of explanations, peripheral questioning, reducing emotional and behavioural investment) to deep interventions (Socratic questioning, reality testing and working with the linked schema). Turkington *et al.* (1996) also redefined the concept of a delusion in line with the evidence base in an attempt to shift dichotomous views of psychopathology. It had been previously assumed that a person was obviously either deluded or not. A view showing delusion on a spectrum with normality seemed necessary to lead to an understanding within psychiatry that CBT might be of benefit and that 'all or nothing' views of psychopathology were not evidence-based (Strauss, 1969). Turkington *et al.* (1996: 127) proposed that

> a delusion is a belief (probably false) at the extreme end of the continuum of consensual agreement. It is not categorically different to overvalued ideas and normal beliefs. It is held in spite of evidence to the contrary but it may be amenable to change when that evidence is collaboratively explored and then the belief may come to approximate more closely to ideas in keeping with the patient's social, cultural, educational and religious background.

This chapter will consider the two main types of delusions and the cognitive models used to explain the emergence of symptoms and their maintenance.

Type I and Type II Delusions

There are two main types of delusion, categorised as Type I and Type II (Turkington *et al.*, 2005). Type I delusions are linked to cognitive deficits and negative symptoms such as affective blunting. These delusions are usually held with less emotional investment and conviction. In Type I delusions patients will often jump to conclusions about bizarre subjective experiences they do not fully understand and grasp at explanations, seizing on current topics which are prominent in newspaper and television reports. Religious delusions used to be common in delusional content but have gradually become replaced by microchips, satellites, mobile phones and aliens as the subject matter for Type I delusions.

By contrast Type II delusions are rarely linked with negative symptoms and usually arise after a period of intense and incremental anxiety, often in mid life, and are typical of a different subgroup of the schizophrenias, the anxiety psychosis. Type II delusions usually presents as a systemised persecutory or grandiose delusion in the absence of negative symptoms. They can also emerge in patients with a history of trauma (see Chapter 13) to protect from the emergence of unbearable affect when further trauma occurs or at times of anniversary or other important symbolic dates.

Cognitive models of psychotic symptom emergence and maintenance

Theory of Mind and cognitive deficits

Theory of Mind (ToM) is essentially the capacity to understand one's own and other people's mental states, such as beliefs, feelings or intentions. A deficit in ToM could lead to an inability to differentiate between subjectivity and objectivity, which, in turn, could help maintain false beliefs in the form of delusions. In particular, a deficit of ToM may account for disorders of self-monitoring such as delusions of alien control, as well as disorders of the monitoring of others, thoughts and intentions, leading to such experiences as delusions of reference and persecution (Frith, 1992). In particular people with delusions of persecution may be unable to understand adequately the motivations, attitudes, and intentions of others (Frith, 2004). Persecutory delusions arise because the person notices that other people's actions have become opaque and surmises that a conspiracy exists. Frith (ibid.) believed that the blunted affect and asocial behaviours linked with negative symptoms of schizophrenia are a further representation of deficits in ToM skills. Abu-Akel and Bailey (2000) expanded upon the original ideas with a suggestion that beside the notion that ToM may be impaired in patients with schizophrenia, there is also the possibility that in some patients there is a hyperactivity in ToM whereby the patient could over attribute intentions to either themselves or others as reflected in certain delusions or simply have an inability to apply knowledge to an intact ToM capability. The evidence base supporting the ToM explanation for delusional symptoms of schizophrenia is not consistent, leading to some controversy over how useful it is. However, recent research supports evidence that ToM deficits are present in schizophrenia, particularly in those who experience negative symptoms, thought disorder and speech difficulties (Freeman and Garety, 1999). Discrepancies in previous research could be accounted for if these deficits are state-specific and also if chronicity and general cognitive impairments or intelligence impacted on the findings. Ability in ToM may also differ from task to task (e.g. previous studies have used both picture and written vignettes). ToM deficits are likely to be

involved in the genesis and maintenance of some delusions with implications for CBT in clinical practice.

Cognitive distortions and delusion formation

Some people may be more prone to certain beliefs, for example that people
are talking about them, when they are in a particularly vulnerable state of
mind. A research question is whether people with schizophrenia have a trait
in which they habitually use less information to arrive at a decision and
'jump to conclusions', forming hasty and often inaccurate beliefs (Garety
and Freeman, 1999). These beliefs may change quickly if evidence is
presented that contradicts them. The 'beads test' is a particular means of
researching this.

The beads test

One bead at a time is drawn from one of two hidden jars, one containing 85:15
black to white beads and the other the opposite ratio. Although they are told
they may take as long as they like, participants who suffer from delusions tend
to make the decision about which jar the beads are from after only a few beads
are presented to them while other participants wait longer before reaching a
hypothesis (Peters and Garety, 2006). Research by Van Dael et al. (2006)
indicates jumping to conclusions may be present in people who are prone to
develop schizophrenia and in close relatives. Further research is needed as to
whether this is restricted to particular types of delusion.

Depressive attributional style and delusion formation

For patients who experience delusions, attributional style may be considered
to be a possible defence mechanism protecting against perceived differences
between how they believe they are viewed by others and how they would like
to be seen. The externalisation of causal attributions such as persecutory
delusions may mask underlying negative self beliefs and representations,
thus protecting against unbearable affect or loss of self esteem arising from
accumulations of life events. These delusions are marked by systematisation
and grandiosity and often occur after key compensatory schemas have been
repeatedly invalidated. The systematised delusion has been traditionally
defined as being based upon either a delusional mood with delusional
perception with the remainder of the belief system being logically built on
this error or an accumulation of secondary delusions resulting in a complicated delusional system in which each delusional statement can be
understood as following from the one before. These fit into an overall plan

that within itself maintains logic, order and consistency. Systematisation is not just present or absent but found to a lesser or greater degree. In particular, Type II delusions focus on underlying schematic issues in terms of content. These would include beliefs such as 'I am worthless, I am damaged, I am unlovable and I am evil'. Linked to these negative beliefs about the self are cognitive distortions including a tendency to externalise praise for good events or blame for negative events and to personalise that praise or blame to one individual or group.

Externalisation and personalisation are linked to a theory of mind deficit which is probably best described as a pervasive problem in empathy, i.e. of perceiving the other to be unable to be empathic to the self. This model of paranoid delusional emergence and maintenance leads to the prospect of a clearly focused mode of intervention. This is based on reality testing, correction of cognitive distortions, role play and role reversal to help with problems of empathy, as well as schema-focused work to help make very negative core beliefs about the self more functional and less distressing (Turkington and Siddle, 1998). An example of this would be to work on the core belief 'I am evil': using positive logging the patient would record just how many evil things she actually did in one day. The continuum could be used with a variety of historical and fictional characters being placed at various points on the continuum from totally 100 per cent evil at one end to totally 100 per cent good at the other extreme. The patient is then encouraged to reconsider their place on the continuum and to change their personal rating of evil if this is indicated. Operationalising a negative construct can be helpful, for example what would an evil person do with their time? This model paves the way for the application of a variety of cognitive and behavioural techniques, as described above, which can reduce the distress and at times also the conviction of the paranoid delusion.

Consider the person who holds the core maladaptive schema 'I am worthless'. To compensate for such a negative belief about the value of the self they work every hour of the day and most of the weekend to be successful in business. Linked to this they continue to seek approval from others by giving them lavish presents. All goes well until the business starts to struggle and the cash flow begins to fail. Increasing their workload and suffering from sleep deprivation such a person begins to suffer from increasing anxiety. Perceived failure and loss of approval are warded off as long as possible but there is a lack of more positive views of the self which might have allowed him to tolerate such high levels of anxiety or the emergence of depression. Following a period of delusional mood the compensatory schema is distorted into a grandiose delusion which resolves the anxiety and protects against the emergence of depression. Prior to the full emergence of the delusion a delusional perception occurs and on seeing a dollar sign flashing in a shop window he realises that he is the long lost heir of the Getty fortune. The implications for cognitive therapy in such a case are that Socratic questioning and reality testing will probably not be helpful and a close examination of the antecedents leading to the development of a jointly shared formulation of belief onset is crucial. This can then be followed by work underneath the delusional system at the schema level. If the patient described a perusal of the family photograph album linked to recall of family interactions led the patient to believe that he had concluded that he was worthless on false premises. As such, when delusional systems weaken during CBT underlying affects such as guilt, shame, sadness or anger can emerge and need to be worked with.

Stigma, worry and rumination

Stigma is an ongoing and sadly a particularly common problem for people with mental health problems in the Western world. Schizophrenia is reported to be one of the most stigmatised disorders where negative stereotypes of people are formed and held by the media and society in general, which in turn leads to a loss of status and discrimination. Although most research focuses upon the importance of external or public stigma, internalised stigma or self-stigma may be an issue even when there is little or no objective level of public stigma present. Self-stigma is the subjective perception of being devalued and marginalised regardless of the objective level of discrimination. The individual feels devalued and ashamed and attempts to hide their problem through secrecy and withdrawal as a result of applying prejudices and stereotypes to oneself (Corrigan, 1998). However, the experience of transient psychotic symptoms such as paranoid ideas and auditory hallucinations is surprisingly common in apparently healthy community samples (Johns and van Os, 2001). Such psychotic symptoms are as common as obsessional thoughts and are usually interpreted in a similarly negative manner which is influenced by the highly stigmatised nature of Western culture. A person who develops pseudo-hallucinations due to sleep disturbance linked to pressure of work could interpret the transient symptoms as follows: 'I'm sure I heard a voice just now . . . it seemed to be calling my name . . . I'm starting to go nuts . . . If I have a breakdown I will lose my job . . . maybe I will be put in a mental hospital . . . I will be injected . . . I will be a danger to others . . . life will be unbearable.' This metacognitive style of worry and rumination about thought based on negative stigmatic beliefs is typical of the stigma model. This sequence of increasingly anxious interpretations of the original pseudo-hallucination can lead to increasing anxiety and further sleep deprivation. This can act to maintain and exacerbate the hallucinatory experience. This stigma model gives a clear rationale for the use of normalising explanations as an early strategy in the engagement of the psychotic patient. It leads to reduced anxiety and improved collaboration, and can lead to an early success experience due to some degree of reduction of hallucinatory intensity by reducing the anxiety which can be acting as a maintaining variable. Other psychotic symptoms (e.g. delusions of thought insertion and ideas of reference) are often the subject of similar catastrophisation and can be helped using normalising explanations.

'Culture-syntonic' delusions

Patients with certain paranoid delusions (Type I) display typical cognitive distortions. These typical distortions include arbitrary inference (drawing a conclusion with inadequate information) and magnification (holding that conclusion more firmly than would others). Such delusions are formed due to attempts by patients who are suffering puzzling psychotic symptoms to make sense of them in an absence of real world knowledge. Such delusions are typically much more culture-syntonic (alien abduction, satellite control, torment with lasers, etc.) and non-Jasperian in character (Kingdon and Turkington, 1994). They often develop in a setting of poor attention due to cognitive deficit and are often surprisingly open to educational work, reality testing homework and the generation and testing of alternative hypotheses.

Avoidance model

Instead of catastrophising about psychotic symptoms, some patients become actively involved in pursuing safety behaviours. For these people the symptom is a danger signal which needs to be controlled. Such people will take no engagement or ownership of the experience and will avoid any situation where the paranoid thoughts might occur. If the paranoid thoughts tends to occur in social situations then the patient will strenuously avoid social contact. When safety behaviours are deployed in this way the paranoid thoughts never have the chance to extinguish and are actively maintained by the coping style of the patient. When there is prominent exacerbation of the experience of the psychotic symptoms by catastrophisation and the use of safety behaviours is very intense and disabling, paranoid delusions can develop. The dropping of safety behaviours is only started when more functional coping strategies have been collaboratively developed and have shown efficacy in symptom management when used in graded homework exercises or during the session itself. Normalising explanations and the use of thought diaries, which encourage engagement and the gradual dropping of safety behaviours, can then be effectively used together. This type of model, which was first developed with hallucinations, also applies to certain delusions.

Traumatic model

Patients with critical and abusive auditory hallucinations, or visual and/or somatic hallucinations, with linked depression and low self-esteem, often disclose during therapy that they have been the victim of childhood sexual abuse or adolescent trauma (Kingdon and Turkington, 1998). Interpersonal trauma (abuse or bullying) has been linked to positive symptoms in schizophrenia (Read *et al.*, 2005). In such cases it is usually a further negative life event which triggers abusive voices or the development of a delusion. Trauma-related intrusive memories may be misinterpreted and be perceived as hallucinations if the patient is unable to appraise the situation and identify the link between the intrusive thought and the past trauma (Steel *et al.*, 2005). There is often strong avoidance by clinical staff of enquiry/ disclosure or of working with the traumatic material for fear of exacerbating depressive mood swings. The increased arousal of the traumatised state worsens psychotic symptoms, as does the linked sleep deprivation. Delusional content is usually persecutory and relates to the world outside of the person. However, delusions about the self also occur, such as delusions of emitting a powerful odour or compensatory delusions of grandeur. In such cases a systematic guided formulation linked with the abuse congruence of the psychotic symptom content will often allow the patient to begin the process of reliving and re-evaluating the trauma and of working with the linked distress at the schema level. Such patients often have repeated readmissions and are a high suicide risk due to the combination of persecutory delusions, critical and command hallucinations, and linked depression. Trauma can also follow the experience of psychosis via the mechanism of victimisation. Many vulnerable patients are targets for muggings, beatings and sexual assaults. Again these are often not disclosed but act to exacerbate hallucinations, persecutory delusions and negative symptoms. Delusions within traumatic psychosis often require to be dealt with using cognitive restructuring or reliving approaches (see Chapter 13).

Anxiety model

This model considers the importance of anxiety in the formation and maintenance of delusions, in particular paranoia. Anxious thoughts involve the anticipation of threat and fears of physical, social or psychological harm, and as such provide a foundation for thoughts of a paranoid nature. Such threat beliefs may emerge as a response to interpersonal stressors or trauma. Pre-existing negative beliefs about the self as a vulnerable or weak person could combine with threatening appraisals of others, such as that they are dangerous or untrustworthy, giving rise to feeling threatened and paranoid (Freeman *et al.*, 2002) – so paranoid delusions may be the response of psychological defences due to learning mechanisms and as a reaction to heightened anxiety. Freeman and Garety (1999) suggest that most people who experience persecutory delusions also have a thinking style characterised by excessive worry, even in matters that are not related to paranoia, with such worries having a higher level of distress. The heightened levels of anxiety associated with persecutory delusions leads to anxiety-related processes such as 'safety behaviours', acts carried out that are perceived to prevent the feared catastrophe from occurring (Freeman *et al.*, 2001; Freeman *et al.*, 2007). Such behaviour is a maintaining factor as the person adopting it believes that threats can genuinely be averted, e.g. 'The reason I wasn't attacked was because I left the street in time and made it back home' – which means that the threat beliefs persist partly due to this failure to obtain and process evidence to the contrary.

Delusions masked by thought disorder

Patients with thought disorder, including Knight's move thinking, fusion of themes and neologisms, are usually highly aroused by one specific issue. The concept here is that one core theme drives disorganisation of thought and that if the patient can be helped to focus on this using thought linkage and explanation, increased coherence can occur (Turkington and Kingdon, 1991). By repeatedly asking the patient how they got from X to Z, they can be encouraged to get into the habit of putting in the Y. Similarly, neologisms are challenged during speech and explanations are requested. The underlying driving theme is usually one of threat and is often delusional. Once this is identified and focused on, this allows a reduction in arousal and increased coherence of speech. The underlying perceived dangers and threats have often been misperceived or magnified and can be gradually corrected during therapy.

Delusions linked to primary negative symptoms

This cognitive model of the emergence of primary negative symptoms (alogia, affective blunting and autism) echoes the work of Bleuler (1911). Bleuler viewed these as being the primary symptoms of schizophrenia (along with ambivalence and disturbance of association) and believed that they represented a defensive position in relation to unbearable levels of stress. Such symptoms are indeed commoner in patients with high levels of vulnerability and a low capacity to cope with stress. As a secondary phenomenon such patients often become socially phobic, agoraphobic and institutionalised. It has long been known that such patients do gradually 'warm up' with gentle, supportive psychotherapy. CBT can be useful if carried out using a gentle, slow conversational style with activity scheduling with minimal targets. As patients slowly begin to recognise and work with affect and begin to allow more linked thinking, work with any coexisting phobia is indicated. Negative symptoms are usually improved with parallel work on coexisting positive symptoms (Kingdon and Turkington, 1994), starting with those that are not too heavily emotionally invested, i.e. Type I delusions.

An integrated cognitive model of delusions

An integration of the above elements was published by Garety *et al.* in 2001. This synthesis was based on a bio-psychosocial model and attempted to include and explain all recent research findings. Schizophrenia certainly has a genetic component in terms of vulnerability. This has been shown to be due to a small number of genes acting independently on a 'multiple hit' (cumulative) basis. Schizophrenia carries a biological predisposition linked to birth trauma and maternal viral infection. Schizophrenia is also commoner in those born in cities rather than in rural areas and this seems to hold true even for people who move from cities into the country. It would appear then that the summation of these vulnerabilities is most likely to occur in run-down inner city areas where there is poor access to or uptake of obstetric facilities. Such areas also tend to have high levels of deprivation and abuse of various types leading to the formation of negative schemas which tend to perpetuate psychotic symptoms. These are also the very areas where there is easier access to hallucinogenic drugs, which can also act to activate and perpetuate paranoid ideas and delusions. Such areas are often the only possible locations for new immigrants and asylum seekers and they are known to have a higher incidence of schizophrenia, particularly in second-generation immigrants who struggle in relation to cultural conflicts and support (Murray, 2002). As such, the stress vulnerability hypothesis would predict different prevalence of schizophrenia in different environments and this has been found to be the case across the UK. Such people, coming from backgrounds with genetic weighting (due to drift into the inner cities), poor obstetric care and negative schemas, are tipped into psychosis by environmental stressors such as drug use, trauma or accumulations of social problems. The negative schemas, lack of support, hallucinogen use, and generally impoverished social environment leading to victimisation act to initiate and maintain psychotic symptoms including delusions.

From models to CBT

In any particular situation where delusions emerge any of the above models might predominate or contribute. The case vignette below gives a typical example which illustrates how the model is crucial for the development of a CBT intervention.

Case Vignette – Jack

Presenting difficulties

At the time of initial contact, Jack believed he had a device implanted in his chest which was able to track all his movements and social activities.

He related his experiences to several years ago when he had a minor operation under general anaesthetic and became convinced that someone implanted the device during his operation, enabling that person to control his life.

Jack was certain the device could control his thought process and to some extent body movements and behaviours. He stopped going out socially and began avoiding situations where he feared the device would be activated (safety behaviours). Jack remained concerned that his family/ friends were involved in some way in the implantation and this led to frequent attempts from him to insist they divulged who was involved in the conspiracy so that he could 'sort them out'. His relationship with his parents was very strained and the level of tension in the household was high. His work relationships were suffering and he felt that no one would listen to his predicament. Jack's parents repeatedly challenged his beliefs (confrontation) which resulted in Jack becoming angry and more resistant to exploring alternative explanations.

Jack was extremely sensitive to suggestions that he was experiencing mental health difficulties and previous attempts resulted in him becoming verbally abusive, angry and disengaged (stigma). He refused to take any form of psychiatric medication and was adamant that the only thing that would be beneficial was to have the device removed.

Jack was very reluctant to engage in talking therapy and he described previous experiences of this, when his beliefs had been dismissed and his experiences invalidated. He conveyed his feelings of no longer trusting anyone, but agreed to engage in a psychological approach on the premise that it may enable him to explore the function of the device further and provide opportunity to talk about his fears and perhaps get his family to listen.

Personal history

Jack was in his late thirties and lived with his parents, who ran a family building business in a small town. He had an older sister who was married. Both his parents were described as very hard-working individuals who 'just got on with life no matter what'. Jack talked about feeling humiliated and embarrassed as a child (schematic vulnerability). Jack attended the local school and described his father as a very controlling, strong-minded individual who often expressed strongly to him the way that Jack should work. Jack described lack of emotional comfort from his parents and stated that both he and his father are very stubborn individuals.

Jack had been on long-term antibiotics for the year prior to his operation and had recently separated from his partner. His parents' health had deteriorated and they had spoken to him about him running the family business to enable them to retire. Jack had begun to work long hours to ensure work tasks were completed and was struggling to get adequate sleep.

Case formulation

Jack felt very controlled and dominated by his father and he constantly measured his own work abilities against those of his father. His early life experiences appeared to have been influential in developing his core mal-adaptive schema that he was weak and not in control. To compensate, Jack developed the dysfunctional assumption that 'I must always be strong to be in control'. He tried to protect his maladaptive schema (I am weak) by ensuring that he never expressed emotions, as he perceived this to be a sign of weakness.

Jack had an operation as a child which was a traumatic experience involving a prolonged period of painful dependence upon others and feel-ings of vulnerability. His recent operation appeared to be a critical incident that activated his fears of not being in control and his attempts to suppress his emotions may have increased his stress levels, influencing his vulner-ability to psychosis.

One possibility is that the hospital environment reactivated traumatic memories and emotions from his childhood that he was unable to process, leading to high levels of anxiety and distress and misinterpretation of events. His parents' decision to retire provoked immense anxiety, which added to current activation of maladaptive schema (not being in control).

Jack began to search for explanations for changes in his emotional well-being and in an attempt to seek further clarity he drove to the hospital to speak to them about his concerns. A cognitive mini-formulation (see Figure 3.1 below) focusing primarily on his thoughts, feelings, behaviours and physiology indicates that he experienced physiological symptoms of anxiety (tightness in chest) on the way to the hospital. Jack misattributed the physical sensations leading to the belief (delusion) that he was being externally controlled by a device. The diagrammatical linear formulation in Figure 3.2 provides illustration of this.

Since this incident Jack had remained hypervigilant, leading to the accumulation of substantial evidence to confirm his delusion, serving only to increase his anxiety and maintain cognitive distortions (confirmatory bias). Jack's level of anxiety was further maintained by avoidance of situ-ations or social encounters he perceived would activate 'the device'. The safety behaviours intermittently reduced his emotional discomfort; how-ever, they maintained his delusion and prevented him from unearthing evidence to the contrary.

It is hypothesised that his beliefs about being externally controlled served to provide a protective mechanism for his schema, enabling him to avoid situations that evoked emotional discomfort, fear and anxiety. His beliefs

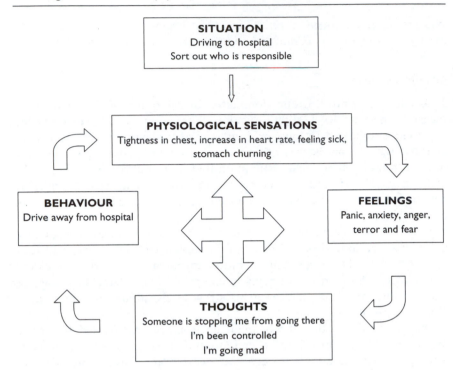

Figure 3.1 Cognitive mini-formulation of Jack's delusional thoughts

were also providing the opportunity for him to externalise and project the anger and frustration he experienced during the prolonged times he felt helpless as a child. A more detailed formulation related to maintenance of Jack's delusion is illustrated in Figure 3.2.

Process of therapy

Initially the sessions focused on allowing Jack to talk openly about his beliefs in relation to the 'device'. This enabled his experiences to be validated and helped the therapist to collate information to develop a preliminary formulation. Jack was able to identify how his beliefs were affecting his emotions and behaviours and the formulation provided ample opportunity to normalise Jack's responses. The normalising process appeared to increase the therapeutic alliance and provided a safe environment to explore his emotions.

The individual sessions continued to focus on a process of guided exploration/discovery, providing Jack with the opportunity to re-evaluate distorted cognitions and explore alternative explanations for feeling different after his operation. He came up with the following:

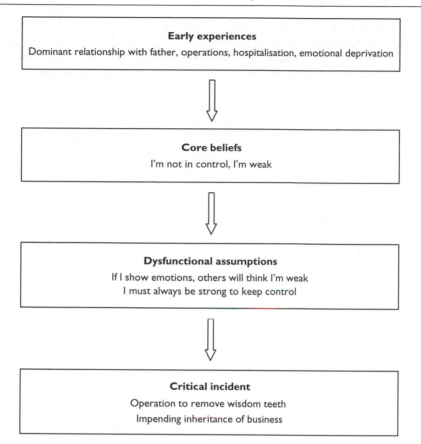

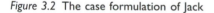

Figure 3.2 The case formulation of Jack

1   Overdose of sedatives
2   Too many antibiotics
3   No pre-op
4   Someone had drugged him.

At times he was reluctant to continue to explore these alternative explanations and attempts to continue resulted in him becoming angry with threats of discontinuing the sessions. In understanding this psychological process further the formulation indicates that when he gave consideration to alternative possibilities this activated his core beliefs of being weak and out of control. In view of this the sessions remained focused on engagement. He steered the therapy towards his agenda and need to discover who would want to control him and why. He frequently expressed his frustrations that he wanted answers which were not being found. At such times the therapist helped Jack to explore his options in dealing with his predicament when using a traditional approach to exploring alternative ways of thinking resulted in anger and disengagement. Acknowledging the emotional distress associated with his concerns was effective in gaining his trust and confidence. Jack remained very focused on wanting the device removed and helping him to explore options at this point appeared a helpful process of maintaining engagement. He demanded scans and meetings with police and his GP in an attempt to have them answer his questions and supporting him during this period improved the therapeutic relationship.

Jack's ultimate agenda for engaging became clear as the therapy progressed: he wanted the 'device removed from my chest'. However, his attempts to talk to people about this resulted in them indicating he had a mental health problem. He identified the following options in relation to his device:

1   Get it removed
2   Leave the country
3   Go to the police
4   Grin and bear it (acceptance).

The therapy continued to explore ways in which Jack could 'grin and bear' the device and he eventually reached a point where he was able to engage in experiments to test out how much control the device had.

The therapeutic relationship improved, which helped the process of therapy. Sessions focused on finding out more about the device and the times it was activated. Jack was encouraged to keep a record of device activation and we were able to explore this further using a cognitive formulation. Jack acknowledged the level of fear and anger associated with potential activation of the device and he established mechanisms for dealing with these strong emotions which appeared to reduce his overall level of arousal.

The timeline was used as a therapeutic tool to develop a collaborative formulation. Constructing a timeline involves reviewing a patient's life history from birth up to the onset of the psychosis. Eventually Jack started to talk about his relationships and emotions, expressing that it felt alien to him to 'have emotions'. Jack spent many sessions talking about his early experiences and relationship with his father and how he had felt controlled as a child.

Jack's level of distress and anxiety associated with the device decreased dramatically; although he still remains convinced that he has a tracking device in his chest, it is no longer activated and doesn't interfere with his life. Jack expresses that he has accepted the implant and has now learnt to 'grin and bear it'. The device is no longer activated several times a day and over the last six months has not been activated at all. He believes that the battery linked to the implant has now run out.

His improvements in emotional well-being are evident in all aspects of his life. Jack is busy at work and has now started to take over the family business. His level of confidence in his own abilities appears to have increased dramatically and Jack is now back to juggling the work/social life balance. Family work increased his parents' understanding of Jack's fears and his father started to involve him more in decisions in relation to the business. Jack's parents have now discovered how capable Jack is of running the business and are now retiring.

Jack and his consultant psychiatrist decided to 'disagree in relation to his beliefs' however, he recently started to take a small amount of antipsychotic medication on a daily basis and he perceives that this has helped him to cope with the emotional effects of the device. It seemed that the models involved here were of depressive attributional style (I am weak, external forces are to blame if things go wrong), anxiety and avoidance.

Conclusions

No simple model explains the emergence and maintenance of delusions in psychosis. It is likely that in any individual person the various vulnerabilities described above interact with their specific life stressors, schema profile and metacognitive style to initiate and maintain their delusion. However, a knowledge of the different models allows the use of model-congruent CBT techniques. Further research is needed on the various models described and a focus needs to be taken on single-case and cohort methodologies which will improve our understanding of which models relate to which types of delusions and which CBT techniques to use in these presentations.

References

Abu-Akel, A. and Bailey, A. L. (2000). The possibility of different forms of theory of mind. *Psychological Medicine, 30,* 735–738.

Bleuler, E. (1911). *Dementia Praecox or the group of Schizophrenias.* New York: International University Press.

Corrigan, P. W. (1998). The impact of stigma on severe mental illness. *Cognitive and Behavioural Practice, 5,* 201–222.

Freeman, D. and Garety, P. A. (1999). Worry, worry processes and dimensions of delusions: An exploratory investigation of a role for anxiety processes in the maintenance of delusional distress. *Behavioural and Cognitive Psychotherapy, 27,* 47–62.

Freeman, D., Garety, P. and Kuipers, E. (2001). Persecutory delusions: Developing the understanding of belief maintenance and emotional distress. *Psychological Medicine, 31,* 1293–1306.

Freeman, D., Garety, P., Kuipers, E., Fowler, D. and Bebbington, P. (2002). A cognitive model of persecutory delusions. *British Journal of Clinical Psychology*, *41*, 331–347.

Freeman, D., Garety, P. A., Bebbington, P. E., Smith, B., Rollinson, R., Fowler, D. and Kuipers, E. (2005). Psychological investigation of the structure of paranoia in a non-clinical population. *British Journal of Psychiatry*, *171*, 420–426.

Freeman, D., Garety, P., Kuipers, E., Fowler, D., Bebington, P. and Dunn, G. (2007). Acting on persecutory delusions: The importance of safety seeking. *Behaviour Research and Therapy*, *45*, 89–99.

Frith, C. D. (1992). *The Cognitive Neuropsychology of Schizophrenia*. Hove: Lawrence Erlbaum.

Frith, C. D. (2004). Schizophrenia and theory of mind. *Psychological Medicine*, *34*, 385–389.

Garety, P. and Freeman, D. (1999). Cognitive approaches to delusions: A critical review of theories and evidence. *British Journal of Clinical Psychology*, *38*, 113–154.

Garety, P., Kuipers, E., Fowler, D., Freeman, D. and Bebbington, P. E. (2001). Cognitive model of the positive symptoms of psychosis. *Psychological Medicine*, *31*(2), 189–195.

Hamilton, M. (1984). *Fish's Schizophrenia* (3rd ed.). Bristol: Wright.

Johns, L. C. and van Os, J. (2001). The continuity of psychotic experiences in the general population. *Clinical Psychology Review*, *21*, 1125–1141.

Kingdon, D. and Turkington D. (1994). *Cognitive Behavioural Therapy of Schizophrenia*. Guilford Press, Hove.

Kingdon, D. and Turkington, D. (1998). Cognitive behavioural therapy of schizophrenia: Styles and methods. In T. Wykes, N. Tarrier and S. Lewis (Eds.), *Outcome and Innovation in Psychological Treatment of Schizophrenia*. Chichester: Wiley.

Kingdon, D., Turkington, D. and John, C. (1994). Cognitive behaviour therapy of schizophrenia. *British Journal of Psychiatry*, *164*, 581–587.

Peters, E. and Garety, P. (2006). Cognitive functioning in delusions. *Behaviour Research and Therapy*, *44*, 481–514.

Read, J., van Os, J., Morrison, A. P. and Ross, C. A. (2005). Childhood trauma, psychosis and schizophrenia: A literature review with theoretical and clinical implications. *Acta Psychiatrica Scandinavica*, *112*, 330–350.

Roberts, G. A. (1991). Delusional systems and meaning in life – a preferred reality? *British Journal of Psychiatry*, *14*, 20–29.

Steel, C., Fowler, D. and Holmes, E. A. (2005). Trauma related intrusions and psychosis: An information processing account. *Behavioural Cognitive Psychotherapy*, *33*, 139–152.

Strauss, J. S. (1969). Hallucinations and delusions as points on continua function. *Archives of General Psychiatry*, *21*, 581–586.

Turkington, D. and Kingdon, D. G. (1991). Ordering thoughts in though disorder. *British Journal of Psychiatry*, *158*, 160–161.

Turkington, D. and Kingdon, D. G. (1996). The use of a normalizing rationale in schizophrenia. In G. Haddock and P. D. Slade (Eds.), *Cognitive Behavioural Interventions with Psychotic Disorders*. Chichester: Wiley.

Turkington, D. and Siddle, R. (1998). Cognitive therapy for the treatment of delusions. *Advances in Psychiatric Treatment*, *4*, 235–242.

Turkington, D., John, C. H., Siddle, R., Ward, D. and Birmingham, L. (1996). Cognitive therapy in the treatment of drug resistant delusional disorder. *Clinical Psychology and Psychotherapy*, *3*, 118–128.

Turkington, D., Martindale, B. and Bloch-Thorsen, G. R. (2005). Schizophrenia. In G. Gabbard, J. S. Beck and J. Holmes (Eds.), *Oxford Textbook of Psychotherapy*. Oxford: Oxford University Press.

van Dael, F., Versmissen, D., Janssen, I., Myin-Germeys, I., van Os, J. and Krabbendam, L. (2006). Data gathering: Biased in psychosis? *Schizophrenia Bulletin*, *32*, 341–351.

Chapter 4

Assessment for symptoms of psychosis

Emmanuelle Peters

Introduction

The term psychosis is used clinically as a generic term to refer to the positive symptoms of psychotic disorders, namely unusual beliefs (delusions) and anomalous experiences (hallucinations and other perceptual abnormalities), as well as disturbances of thought and language. Recent years have seen a growing and fruitful debate on the merits of using a symptom-based approach to psychosis instead of the traditional diagnostic categories favoured by the medical profession (Bentall, 2003; van Os *et al.*, 1999). Assessment tools in psychosis reflect these developments in the academic literature, as well as the recent mushrooming of cognitive behavioural interventions for individuals with distressing psychotic experiences. In this chapter the assessment of psychosis will be considered in terms of: (1) symptom-based measures, with an emphasis on hallucinations and delusions; (2) important areas of assessment in cognitive behavioural therapy (CBT) for psychosis. Two different assessment approaches will be illustrated with two case studies.

Symptom measures

The recent symptom approach has led to the emergence of a number of self-report scales and interviews concentrating on single symptom dimensions. The most widely used currently is the Psychotic Symptom Rating Scales (PSYRATS; Haddock *et al.*, 1999), which is a semi-structured interview measuring psychological dimensions, rather than categorical types, of delusions and hallucinations. The auditory hallucinations subscale has 11 items (including frequency, intensity, duration, disruption and beliefs about origin and control), and the delusion subscale has six items (including conviction, preoccupation, disruption to functioning, and distress). All items are rated by the interviewer on a five-point ordinal scale. The PSYRATS is the most useful scale currently available to assess dimensional change in psychosis, although the ordinal scales for some of the items lack sensitivity to change, e.g. one rating for delusional conviction spans 51–100 per cent. The Personal Questionnaires (PQs; Brett-Jones *et al.*, 1987) also assess psychological dimensions such as conviction, preoccupation and distress for delusions, and frequency, intensity and distress for hallucinations. PQs differ from other questionnaire forms in that they are devised for each individual, using that person's words to describe their beliefs, experiences or feelings.

Delusions-specific measures

In addition to the PSYRATS, measures to assess delusions specifically include the Maudsley Assessment of Delusions Schedule (MADS; Buchanan *et al.*, 1993), the Delusions-Symptoms-States Inventory – Revised (DSSI-R; Foulds and Bedford, 1975), the Brown Assessment of Beliefs Scale (BABS; Eisen *et al.*, 1998), and the Conviction of Delusional Beliefs Scale (CDBS; Combs *et al.*, 2006), each focusing on different aspects of delusions.

The MADS is an in-depth interview covering various aspects of delusional phenomenology, including conviction, belief maintenance factors, affect related to beliefs, action, preoccupation, systematisation, and insight. Although it is a lengthy interview, particular sections can be used in isolation. The two most important aspects for psychological intervention purposes are "reaction to hypothetical contradiction", and "accommodation", which assess potential or actual impact of information incompatible with the person's delusion.

The DSSI-R is a self-report inventory based on Foulds and Bedford's (1975) four hierarchical classes of personal illness (with dysthymic states at the bottom of the hierarchy, followed by neurotic symptoms, integrated delusions, and delusions of disintegration). The integrated delusions consist of delusions of persecution, grandeur, and contrition, and the delusions of disintegration stand alone at the top of the hierarchy (seven items for each type of delusion). They are scored in terms of True–False responses with an added conviction rating. This scale is not widely used in clinical practice, and individuals with delusions other than the four types included in the scale would not score on it. However, it can be useful as a general psychopathology scale for individuals who have difficulties in verbal communication.

The BABS is a clinician-administered scale designed to assess 'delusionality' of beliefs across a wide range of psychiatric disorders, for instance obsessive compulsive disorder, body dysmorphia, mood disorders with psychotic features, anorexia nervosa, etc. The dominant belief (obsession, concern, idea, worry, or delusion) is first elicited, and seven items related to the belief are assessed by specific probes and scored on a five-point scale ranging from non-delusional/least pathological to delusional/most pathological. The seven items consist of conviction, perception of others' views of beliefs, explanation of differing views, fixity of ideas, attempt to disprove beliefs, insight, and ideas/delusions of reference. Finally, the CDBS assesses the dimension of delusional conviction specifically, incorporating cognitive, emotional, and behavioural items.

A number of other scales were designed to measure delusional ideation and paranoia in the general population. The Peters *et al.* Delusions Inventory (40-item PDI; Peters *et al.*, 1999b; 21-item PDI; Peters *et al.*, 2004) is based on the Present State Examination (Wing *et al.*, 1974), and also assesses levels of distress, preoccupation and conviction on a five-point scale for each item endorsed. Other measures have concentrated on specific types of delusional thinking, such as the Magical Ideation Scale (Eckblad and Chapman, 1986), which assesses predominantly superstitious thinking, and the Referential Thinking Scale (Lenzenweger *et al.*, 1997).

The assessment of paranoia has generated the greatest number of scales. The Paranoia Scale (Fenigstein and Vanable, 1992) and the Paranoia and Suspiciousness Questionnaire (PSQ; Rawlings and Freeman, 1996) were designed to measure paranoia in college students, although some of the items are not persecutory and relate more to the self-consciousness and interpersonal difficulties typical of neurotic disorders. The Persecutory Ideation Questionnaire (PIQ; McKay *et al.*, 2006) is a ten-item scale, constructed to tap more specifically into ideas of persecution, rather than the broader concept covered by paranoia. From a slightly different perspective, Morrison *et al.* (2005) developed a self-report measure to assess metacognitive beliefs about paranoia, which includes four factors: negative beliefs about paranoia, beliefs about paranoia as a survival strategy, general positive beliefs, and normalising beliefs.

Freeman and his colleagues have published a number of paranoia measures. The Paranoia Checklist (Freeman *et al.*, 2005) was designed to investigate paranoid thoughts of a more clinical nature than the Paranoia Scale, and to provide a multidimensional assessment of paranoid ideation. All items are rated on a five-point scale for frequency, conviction, and distress. Freeman *et al.* (2007) also published the State Social Paranoia Scale to assess state paranoia specifically, which they suggest will be useful in experimental studies wanting to investigate moment-by-moment variations in paranoia. The most comprehensive measure of paranoia to date is the Green *et al.* Paranoid Thoughts Scale (Green *et al.*, 2007), which assesses ideas of social reference and persecution. Similarly to the PDI, it also incorporates dimensions of conviction, distress and preoccupation.

Hallucinations-specific measures

In addition to the PSYRATS, measures to assess hallucinations specifically include the Auditory Hallucinations Record Form (AHRF; Slade, 1972) and Self-Report Form (Hustig and Hafner, 1990), and the Mental Health

Research Institute Unusual Perceptions Schedule (MUPS; Carter *et al.*, 1995). A number of measures also exist to measure hallucinations in the general population, namely the Launay-Slade Hallucination Scale (LSHS; Launay and Slade, 1981), the Structured Interview for Assessing Perceptual Anomalies (SIAPA; Bunney *et al.*, 1999), and the Cardiff Anomalous Perceptions Scale (CAPS; Bell *et al.*, 2006).

The AHRF was designed to identify triggers to voices, and needs to be completed over a period of a few weeks. The patient records on the form, at pre-determined times, the presence/absence of voices, their intensity, a series of subjectively assessed environmental variables (e.g. noise, people, activity), mood state and 15 semantic differential scales to assess the "quality" of the voices. Hustig and Hafner's Self-Report Form assesses dimensions of hallucinatory experience on visual analogue scales. It includes loudness, clarity, distress and distractibility of the voices, and mood and delusional conviction are also self-rated.

The MUPS is a comprehensive instrument developed to record people's experiences of auditory hallucinations as completely as possible. The schedule comprises a semi-structured interview and documents the physical characteristics of auditory hallucinations, including their onset and course, number, volume, tone, location, as well as other phenomena associated with them, such as delusions. In addition, other aspects of hallucinations, such as coping strategies, contributing factors and patients' personal views and reactions are also explored. It is too lengthy to be used in routine clinical practice, but subsections can be used independently.

The LSHS has been used extensively in research looking at hallucinatory activity in the general population, and is a relatively brief (12 items) scale measuring visual and auditory hallucinations, as well as the vividness and intrusiveness of cognitive experiences. More recent scales have broadened their remit to include other sensory modalities. SIAPA is a structured interview to assess subtle perceptual and attentional anomalies distinct from hallucinations across sensory modalities (auditory, visual, tactile, olfactory, and gustatory). It is useful for research purposes, but the five-point rating scale is problematic (jumps from never and rarely, to half the time, often and always). The CAPS is a more useful scale for assessing anomalous perceptions in all modalities (Bell *et al.*, 2006). The CAPS is the hallucinations version of the PDI, and includes subscales measuring distress, intrusiveness, and frequency.

An important dimension of hallucinations is the beliefs people hold about their voices (Chadwick and Birchwood, 1994). The Beliefs about Voices Questionnaire – Revised (BAVQ–R; Chadwick *et al.*, 2000) and the Cognitive Assessment of Voices Interview Schedule (CAVIS; Chadwick *et al.*, 1996) assess this dimension specifically. The BAVQ–R consists of 35 items with five subscales relating to voices' identity (malevolence/ benevolence) and power (omnipotence), and consequences of obedience (engagement/resistance), rated on a four-point scale. The CAVIS enquires about the voice, the individual's feelings and behaviour in relation to the voice, and his or her beliefs about the voice's identity, power, purpose or meaning, and about the likely consequences of obedience and disobedience. The CAVIS can be useful to use as a guideline for the clinical assessment of an individual hearing voices. Morrison *et al.* (2002) have also designed a scale to measure interpretations of voices, for use in non-clinical populations – the Interpretations of Voices Inventory (IVI). It has three subscales relating to positive beliefs about voices, metaphysical beliefs about voices, and interpretations of loss of control.

A number of measures have been used specifically with command hallucinations. The Voice Acceptance and Action Scale (VAAS; Shawyer *et al.*, 2007) is a 31-item instrument designed to measure the psychological impact of hallucinations. It assesses acceptance-based attitudes and actions (derived from Action and Commitment Therapy; Hayes *et al.*, 1999) in relation to auditory and command hallucinations. Birchwood *et al.* have also proposed a number of assessments to capture compliance with commands (the Voice Compliance Scale; Trower *et al.*, 2004) and perceived power of the voices (Voice Power Differential Scale; Birchwood *et al.*, 2004).

The "Interview with a person who hears voices" (Romme and Escher, 2000) is a clinical tool based on Romme and Escher's and the Hearing Voices Network's "empowerment" model. The interview is comprehensive, but can be used in parts. Although it has a high utility factor to guide the assessment process within a clinical context, there are no data available on reliability or other psychometric properties. Subsections include the nature of the experience; characteristics of the voices; personal history of hearing voices; triggers; content of voices; beliefs re origin of voices; impact of voices on quality of life; relationship with voices; coping strategies; childhood experiences; treatment history; and social network.

One other measure, the La Trobe University "Coping with Auditory Hallucinations" Interview Schedule (Farhall and Gehrke, 1997), is worth mentioning, although it has not been used particularly widely since its publication. It consists of a rather lengthy structured interview concentrating on how patients cope with their hallucinations, based on the Lazarus and Folkman (1984) theoretical framework of stress and coping.

Thought-disorder-specific measures

Thought disorder has not received as much attention as delusions and hallucinations in the research literature, and this is reflected by the smaller number of scales available. The only widely used scales are the Scale for the Assessment of Thought, Language and Communication (Andreasen, 1986), where ratings are made during a psychiatric interview, and the Comprehensive Index of Positive Thought Disorder (Marengo *et al.*, 1986), which uses the comprehension subtest of the WAIS-R and a proverbs test to elucidate bizarre thinking.

Negative-symptoms-specific scales

Similarly, apart from general psychiatric measures, there are few specific negative symptoms scales. One notable exception is the Subjective Experience of Negative Symptoms Scale (SENS; Selten *et al.*, 1993), which is a self-rating scale measuring the severity and related distress of negative symptoms as perceived by the person. It requires respondents to compare themselves with others of their own age on a number of indices of motivation, enthusiasm and social function, and to rate their distress with their perceived level of function. Otherwise, clinical researchers have used assessment tools measuring social functioning and quality of life, both related to negative symptoms.

Single scores can be obtained from the Global Assessment of Functioning Scale (GAF; DSM-III-R, APA, 1987), and an adapted version of the GAF, the Social and Occupational Functioning Assessment Scale (SOFAS; Goldman *et al.*, 1992). The Social Behaviour Scale (Wykes and Sturt, 1986) covers 21 items that measure the behavioural consequences of symptoms, chosen because they were identified as providing a barrier to successful resettlement in the community. The items are rated from information provided by a key informant, on a five-point scale. The scale can be used to provide an overall score by adding up all items that score two or more points, or it can be used to monitor change using the individual five-point scale ratings. The Social Functioning Scale (Birchwood *et al.*, 1990) measures social performance in a number of areas. It can be completed by the client, a carer, or a key worker (different forms are available), and norms are given for comparable samples (e.g. the unemployed).

Quality of life scales are numerous, but tend to be too lengthy for use with psychotic populations. One exception is the Manchester Short Assessment of Quality of Life (MANSA; Priebe *et al.*, 1999), which assesses satisfaction in areas such as employment, finances, leisure, friendships, relationships, accommodation and physical and mental health.

Cognitive behavioural therapy for psychosis

The two most important areas to identify when working psychologically with psychotic individuals are the distressing experiences they bring to the therapy, and the sense they make of them, i.e. what "model" or perspective they have about their experiences. From the start of the assessment it is vital to use the person's own terminology for their psychotic experiences, rather than using psychiatric jargon such as "voices" or "delusions". For instance, the person may not recognise that they are "hearing voices" if what they are hearing is their father talking to them, or are hearing spirits accompanied by their visual appearance. Words such as "schizophrenia" or "mental illness" may be offensive to the person and should not be used unless the person is happy with a medical model explanation.

Throughout the assessment it is crucial to remember that the ultimate goal of the therapist is to try to understand, rather than to try to make the person change their mind by challenging the reality of their voices and delusions. Rather than challenging, empathy with the distress caused by the experiences is an important therapeutic tool in early stages of assessment and engagement.

The "funnel" method of assessment is a useful model to follow. In the first instance an overview assessment of distressing experiences is carried out, which might include positive and negative symptoms, as well as emotional disorders and general quality of life. Once specific problems have been identified, they can then be assessed in more depth.

For hallucinations, a useful place to start is by identifying the physical characteristics of the voices (although note that hallucinations in other modalities are also common: visions, and somatic and tactile hallucinations). Important factors include the frequency of the voices, and their duration, loudness, number, location, and type. The content of the voices should be identified, although some clients may not be ready to disclose this until trust in the therapist has been established, for instance if the content of the voices is shaming or dangerous. The PSYRATS (Haddock *et al.*, 1999) or Romme and Escher's (2000) "Interview with a person who hears voices" can be useful guides for this part of the assessment. An ABC assessment will also be helpful, i.e. identifying antecedents or triggers, and consequences. Triggers can be both environmental (where, when, etc.) and internal or emotional (e.g. anxiety). Consequences to look out for should be both behavioural and emotional, with additional focus on the general impact on functioning. The extent to which people resist or comply with their voices, especially in the case of command hallucinations, is an important factor to identity. Voice diaries can be useful to identify the ABCs outside of the sessions.

It is also crucial to assess the beliefs people hold about their voices (Chadwick and Birchwood, 1994), since much of the psychological work will attempt to modify those beliefs to reduce emotional distress and enhance feelings of control, rather than reducing the frequency of hallucinations per se. Crucial dimensions include the identity (Who are they? Are they beneficial or harmful?), the perceived cause (What causes them?), their power (How powerful are they?), and control (How much control do they have over the voices? How much control do the voices have over them?). The type of relationship the person has with his or her voices is also a key feature (Birchwood *et al.*, 2000). Again, useful guides for the cognitive and interpersonal aspects of voices include Romme and Escher's (2000) "Interview with a person who hears voices" and the PSYRATS, as well as Chadwick et al.'s (1996) Cognitive Assessment of Voices Interview Schedule.

It is important to view delusions as lying on more than one dimension rather than being all-or-nothing false beliefs (Peters et al., 1999a). Once the content and number of delusions have been identified, the crucial dimensions to assess are conviction (How much do they believe it?), preoccupation (How much time do they think about it?), distress (How upsetting are the beliefs?), and disability (What impact does it have on their lives?). The PSYRATS covers these dimensions, or, alternatively, patients can be asked to rate conviction, preoccupation, and distress on a scale of 0–100 per cent, or any kind of Likert scale, on a session-by-session basis.

Similarly to voices, delusions are often inextricably linked with emotional factors (Freeman and Garety, 2003) and potential maintaining factors, such as safety behaviours, should also be identified. Delusions, especially those of a persecutory or grandiose nature, can also be linked with self-esteem, and such associations should be explored before attempting to reframe the beliefs. The links may be either direct (i.e. reflecting low self-esteem; Freeman et al., 1998) or indirect (i.e. protecting against low self-esteem; Bentall et al., 2001). Finally, it can be useful to assess cognitive flexibility about delusions (i.e. the extent to which the client is willing to entertain the idea that there may be an alternative explanation, even if alternative explanations are not actually available to the client), since there is some preliminary evidence that flexibility is associated with good outcome in cognitive behavioural therapy (Garety et al., 1997).

In clinical practice there are no clear-cut distinctions between engagement, assessment and intervention in psychological interventions for psychosis, with engagement and assessment remaining key therapeutic factors throughout therapy. In terms of evaluating the outcome of therapy, the PSYRATS is the most useful scale to measure psychotic symptom change. However, additional areas should also be evaluated, such as emotional problems, functioning, and quality of life, as well as satisfaction with therapy. A recent measure, CHOICE (CHoice of Outcome In Cognitive behavioural therapy for the psychosEs; Greenwood et al., 2010), has been developed specifically to cover a wider area of outcomes than merely symptom change. It was designed in consultation with service users, with the aim of deriving a new service-user-focused outcome measure that more closely reflects the priorities of service users and the aims of cognitive behavioural therapy for psychosis. It includes 24 potential outcome items, rated on a ten-point scale on dimensions of severity and satisfaction. Outcome items include "The ability to approach problems in a variety of ways"; "Knowing I am not the only person who has unusual experiences"; "The ability to step back from overwhelming experiences (e.g. thoughts or voices)"; "The ability to question the way I look at things"; "Facing my own upsetting thoughts and feelings"; "Understanding myself and my past"; "A positive purpose and direction in life"; and two further individual goals of therapy.

Summary of areas of assessment for cognitive behavioural therapy for psychosis

1   Delusion-specific
   i   Content
   ii   Conviction, preoccupation, distress
   iii   Behavioural impact
   iv   Initial formation (e.g. life events)
   v   Day-to-day examples
   vi   Triggers and consequences (ABCs)
   vii   Coping strategies
   viii Clarify thoughts/beliefs/emotions/behaviours (within context of internal/external events, and what is psychotic and what is normal)
   ix   Maintenance factors (including other psychotic symptoms, emotional processes, safety behaviours, environment, and drug and alcohol abuse)
   x   Change over time (including adaptation to symptoms)
   xi   Meaning of belief (for self and others)
   xii   View of self without delusions (e.g. being persecuted may be better than being mad)
   xiii Develop hierarchy of distressing beliefs (if necessary)
2   Voice-specific
   i   Triggers: environmental (where, when, etc.) and internal or emotional (e.g. anxiety)
   ii   Consequences: behavioural and emotional, as well as general impact on functioning
   iii   Frequency
   iv   Content
   v   Number
   vi   Location
   vii   Type
   viii Resistance vs compliance with the voices
   ix   Coping strategies
   x   Beliefs about voices:
         a   identity (who are they? Are they beneficial or harmful?)
         b   cause/origin (what causes them? Where do they come from?)
         c   power (how powerful are they?)
         d   control (how much control do they have over the voices?)

3   Psychosis-specific
   i   Cognitive biases: jumping to conclusions, theory of mind deficits, attributional biases (personal or externalising bias, but also normal biases in belief formation)
   ii   Cognitive deficits (difficulties in concentration, memory, planning, and ability to manage complex information)
   iii   Illness model
   iv   Attitude towards medication
   v   Risk (for instance, of complying with voices, of acting on delusions)

4   Person-specific
   i   Personal beliefs (e.g. religion)
   ii   Relationship with services
   iii   Social support and social relationships
   iv   Short- and long-term goals and plans
   v   Core beliefs, dysfunctional assumptions and schemas (sometimes)
   vi   Life history (sometimes)
   vii   Daily activities

5   Secondary disturbances
   i   Other emotional problems (low mood, anxiety, worry, intrusive thoughts)
   ii   Cognitive distortions (as found in depression and anxiety)
   iii   Substance use

6   Look out for
   i   Reaction to hypothetical contradiction (some flexibility about delusions potential is a predictor of good outcome)
   ii   Accommodation (i.e. incorporation of experiences into delusion)
   iii   Cognitive flexibility

Case examples

The first example below is an assessment report illustrating how a combination of standardised scales can be used to assess overall presentation in a number of areas, giving some indication of specific difficulties that can then be followed up with a more thorough CBT assessment. There are a number of advantages to using standardised measures. Such an assessment can be carried out routinely by an assistant clinical psychologist before therapy starts, saving the therapist time, so that they can concentrate on engagement and proceed directly to a CBT assessment. Alternatively the measures can provide a useful guide of areas to cover for novice clinicians. The assessment described below provides a useful combination of qualitative and quantitative data that can be easily communicated to referrers or other members of the multidisciplinary team. Importantly, a repeat assessment at the end of therapy allows for an objective evaluation of the outcome of therapy. The second example does not involve the use of standardised assessments, but illustrates a thorough CBT assessment of auditory hallucinations.

Case example 1: General assessment using a variety of standardised measures

Thank you for referring X for cognitive behavioural therapy. This report summarises the findings of the initial assessment, which was carried out using a range of standardised measures. The assessment will be repeated at the end of therapy to report on any changes made during therapy.

X engaged cooperatively with the assessment process, and maintained good eye contact and concentration. However, he clearly found talking about his experiences distressing, and became tearful on a number of occasions.

The PSYRATS–Beliefs questionnaire (total score = 19) revealed that X believes people are plotting against him. He fears that people are "playing with his mind" and talk in codes, with their conversations with him being peppered with "hidden meanings". He rated his conviction as 50 per cent, in the sense that at times he is able to refer to these events as "distressing thoughts", while at other times he believes them with 100 per cent absolute conviction, depending on what is happening and how he is feeling. Although the thoughts are always there in the background, he has varying amounts of control over them. When the thoughts "come to the surface" he feels guilty and believes he deserves to be punished. When they occur they last for hours or days at a time, are extremely distressing, and cause a moderate amount of disruption to his life. For instance, he reports not answering the telephone because he feels people are using the phone to play with his mind, and isolating himself from friends and family to try not to trigger the onset of the thoughts. He is currently on sick leave from work, although with the support of his wife he feels he is able to manage in the community.

X did not describe any experiences of voices so the PSYRATS–Voices questionnaire was not administered.

In terms of general distress, X scored 39 on the Beck Depression Inventory and 49 on the Beck Anxiety Inventory, placing him in the severe range for both depression and anxiety. His responses on the Beck Depression Inventory indicated that he has feelings of guilt and of being punished, as well as blaming himself for everything bad that happens. Although he has felt suicidal in the past, he is not considering suicide at the moment. On the Beck Anxiety Inventory X reported suffering from panic attacks (with two attacks in the last month), being unable to relax, and fearing the worst happening. His responses on the Beck Cognitive Insight Scale indicated that he recognises that sometimes he jumps to conclusions too fast, and is willing to consider other perspectives on his problems.

On the SENS, X described feeling little motivation to do things and having low energy levels, although he still manages to keep busy during the day. He reported needing little contact with other people, because he feels people play with his mind, but needing lots of contact with his wife.

The MANSA revealed that overall he has mixed feelings about his life. He is dissatisfied with his employment and friendships, as he has become very isolated from his friends. He is very dissatisfied with his mental health, but is satisfied with his physical health. He is satisfied with his relationship with his wife and his accommodation.

X is keen to engage in therapy. On the CHOICE questionnaire he identified a number of goals for therapy, specifically getting rid of his distressing thoughts, reducing his isolation, and regaining his strength and confidence.

Case example 2: A cognitive behavioural therapy assessment of auditory hallucinations

1   *Physical characteristics*: X's voices consist of men, women and children, some of whom she recognises (e.g. parents, sister), and some she does not. One particular female voice is predominant, and they feel "familiar" to her although she does not know them "face to face". They tend to be fairly loud, and she can communicate back to them with her brain. They also sometimes speak to other people (e.g. her Mum and Dad), although she recognises that they do not hear the voices.

2   *Content*: The voices are invariably nasty, and say things such as "She's having us on"; "We'd be pleased to get rid of her"; and "She's showing off". Sometimes they threaten her with physical violence, e.g. "We'll beat you up", or threaten to harm others, e.g. her parents. They also sometimes tell her to do things, usually trivial things such as not watching television. Their most common theme of abuse concerns her continuing unemployment, which she feels ashamed about, and seems to be a large contributor to her low self-worth. She does report them being somewhat nicer since her inpatient admission.

3   *Antecedents*: X found it difficult to identify any potential antecedents involved in triggering the voices, since she hears them almost continuously. However, they are worse when she is at home, and although they get better if she goes out they will be even worse on her return, so most of the time she will avoid going out. When going to new places they also tend to get better, although they usually come back after a while, so that she worries constantly about them coming back even if she does not hear them. They also seem to be influenced by her emotional states, inasmuch as she describes that they can react to the way

she is feeling, e.g. if she is in a depressed state they will say "We'd be pleased to get rid of her", while if she is in a happy state they will say "She's showing off".

4   *Emotional impact*: X describes how they put her in a "funny frame of mind", that she becomes "depressed" (e.g. sometimes tearful, sometimes angry), that they "just wear her down" and that they cause "mental strain". She also describes how they make her "a not nice person", both because they do not like her being nice, and because they put her in a funny frame of mind, which in turn leads to her not being a nice person. She is also genuinely scared of them, describing how she sometimes locks all the windows and doors because they say they are going to get her. Overall they give her no peace of mind – every day is a struggle.

5   *Behavioural impact*: Her voices appear to be the main reason for her isolation. She does act on them, but usually only in relation to trivial things such as not watching TV. She also tends to go to bed early to get rest from her voices. She has in the past confronted her neighbours, as she felt it may be them saying things to her rather than voices. She also feels that her voices lead to her checking (X also has an obsessive compulsive disorder problem), inasmuch as she has to constantly be "on guard" and feel her "mind is clear" (which she achieves through checking), otherwise the voices get worse.

6   *Beliefs about voices*: X is confused about the voices' origin. On the one hand her beliefs about demons and Satan (she is a Jehovah's Witness) would accommodate the voices being demons, however she has never done anything which would have summoned them (such as doing a Weegee board), so she cannot reconcile herself to them being actual demons. On the other hand, although she is willing to say that "there is probably something wrong with her brain", this is more because that is what other people have told her rather than her own belief. She does believe that they have power over her ("They are stronger than I am") and have malevolent intentions towards her. She does not feel there is anything she can do to control them. They are omniscient in the sense that they react to how she thinks, and although she at times resists them she believes that if she does not obey them they will just get worse and worse. She describes how they feel so real it is hard to believe other people do not hear them.

7   *Coping strategies*: It was difficult to elicit any coping strategies since she reports there is nothing she can do as her voices are so overwhelming. She finds going to bed helpful, and going to her sister's but, as mentioned above, they get worse when she returns. She also finds that she hardly hears them when on holiday, although again she spends her time worrying about them coming back (and developing new ones) on her return. Nevertheless, she does still go to her sister's and on holiday

for a "mind rest", but avoids all other types of going out. She also described how seeing a psychologist previously gave her "mind rest" at least for the hour that she spent in the session. She finds it impossible to distract herself from them, and things like listening to music on headphones make them worse. Getting angry and shouting back at them also makes them worse.

8 *Goals*: X could not envisage how therapy would help with the voices. However, she would like to use therapy to increase her confidence and self-esteem, with the ultimate goal of getting a job and "just having a normal life".

References

Andreasen, N. (1986). Scale for the assessment of thought, language and communication. *Schizophrenia Bulletin*, *12*, 473–482.

American Psychiatric Association (APA) (1987). *Diagnostic and Statistical Manual of Mental Disorders (DSM-III-R)* (3rd ed. revised). Washington, DC: APA.

Bell, V., Ellis, H. and Halligan, P. W. (2006). The Cardiff Anomalous Perception Scale: A new validated measure of anomalous experience. *Schizophrenia Bulletin*, *32*, 366–377.

Bentall, R. P. (2003). *Madness explained*. Penguin: London.

Bentall, R. P., Corcoran, R., Howard, R., Blackwood, N. and Kinderman, P. (2001). Persecutory delusions: A review and theoretical integration. *Clinical Psychology Review*, *21*, 1143–1192.

Birchwood, M., Smith, T., Cochrane, R., Wetton, S. and Copestake, S. (1990). The Social Functioning Scale. *British Journal of Psychiatry*, *157*, 853–859.

Birchwood, M., Meaden, A., Trower, P., Gilbert, P. and Plaistow, J. (2000). The power and omnipotence of voices: Subordination and entrapment by voices and significant others. *Psychological Medicine*, *30*, 337–344.

Birchwood, M., Gilbert, P., Trower, P., Meaden, A., Hays, J., Murray, E. *et al.* (2004). The relationship with the dominant voice in voice hearers: A comparison of three models. *Psychological Medicine*, *34*, 1572–1580.

Brett-Jones, J., Garety, P. A. and Hemsley, D. (1987). Measuring delusional experiences: A method and its application. *British Journal of Clinical Psychology*, *26*, 257–265.

Buchanan, A., Reed, A., Wessely, S., Garety, P., Taylor, P., Grubin, D. and Dunn, G. (1993). Acting on delusions. II: The phenomenological correlates of acting on delusions. *British Journal of Psychiatry*, *163*, 77–81.

Bunney, W., Hetrick, W., Bunney, B., Patterson, J., Jin, Y., Potkin, S. and Sandman, C. (1999). Structured Interview for Assessing Perceptual Anomalies (SIAPA). *Schizophrenia Bulletin*, *25*, 577–592.

Carter, D., Mackinnon, A., Howard, S., Zeegers, T. and Copolov, D. L. (1995). The development and reliability of the Mental Health Research Institute unusual perceptions schedule (MUPS): An instrument to record auditory hallucinatory experience. *Schizophrenia Research*, *16*, 157–165.

Chadwick, P. and Birchwood, M. (1994). The omnipotence of voices: A cognitive approach to auditory hallucinations. *British Journal of Psychiatry, 164*, 190–201.

Chadwick, P., Birchwood, M. and Trower, P. (1996). *Cognitive therapy for delusions, voices and paranoia.* Chichester: John Wiley & Sons.

Chadwick, P., Lees, S. and Birchwood, M. (2000). The revised Beliefs About Voices Questionnaire (BAVQ-R). *British Journal of Psychiatry, 177*, 229–232.

Combs, D. R., Adams, S. D., Michael, C. O., Penn, D. L., Basso, M. R. and Gouvier, W. D. (2006). The conviction of delusional beliefs scale: Reliability and validity. *Schizophrenia Research, 86*, 80–88.

Eckblad, M. and Chapman, L. J. (1986). Development and validation of a scale for hypomanic personality. *Journal of Abnormal Psychology, 95*, 217-233.

Eisen, J., Phillips, K., Baer, L., Beer, D., Atala, K. and Rasmussen, S. (1998). The Brown Assessment of Beliefs Scale: Reliability and validity. *American Journal of Psychiatry, 155*, 102–108.

Farhall, J. and Gehrke, M. (1997). Coping with hallucinations: Exploring stress and coping framework. *British Journal of Clinical Psychology, 36*, 259–261.

Fenigstein, A. and Vanable, P. A. (1992). Paranoia and self-consciousness. *Journal of Personality and Social Psychology, 62*, 129–138.

Foulds, G. A. and Bedford, A. (1975). Hierarchy of classes of personal illness. *Psychological Medicine, 5*, 181–192.

Freeman, D. and Garety, P. A. (2003). Connecting neurosis and psychosis: The direct influence of emotion on delusions and hallucinations. *Behaviour Research and Therapy, 41*, 923–947.

Freeman, D., Garety, P., Fowler, D., Kuipers, E., Dunn, G., Bebbington, P. and Hadley, C. (1998). The London–East Anglia randomised controlled trial of cognitive behaviour therapy for psychosis. IV: Self-esteem and persecutory delusions. *British Journal of Clinical Psychology, 37*, 415–430.

Freeman, D., Garety, P. A., Bebbington, P. E., Smith, B., Rollinson, R., Fowler, D., Kuipers, E., Ray, K. and Dunn, G. (2005). Psychological investigation of the structure of paranoia in a non-clinical population. *British Journal of Psychiatry, 186*, 427–435.

Freeman, D., Pugh, K., Green, C., Valmaggia, L., Dunn, G. and Garety, P. A. (2007). A measure of state persecutory ideation for experimental studies. *Journal of Nervous and Mental Disease, 195*, 781–784.

Garety, P. A., Fowler, D., Kuipers, E., Freeman, D., Dunn, G., Bebbington, P., Hadley, C. and Jones, S. (1997). London–East Anglia randomised controlled trial of cognitive behavioural therapy for psychosis. II: Predictors of outcome. *British Journal of Psychiatry, 171*, 420–426.

Goldman, H. H., Skodol, A. E. and Lave, T. R. (1992). Revising Axis V for DSM-IV: A review of measures of social functioning. *American Journal of Psychiatry, 149*, 1148–1156.

Green, C. E. L., Freeman, D., Kuipers, E., Bebbington, P., Fowler, D., Dunn, G. and Garety, P. A. (2007). Measuring ideas of persecution and social reference: The Green *et al.* Paranoid Thoughts Scale (GPTS). *Psychological Medicine, 38*, 101–111.

Greenwood, K. E., Sweeney, A., Williams, S., Kuipers, E., Garety, P., Scott J. and Peters, E. (2010). CHoice of Outcome In Cbt for psychosEs (CHOICE): The development of a new service-user-led outcome measure of CBT for Psychosis. *Schizophrenia Bulletin, 36,* 126–135.

Haddock, G., McCarron, J., Tarrier, N. and Faragher, E. B. (1999). Scales to measure dimensions of hallucinations and delusions: The psychotic symptom rating scales (PSYRATS). *Psychological Medicine, 29,* 879–889.

Hayes, S. C., Strosahl, K. D. and Wilson, K. G. (1999). Acceptance and commitment therapy: An experiential approach to behavior change. New York: The Guilford Press.

Hustig, H. H. and Hafner, R. J. (1990). Persistent auditory hallucinations and their relationship to delusions and mood. *Journal of Neurology and Mental Disorders, 178,* 264–267.

Launay, G. and Slade, P. D. (1981). The measurement of hallucinatory predisposition in male and female prisoners. *Personality and Individual Differences, 2,* 221–234.

Lazarus, R. S. and Folkman, S. (1984). *Stress, appraisal and coping.* New York: Springer Publishing Company.

Lenzenweger, M. F., Bennett, M. E. and Lilenfeld, L. R. (1997). The Referential Thinking Scale as a measure of schizotypy: Scale development and initial construct validation. *Psychological Assessment, 9,* 452–463.

McKay, R., Langdon, R. and Coltheart, M. (2006). The Persecutory Ideation Questionnaire. *Journal of Nervous and Mental Disease, 194,* 628–631.

Marengo, J., Harrow, M., Lanin-Kettering, I. and Wilson, A. (1986). Comprehensive Index of Thought Disorder. *Schizophrenia Bulletin, 12,* 497–509.

Morrison, A. P., Wells, A. and Nothard, S. (2002). Cognitive and emotional predictors of predisposition to hallucinations in non patients. *British Journal of Clinical Psychology, 41,* 259–270.

Morrison, A. P., Gumley, A. I., Schwannauer, M., Campbell, M., Gleeson, A., Griffin, E. and Gillan, K. (2005). The Beliefs about Paranoia Scale: Preliminary validation of a metacognitive approach to conceptualising paranoia. *Behavioural and Cognitive Psychotherapy, 33,* 153–164.

Peters, E. R., Day, S., McKenna, J. and Orbach, G. (1999a). The incidence of delusional ideation in religious and psychotic populations. *British Journal of Clinical Psychology, 38,* 83–96.

Peters, E. R., Joseph, S. and Garety, P. A. (1999b). The assessment of delusions in normal and psychotic populations: Introducing the PDI (Peters *et al.* Delusions Inventory). *Schizophrenia Bulletin, 25,* 553–576.

Peters, E. R., Joseph, S., Day, S. and Garety, P. A. (2004). Measuring delusional ideation: The 21-item PDI (Peters *et al.* Delusions Inventory). *Schizophrenia Bulletin, 30,* 1005–1022.

Priebe, S., Huxley, P., Knight, S. and Evans, S. (1999). Application and results of the Manchester Short Assessment of Quality of Life (MANSA). *International Journal of Social Psychiatry, 45,* 7–12.

Rawlings, D. and Freeman, J. L. (1996). A questionnaire for the measurement of paranoia/suspiciousness. *British Journal of Clinical Psychology, 35,* 451-461.

Romme, M. and Escher, S. (2000). *Making Sense of Voices. A Guide for Mental Health Professionals Working with Voice-Hearers.* London: Mind Publications.

Selten, J. P., Sijben, N. E., van den Bosch, R. J., Omloo-Visser, J. and Warmerdam,

H. (1993). The subjective experience of negative symptoms: A self-rating scale. *Comprehensive Psychiatry*, *34*(3), 192–197.

Shawyer, F., Ratcliff, K., MacKinnon, A., Farhall, J., Hayes, S. C. and Copolov, D. (2007). The Voices Acceptance and Action Scale (VAAS): Pilot data. *Journal of Clinical Psychology*, *63*, 593–606.

Slade, P. D. (1972). The effects of systematic desensitization on auditory hallucinations. *Behavioural Research Therapy*, *10*, 85–91.

Trower, P., Birchwood, M. and Meaden, A. (2004). Cognitive therapy for command hallucinations: A randomised controlled trial. *British Journal of Psychiatry*, *184*, 312–320.

van Os, J., Gilvarry, C., Bale, R., van Horn, E., Tattan, T., White, I. and Murray, R. (1999). A comparison of the utility of dimensional and categorical representations of psychosis. *Psychological Medicine*, *29*, 595–606.

Wing, J. K., Cooper, J. E. and Sartorius, N. (1974). *Measurement and classification of psychiatric symptoms*. Cambridge: Cambridge University Press.

Wykes, T. and Sturt, E. (1986). The measurement of social behaviour in psychiatric patients: An assessment of the reliability and validity of the SBS scale. *British Journal of Psychiatry*, *148*, 1–11.

Part II

The practice of CBT for persons with psychotic symptoms

Chapter 5

The therapeutic alliance in cognitive behavioral therapy for psychosis

Live E. C. Hoaas, Sara Eidsbø Lindholm, Torkil Berge and Roger Hagen

In recent years it has been the case that more weight is being placed on understanding the factors that contribute to the therapeutic alliance within CBT and on relational factors, such as empathy, goal consensus, colla-boration, warmth, genuineness and positive regard. In order for CBT to be successful, patients need to feel understood and involved in the therapeutic relationship. In this chapter, we will focus on ways in which the therapist can contribute to establishing the therapeutic alliance. We will start by describing aspects of the therapeutic alliance, before discussing the chal-lenges to establishing a good alliance in the therapy of psychotic disorders, and how these challenges can be overcome.

Empirically supported elements of the therapeutic alliance

According to Bordin (1994), the therapeutic alliance consists of three mutually dependent factors:

1 Agreement on therapeutic goals;
2 Which methods and techniques are to be used by each party in reaching these goals; and
3 An emotional bond characterized by warmth, mutual trust and confidence.

Bordin's model takes both the technical–methodical and the emotional aspects of the relationship into account. Although alternative models for the therapeutic alliance have been developed, there is general agreement that these three factors are invariably involved. At the core of the alliance is the degree to which the patient and therapist are involved in collaborative and goal-oriented work.

Research in psychotherapy has unambiguously documented the import-ance of the therapeutic alliance in effective treatment. It is a common finding in the psychotherapy literature that the strength of the therapeutic alliance early in the course of treatment is of great significance for outcome. This seems to be the case regardless of therapeutic orientation, patient groups and diagnostic approaches.

Studies carried out on patients with psychotic disorders are concordant with this finding (McCabe and Priebe, 2004). In a qualitative study exploring patients' understanding and experience of CBT for psychosis, Messari and Hallam (2003) found that most participants emphasized the value of a trusting and respectful therapeutic relationship. Among patients with psychotic disorders, outcomes that are associated with stronger therapeutic alliances include lower levels of patient-perceived problems and severity (Neale and Rosenheck, 1995), higher general and social functioning (Svensson and Hansson, 1999), better homework compliance (Dunn *et al.*, 2006), and lower dropout rates. The quality of the therapeutic alliance has also been found to be a predictor of patients' adherence to anti-psychotic medication regimens (Day *et al.*, 2005) and to rehabilitation outcome and work performance (Davis and Lysaker, 2007). Having described the important main findings from research related to a good therapeutic alliance, we will try to clarify in more depth the central factors which contribute to the alliance.

Therapeutic empathy

A central factor in all good therapy is that the therapist enters the other's world with empathy in order to understand how the person sees him/herself and his/her life. The therapist encourages the patients to verbalize their experience(s) and discover whether the therapist has understood correctly. It is, however, difficult to define the concept of empathy precisely, and a generally accepted definition is lacking. Empathy has both an emotional component (to feel what another person feels; to respond in a caring manner to another person's feelings) and a cognitive component (to understand the way in which the patient experiences the world) (Bohart *et al.*, 2002).

An essential aspect of empathy is, therefore, whether the therapist is able to express a caring attitude towards the patient, and to show that he or she is capable of understanding the patient's experiences.

Empathy can be described as an ideal that is not always possible to attain; one can only do one's best. The therapist's *intention* to understand is often more important than whether or not he or she ultimately does understand everything. In having empathy as a goal, the therapist listens and monitors his or her own impressions while trying, at the same time, to be in touch with his or her own feelings and thoughts. By adopting such a position, the therapist makes a contribution toward creating a climate for reflection, insight and change.

Bohart *et al.* (2002) suggest a number of ways in which empathy can contribute to promoting change in therapy. The feeling of being understood will increase the patient's contentment with the treatment and therefore the patient's willingness to change. Empathy can function as a corrective emotional experience in teaching that the patient deserves respect and deserves to be heard so that the patient is better able to express his or her feelings and needs, while also understanding the feelings and needs of others. In addition, experiencing empathy can increase the patient's feeling of security, thereby encouraging openness in discussing difficult topics. Experiencing empathy can, moreover, strengthen self-discovery and capacity and motivation for emotional work, and help the patient to sort out his or her own thoughts and reflect upon his or her problems.

Empathy is recognized in the psychotherapy outcome literature as a therapeutically important variable that influences the formation of a therapeutic alliance, but it is a relatively unexamined construct in CBT for psychosis. Further investigation in this area will potentially enhance psychological treatment delivery and subsequent outcomes for people who experience hallucinations and delusions. For example, a three-day CBT training course for managing hallucinations and delusions was shown to change attitudes and empathy, by strengthening therapists' understanding of the subjective experience of psychotic symptoms (McLeod *et al.*, 2002).

Positive regard and congruence

Congruence is a person's ability to be his/herself, to be genuine and authentic. This involves self-awareness on the part of the therapist, as well as a willingness to share this awareness in the moment. According to Rogers (1957), the therapist's genuineness is a pre-condition for positive regard and empathy, and the main factor in contributing to change in therapy. Others have claimed that positive regard and genuineness should be understood as aspects of a more fundamental attitude of "openness". Studies on congruence have had mixed results in demonstrating a direct connection with the effect of treatment, but one does find support for this as an important dimension in what is understood as a strong therapeutic alliance (Klein *et al.*, 2002).

In order to be genuine, the therapist must be conscious and willing to share his or her inner experiences here and now. This implies that the therapist must permit him/herself to be moved emotionally by the patient and be able to share these feelings (Klein *et al.*, 2002). It is, however, important that the therapist tailors the degree of genuineness according to the individual patient's therapeutic needs at that moment. Some patients, for example, expect a more formal approach from the therapist. This is discussed further in the section on self-disclosure below.

Rogers (1957) asserts that acceptance means the therapist experiences the patient as a person of unconditional worth, independent of the patient's condition, actions or feelings. This view has a number of implications in regard to therapy with psychotic patients; in offering unconditional accept-ance, the therapist is open in relation to and accepts all aspects of the patient, including that which is challenging and difficult for him or her. This kind of acceptance is only possible if the therapist strives for a non-dominating and non-evaluating attitude. When the therapist accepts the patient, it becomes easier for the patient to accept him/herself. Therapeutic acceptance does not only mean accepting the patient's experiences here and now, but also the right to choose how one will change.

Goal consensus and collaboration

Tryon and Winograd (2002) have reviewed the research on the significance of goal consensus and collaboration, and they found that the therapeutic effect increases when the patient and the therapist are mutually involved in the therapy, and when the patient also works actively with his/her problems between sessions. Based on these findings they offer the recommendation that the patient takes an active part in deciding which goals to pursue in the process of change, because a common understanding of the goals has a therapeutic effect. When the patient comprehends the relationship between tasks and goals, their understanding of the rationale for therapy will increase, providing motivation to see it through.

Early in the course of treatment it is advantageous to base collaboration to a larger degree on the patient's understanding of his/her problems, rather than on the therapist's theoretical point of view. This is in line with findings that point to a negative influence on the therapeutic alliance when the therapist takes too much control in the conversation and attempts, to too great a degree, to put forth his or her own understanding of what should go on in the therapy. Treatment goals and measures should nevertheless remain objects for discussion throughout the entire course of treatment.

Certain patients have vague goals, for example, "wanting to be better", "have fewer problems" or "have a better life". Goals such as these can be difficult to concretize and use as navigational tools. Other patients have completely unrealistic and unattainable goals. The therapist's creative abili-ties are put to the test in discussion of what the goals of therapy should be.

Self-disclosure

Hill and Knox (2002) define self-disclosure as a statement from the therapist that conveys something personal. They divide this into four subgroups:

- Disclosure of facts (I studied at the University of Oslo)
- Disclosure of feelings (When I have been in similar situations, I have been angry)

- Disclosure of insights (When I was in a similar situation after I had moved away from home, I realized that what made moving so difficult was guilt at the thought of leaving my mother alone)
- Disclosure of strategies (When I was in a comparable situation, I made myself go for a walk).

After a research review, Hill and Knox made recommendations about the use of self-disclosure: self-disclosure should be used to validate, normalize, model and strengthen the alliance, or to offer alternative ways of thinking or behaving. It should not be used because the therapist needs it; if it will take the focus off the patient, disrupt the flow of conversation, or be uncomfortable for the patient; if it could erase the professional divide between therapist and patient; or if it could result in over-stimulating the patient. It is important that the therapist closely observes how the patient responds to disclosure, asks the patient how they felt about it, and uses this information in relation to any future disclosures. Self-disclosure has greater impact on some patients than others, for example, in relation to establishing trust.

Stages of change and motivation

Prochaska and DiClemente (1984) recommend taking the patient's stage of change into account when planning a course of treatment. They suggest that the minority of patients who enter therapy are at a stage in which they are ready for behavior modification, concrete advice and therapy involving active measures. The vast majority of patients are either in the *precontemplation stage*, in which they do not acknowledge their own problems or in which the inconveniences associated with behavior modification seem to be greater than the advantages, or within the *contemplation stage*, in which problems are acknowledged but there is great ambivalence towards change and little belief that they will achieve it. If therapy focuses on change when the patient is in these phases, he or she is likely to discontinue therapy. The therapist should therefore evaluate what the patient needs most – for example, increased awareness of "the price" one pays for one's behaviour, rather than suggestions on modification and coping strategies – and thereafter adapt the goals of the therapy. It is important to set realistic goals and tailor the processes to the stage the patient is at to avoid causing the patient unnecessary setbacks and reinforcing demoralization.

A well-documented method in these situations, in which the patient is strongly ambivalent toward the treatment, is the use of motivational interviewing (Arkowitz *et al.*, 2008). Here, the patient's ambivalence is examined in a neutral and systematic manner. This method has also proved to be useful with patients with psychotic disorders.

Resistance or psychological reactance

From a social-psychological perspective, resistance has been reformulated as "psychological reactance" (Brehm and Brehm, 1981). This is a universal way of reacting when one perceives an attempt to influence one and feels that one's freedom of choice could be curtailed. Psychological reactance sometimes leads to the boomerang effect of becoming contrary and doing the opposite of what is being recommended in order to demonstrate one's freedom (Beutler et al., 2006).

Psychological reactance is something the therapist must pay particular attention to when building a therapeutic alliance. Motivation to change must, first and foremost, come from the patient. Persuasion and argumentation can easily increase resistance, whereas the feeling of having freedom of choice can strengthen the commitment to change. It has been asserted that creating resistance in therapy can promote change in the long run, in that one can work on the resistance. Research shows, however, that psychotherapy is most successful when the therapist is able to avoid resistance (Beutler et al., 2006). Effective therapy should therefore be aimed at creating as little psychological reactance as possible, while simultaneously helping the patient toward his or her goals.

Certain people have an especially strong inclination toward psychological reactance. These people value their independence very highly. In the worst cases, the need for independence can have a self-destructive quality, in that one compulsively says the opposite of others. It is especially important in these cases that the therapist chooses the path of least resistance and minimizes pressure on the patient. The goal is to establish a therapeutic space that is characterized by personal freedom and control, bound up with personal responsibility, so that change can occur.

Expectations and preferences

It is important to chart the patient's expectations early on, and to negotiate partial goals and more realistic expectations with the patient. At the same time, the therapist attempts to reinforce the patient's sense of optimism and realistic hopes concerning change. Positive expectations seem, in and of themselves, to promote positive change (Arnkoff et al., 2002). The therapist must be able to give positive expectations and hope, while simultaneously praising and affirming that the patient is doing well. The therapist should not promise dramatic changes early in treatment, but should help the patient to see that small changes are a sign that the therapy is helping. One should convey optimism without becoming unrealistic. If the patient is initially skeptical, one should endeavor to show that therapy works rather than attempting to persuade.

We do not yet know enough about the ways in which expectations influence results in therapy. One study examining CBT in cases of panic disorder and generalized anxiety disorder found that patients who had positive expectations were more active in regard to homework early on in therapy, such as allowing exposure to feared situations. This contributed to the alleviation of symptoms, thereby strengthening both the therapeutic alliance and expectations of future treatment (Westra *et al.*, 2007).

Patient contributions

An important conclusion in psychotherapy research is that patients who are active, and who openly discuss thoughts and feelings, achieve the best results (Bachelor *et al.*, 2007). In contrast, defensiveness and hostility in patients are associated with weaker treatment alliances and poorer results. Patients can make positive contributions to therapy by offering their own topics for discussion, by trusting the therapist, by participating actively in conversation, by following up on both their own and the therapist's suggestions, and by exposing themselves to difficult situations. The therapist can emphasize the patient's importance by continually asking questions, asking the patient to expand on his/her thoughts and asking which measures the patient thinks are beneficial in the current situation. There are many methods in CBT that are directed toward encouraging an increased contribution from the patient.

Repairing alliance ruptures

Therapy is characterized by a continuous and more or less conscious negotiation between patient and therapist concerning treatment tasks and goals. Intermittent cracks or ruptures will occur in the therapeutic alliance, either in relation to the tasks and goals of the treatment, or in the actual bond between therapist and client. An example could be that the patient becomes overwhelmed by the therapist's optimism and loses faith that the therapist comprehends how serious his or her problems are, or that the patient feels pressured to do something he or she does not feel ready for, for example, exposing him/herself to a feared situation. The patient can be passive in conversations, not do homework or be erratic in attending sessions. Research shows that larger or smaller ruptures in the therapeutic alliance are more frequent than many therapists believe, and that they often ignore such ruptures (Katzow and Safran, 2007).

The therapist's best opportunity to discover both small and large alliance ruptures is to ask the patient to give open and direct feedback. This presupposes that the therapist is able to receive criticism without becoming defensive. Repairing alliance ruptures, for example, after failure in empathy, is emphasized in several studies as an important factor in change. A study by

Strauss *et al.* (2006), for instance, examined CBT of avoidant personality disorder and obsessive personality disorder, and found that repairing alliance ruptures was connected to better treatment results.

Challenges in establishing a therapeutic alliance in therapy for psychosis

CBT is built upon both good relations and concrete methods that can help patients understand and master their psychotic experiences. In this type of therapy it is necessary to work actively to engage the patient in a creative and positive manner with the specific challenges that patients with psychosis have. Patients must be able to regard the therapist as trustworthy and feel secure and respected, so that frightening and often shameful experiences and thoughts can be explored. This is often challenging, not least when the patient is suspicious and paranoid, and regards the therapist's questions as threatening.

In our practice, we have experienced that some patients with psychotic disorders have little or no insight into their illness. The patient's various explanations of problems can have helped him/her give meaning to experiences, thereby reducing discomfort. A lack of insight can, therefore, initially have been functional for the patient, but it creates new problems later in life. If the patient does not realize that he/she has a problem, there is little reason for them to engage in therapy. Under these conditions, a good rapport between therapist and patient is often the only reason the patient comes back for the next session.

Patients can experience a diagnosis of psychosis as stigmatizing, because of both their own and others' prejudices. Schizophrenia is a diagnosis that can arouse fear and uncertainty, and which is associated with hopelessness. Stigma is usually defined as something negative whose source is external, over which the person does not have control. The patient is regarded as a passive victim of others' negative attitudes. In relation to schizophrenia, the most destructive effect of stigma is often caused by the subjective internalization of these negative values, and this is a cognitive process that can be both reversed and changed. Modifying the ways in which the patient and his or her family react to stigma is likely to be more effective and more realistic to achieve than large-scale campaigns directed at changing the public's negative attitudes. In addition, many patients experience a double stigma in that they often also have a drug or alcohol use disorder, with all the stereotypes and prejudices associated with these difficulties. Other challenges in relation to establishing a good treatment alliance are cultural differences, cognitive deficits, personality disorders, paranoia, hostility, grandiosity, unwillingness to cooperate, negative attitudes from family and others, committal, severe reclusiveness or being overmedicated.

> I felt that she (the therapist) twisted everything I had said. She said that I was very paranoid. After that, I denied everything. I felt that she had abused my trust, and twisted things I had said in confidence. It was hard to hear that about myself. I felt as if I had been declared incompetent, and was afraid I would never get out again.

The therapist's ability to tolerate, accommodate and accept deviant experiences, such as psychotic symptoms, has great significance in establishing collaboration. It is therefore important that one does not give up if one does not understand the patient. Rather, with ample time, perseverance and help from the patient, the therapist will achieve an increased understanding.

The goal is to meet the other wherever he/she is in life, and to try to see and understand their problems from this standpoint. This builds up the alliance, and the therapist will be perceived as empathetic precisely because he or she is demonstrating an attempt at understanding. As one patient said:

> I think that even with sick people it's possible to have a fruitful dialogue, if one is treated with human compassion, empathy and caring. I am convinced of that! One needs to have people on one's side.

Genuineness, openness and an unconditional positive regard for the person are stressed in therapy. If one is inauthentic, one will easily be seen through and the seeds of suspicion and distrust will be sown or exacerbated. The challenge lies in being honest while, at the same time, showing respect for the patient's assumptions and conceptions and treating the other in an authentic manner.

The therapist can be empathetic with the patient's anger and experience, but without affirming all of the patient's conceptions. A too energetic understanding or expression of empathy can be frightening for some patients, and they can withdraw from therapy. Our experience is that an emotional attunement to the patient's current condition is decisive for success.

The therapist in CBT places emphasis on being clear and concrete and takes an active role. This contributes to predictability and security in the treatment situation and creates a framework that is beneficial for patients with psychotic disorders. By approaching and taking as one's starting point the patient's own experiences and problems within this framework, such as in the quote below, the way is opened to meet challenges such as, for example, lack of insight, disturbances and traumatic experiences.

> At this point, I had lost more and more control over my life, become more and more confused. I had lost myself, I didn't recognize myself

any more; thoughts, ideas and beliefs were blurred. One changes in relation to how one understands oneself. I felt like a stranger.

Through CBT, patients learn to ask questions regarding their own understanding of reality and become open to new assumptions about themselves and their surroundings. Insight plays a central role in the healing process. Socratic dialogue can be positive here in that patients themselves experience that they "own" new insights to a greater degree. Many people with psychosis have a diminished capacity or ability to reason and formulate alternative explanations, or they can have so strong a belief in delusions that they do not understand that it is possible to arrive at alternative explanations. If the patient truly believes that he or she knows the truth, there is maybe no point in trying to see it from another perspective. Because the patient's condition and degree of insight can change rapidly – often from hour to hour – it is important that the therapist is continually aware and asks patients if they have the same perception of hallucinations or delusions that they had the last time they talked about it.

A flexible organization of structure in therapy

An ideal agenda for a session is often unrealistic with patients with psychosis. Emphasis is therefore often placed upon flexibility and on conversation about more everyday topics. An example is beginning to establish contact with a hospitalized patient in the ward, and not in the therapist's office. Another example is to have shorter sessions than usual. In contrast to CBT in cases of anxiety and depression, the therapeutic agenda in the treatment of psychosis will, as a rule, be more implicit in the earliest stages, and evolve over the course of therapy. It is, however, important that the therapist has an agenda in his/her thoughts from which to proceed. Structure and predictability are both beneficial in therapy with psychosis.

It is important to socialize with the patient at the beginning of each session; to talk, for example, about how things have been since the last conversation. The therapist should strive for as natural and friendly an attitude as he/she would have when meeting friends. Then, one should go through any homework. It is important that tasks are prepared together, so that it is possible for the patient to complete them, and so that they are relevant to the patient's needs. Patients with psychosis often have problems carrying out such tasks, especially written ones, and it can be appropriate not to give homework in the beginning. Next, goals for the therapy session should be agreed upon. The object is to engage the patient so that he/she becomes more motivated to change. At the end of the session, the patient is asked to sum up what has been discussed, in order to check what they have gained and correct any misunderstandings. In addition, the patient is asked for feedback regarding the usefulness of the session, and his/her opinion of the quality of collaboration.

How to encourage engagement

The therapist socializes the patient to the CBT model. One technique is to share any positive experiences with CBT or self help, for example with phobias or performance anxiety. One can, moreover, demonstrate that the method's usefulness has been documented by research and, in this way, give the patient greater hope that the method can help him/her to improve their quality of life and social functioning. The fact that CBT is not something that the therapist or the patient does alone is stressed, emphasizing that it is an active collaboration with mutual goals in which the patient gains knowledge about CBT.

Our experience is that the first session can be the most important one, for both patient and therapist. Many patients with psychotic disorders approach the therapist with suspicion and reticence, and disclose very little of what they are struggling with. Patients can have difficulty trusting another person because of the symptoms of psychosis, but also because they may have had negative experiences in previous treatments. Psychotic symptoms can, in and of themselves, contribute to undermining the patient's willingness to engage. A patient can, for example, hear commanding voices that say, "Do not listen to the therapist; she is not to be trusted."

A therapist who is empathetic and interested, and who shows respect will succeed in overcoming the patient's skepticism, mistrust and anxiety:

> I had a very good impression during the first session with the psychologist. I had, of course, had a very bad experience before. She used a careful approach, she took time to listen to me, and I was heard. I was terrified to say anything during the first session. It took some time before I dared to say anything, first about anxiety and depression, and after that about feeling suicidal and other things. I was treated in a friendly way.

The goal is to be open in communication and honest and clear in relation to what one is thinking, and why. It is important that the communication is, as much as possible, between equals, in an atmosphere of relaxation:

> We started to go into things carefully. I used a number of quotes from literature; it was a safe way to describe things. [. . .] It's something you can talk about without it being dangerous. It is important to be able to have a dialogue. It's a long process, gaining someone's confidence and trusting people.

The therapist's goal is that sessions are, as much as possible, positive and even pleasant experiences. A characteristic of psychotic disorders is that patients often handle social situations poorly, and that they have suffered many social setbacks. Because of this, one will occasionally focus conversation on neutral but engaging topics.

The therapist uses language the patient can understand, does not use irony or figurative speech, and avoids being confrontational. Creating a candid relationship, establishing common goals, using appropriate language and providing good explanations of what one is doing and why also help to increase the patient's engagement. The therapist is a friend and is personal to the degree that is possible. Optimal use of self-disclosure can contribute toward making the therapist an unambiguous person for the patient, and thereby also less dangerous and frightening. The therapist can function as a role model for the patient, and the patient can, through model learning, learn to tackle difficult situations.

One must often take the initiative to visit patients with psychosis in the early stages of therapy, as these patients often lack insight into their illness and are unmotivated. Good preliminary work is important as well as good charting and collecting relevant information from the patient, his/her family and from other relevant sources. The therapist should be curious and familiarizes him/herself with and keep up to date with the patient's concerns. Attention is directed towards whichever stage in the process of change at which the patient finds him/herself.

The therapist's beliefs and assumptions can weaken the therapeutic relation and undermine progress in therapy. In order to avoid one's own assumptions interfering to too great a degree in the therapy, it can be advisable for the therapist, in preparation for a session, to examine his/her own feelings and expectations in relation to what will happen during the session.

Some patients do not wish to collaborate. They may have been committed against their will and lack insight into their illness. They perceive that the therapist is against them, is keeping them in hospital and forcing them to take medication. In order to understand the connection between the patient's earlier experiences and their attitudes towards and expectations of treatment, it can be helpful in the course of the first sessions to go through the patient's positive and negative experiences with treatment. It will occasionally be appropriate for the therapist to try to distance him/ herself from the rest of the system in order to create an alliance. Formulations such as "I had nothing to do with your committal" or "I'm not the one deciding which medications you'll take" can help in achieving this kind of distancing. The relation develops through showing interest and caring. Helping the patient with more practical goals can often be very useful in the beginning phase, even though this may not be part of the usual areas of responsibility for the therapist. By doing this him/herself, rather than delegating to other members of staff, the therapist demonstrates through action that he/she actually cares about and wishes to help the patient.

Cognitive deficits can pose a particular challenge in terms of the patient achieving engagement. Because many patients struggle with remembering appointments, it can be an advantage to schedule therapy sessions at the same times and to refrain from giving homework, as this can create the experience of one more thing the patient cannot master. It is also important that one is flexible in terms of the form and duration of therapy sessions. For some patients, fifteen minutes is more than enough, whereas others possibly need longer sessions on day-to-day topics before they are ready to talk about more difficult topics.

As a therapist, one must be persistent, but also be able to withdraw if the patient becomes too uneasy. It is important to have flow in the conversation, so that the patient does not regard the therapy as some sort of interrogation or, in contrast, as boring or uninteresting. Patients can have different degrees of tolerance for quietness. Some cannot cope with long, silent breaks and react with anxiety that may worsen symptoms of psychosis.

Normalization

Normalization is one of the most important components for success in CBT for psychosis, and reflects a therapeutic attitude characterized by empathy (see Chapter 6). This will counteract stigmatization. Psychotic symptoms are discussed as being on a continuum with normal reactions. Many people experience psychotic symptoms as dramatic, causing distress and anxiety. To realize that one is not in control of one's own life, thoughts and feelings is frightening. It is this experience the therapist must deal with by emphasizing that the experience of emotional distress is both normal and understandable, and by helping the patient to see that he or she is not alone with their thoughts and feelings.

One approach is to normalize by means of emphasizing the effect different stress factors can have on the development of psychotic symptoms. The stress-vulnerability model, which states that vulnerability factors in combination with stress can lead to psychotic symptoms, can help the patient find alternative explanations. One can also refer to scientific evidence of normal conditions in which psychotic symptoms can occur, such as: conditions of deprivation; the absence of sleep and sensory impressions; fear, i.e. hostage situations; sexual and physical abuse; or organic, i.e. medication-induced psychosis. Other possible triggering factors that can be topics in discussions such as these are: drug and alcohol use; withdrawal; brain stimuli; loss; grieving; hypnagogic or hypnopompic hallucinations (immediately before and after sleep); and states of trance, for example in religious ceremonies. What separates these experiences from psychotic disorders is that they do not last, but beyond this there are many similarities. One might also show that unusual assumptions are very widespread in the population, making it difficult to draw the line with the patient's beliefs.

The greatest risk with normalization is an unfavorable belittling of the patient's problems. If normalization is carried out in an insensitive and non-validating manner, the patients might believe that others master similar experiences without difficulties and that there is therefore something wrong with them.

Conclusion

We have argued that CBT in cases of psychosis can create a foundation for the establishment of a good therapeutic alliance. The approach builds on a view of humanity characterized by respect, individualization, normalizing and inclusion. One is concerned with the individual rather than the diagnosis, and has specific methods for reducing the damaging effects of prejudices and stigma. Moreover, it is a fundamental condition for CBT that the patient and therapist are of equal value and active collaborators in the therapeutic process.

Despite the fact that CBT in cases of psychosis has shown promising results, this therapeutic approach does not work for all patients, and not all therapists master this method equally well. It is important to be clear-headed in relation to what is possible to achieve through individual therapy. But a good therapeutic relation and alliance and the interest, respect and caring the therapist shows toward the patient can, in and of themselves, contribute to the reduction of the negative effects of serious psychotic illness in relation to the patient's life and social network.

References

Arkowitz, H., Westra, H. A., Miller, W. R. and Rollnick, S. (Eds.). (2008). *Motivational Interviewing in the Treatment of Psychological Problems*. New York: Guilford Press.

Arnkoff, D. B., Glass, C. R. and Shapiro, S. J. (2002). Expectations and preferences. In J. C. Norcross (Ed.), *Psychotherapy Relationships That Work: Therapist Contributions and Responsiveness to Patients* (pp. 335–356). New York: Oxford University Press.

Bachelor, A., Laverdière, O., Gamache, D. and Bordeleau, V. (2007). Clients' collaboration in therapy: Self-perceptions and relationships with client psychological functioning, interpersonal relations and motivation. *Psychotherapy: Theory, Research, Practice, Training, 44*, 175–192.

Beutler, L. E., Blatt, S. J., Alimohamed, S., Levy, K. N. and Angtuaco, L. (2006). Participant factors in treating dysphoric disorders. In L. G. Castonguay and L. E. Beutler (Eds.), *Principles of Therapeutic Change That Work* (pp. 13–63). New York: Oxford University Press.

Bohart, A., Elliott, R., Greenberg, L. A. and Watson, J. C. (2002). Empathy. In J. C. Norcross (Ed.), *Psychotherapy Relationships That Work: Therapist Contributions and Responsiveness to Patients* (pp. 89–108). New York: Oxford University Press.

Bordin, E. S. (1994). Theory and research on the therapeutic working alliance: New directions. In A. O. Horvath and L. S. Greenberg (Eds.), *The Working Alliance. Theory, Research and Practice* (pp. 13–37). New York: John Wiley.

Brehm, S. S. and Brehm, J. W. (1981). *Psychological Reactance: A Theory of Freedom and Control.* New York: Academic Press.

Davis, L. and Lysaker, P. (2007). Therapeutic alliance and improvements in work performance over time in patients with schizophrenia. *The Journal of Nervous and Mental Disease, 195,* 4.

Day, J. C., Bentall, R. P., Roberts, C., Randall, F., Rogers, A., Cattell, D. *et al.* (2005). Attitudes toward antipsychotic medication. *Archives of General Psychiatry, 62,* 717–724.

Dunn, H., Morrison, A. P. and Bentall, R. P. (2006). The relationship between patient suitability, therapeutic alliance, homework compliance and outcome in cognitive therapy for psychosis. *Clinical Psychology and Psychotherapy, 13,* 145–152.

Hill, C. E. and Knox, S. (2002). Self-disclosure. In J. C. Norcross (Ed.), *Psychotherapy Relationships That Work: Therapist Contributions and Responsiveness to Patients* (pp. 255–267). New York: Oxford University Press.

Jackson, C., Knott, C., Skeate, A. and Birchwood, M. (2004). The trauma of first-episode psychosis: The role of cognitive mediation. *Australian and New Zealand Journal of Psychiatry, 38,* 327–333.

Katzow, A. W. and Safran, J. D. (2007). Recognizing and resolving ruptures in the therapeutic alliance. In P. Gilbert and R. L. Leahy (Eds.), *The Therapeutic Relationship in the Cognitive Behavioral Psychotherapies* (pp. 90–105). London: Routledge.

Klein, M. H., Kolden, G. G., Michels, J. L. and Chisholm-Stockard, S. (2002). Congruence. In J. C. Norcross (Ed.), *Psychotherapy Relationships That Work: Therapist Contributions and Responsiveness to Patients* (pp. 195–216). New York: Oxford University Press.

McCabe, R. and Priebe, S. (2004). The therapeutic relationship in the treatment of severe mental illness: A review of methods and findings. *International Journal of Social Psychiatry, 50,* 115–128.

McLeod, H. J., Deane, F. P. and Hogbin, B. (2002). Changing staff attitudes and empathy for working with people with psychosis. *Behavioural and Cognitive Psychotherapy, 30,* 459–470.

Messari, S. and Hallam, R. (2003). CBT for psychosis: A qualitative analysis of clients' experiences. *British Journal of Clinical Psychology, 42,* 171–188.

Neale, M. S. and Rosenheck, R. A. (1995). Therapeutic alliance and outcome in a VA intensive case management program. *Psychiatric Services, 46,* 719–721.

Prochaska, J. O. and DiClemente, C. C. (1984). *The Transtheoretical Approach: Crossing Traditional Boundaries of Therapy.* Homewood, IL: Dow Jones-Irwin.

Rogers, C. R. (1957). The necessary and sufficient conditions of therapeutic personality change. *Journal of Consulting Psychology, 21,* 95–103.

Shevlin, M., Houston, J. E., Dorahy, M. J. and Adamson, G. (2008). Cumulative traumas and psychosis: An analysis of the National Comorbidity Survey and the British Psychiatric Morbidity Survey. *Schizophrenia Bulletin, 34*, 193–199.

Strauss, J. L., Hayes, A. M., Johnson, S. L., Newman, C. F., Brown, G. K., Barber, J. P., Laurenceau, J.-P. and Beck, A. T. (2006). Early alliance, alliance ruptures, and symptom change in a non-randomized trial of cognitive therapy for avoidant and obsessive-compulsive personality disorders. *Journal of Consulting and Clinical Psychology, 74*, 337–345.

Svensson, B. and Hansson, L. (1999). Therapeutic alliance in cognitive therapy for schizophrenic and other long-term mentally ill patients: Development and relationship to outcome in an inpatient treatment program. *Acta Psychiatrica Scandinavia, 99*, 281–287.

Tryon, G. S. and Winograd, G. (2002). Goal consensus and collaboration. In J. C. Norcross (Ed.), *Psychotherapy Relationships That Work: Therapist Contributions and Responsiveness to Patients* (pp. 109–125). New York: Oxford University Press.

Westra, H. A., Dozois, D. J. A. and Marcus, M. (2007). Expectancy, homework compliance, and initial change in cognitive behavioral therapy for anxiety. *Journal of Consulting and Clinical Psychology, 75*, 363–373.

Chapter 6

Using normalising in cognitive behavioural therapy for schizophrenia[1]

Robert Dudley and Douglas Turkington

The role of normalising in cognitive therapy

Normalisation is a central process within cognitive behavioural therapy (CBT) and not just CBT for psychosis (CBTp). This is because CBT is based on the cognitive model which emphasises that the appraisal of an internal or external event determines emotion and behaviour (Beck, 1995). Central to the model is the notion that if we understand the cognition or appraisal, the emotion and behaviour will make sense to us. In fact, if we believed the same thought there is a good chance we would feel and act in the same way. The goal of treatment in CBT is to help the person appraise the world, other people and the self as they really are and to not over-estimate threat (e.g. my palpitations are normal and a reaction to arousal not a sign of a heart attack), or overvalue the event if it has happened (e.g. just because I lost a job it does not mean I am a failure).

Normalising is used in CBT in a number of different ways. For instance, by drawing on the cognitive model we regard the distress arising from the experience as normal and understandable. The therapist will say to a person with compulsive washing something like "So you believed you had poison on your hands and that you would be responsible for killing your children, well no wonder you felt anxious, and wanted to wash your hands." This style is evident from the first session and is a powerful form of normal-isation. Furthermore, the therapist helps the clients see that they are not alone in experiencing certain feelings or thoughts, and this can enhance feelings of self-esteem, facilitate improved coping and reduce stigmatisa-tion. Normalising can help reduce secondary emotional reactions such as being anxious about anxiety or depressed about being depressed. Secondary behaviours which perpetuate the primary symptom are also reduced, e.g. safety behaviours and social withdrawal. This process can be carried out through the therapist providing the client with reading material (e.g. fight/flight response material to normalise physical sensations in anxiety and examples of people also suffering depressive symptoms after losing their job).

Personal disclosure is also potent in the process of normalising. For instance, the therapist might describe how they had a phobia of public speaking and how they overcame this or perhaps reveal one of their own experiences of intrusive thoughts when working with a person with obsessions (Salkovskis, 1999). Normalisation can also be seen as an active element within group CBT as people can relate to one another within the group and see that other people experience similar problems.

Normalising experience is also at the heart of current appraisal models of anxiety disorders. In these problems, central to treatment is creating a change in catastrophic or unhelpful appraisals of normal phenomena such as bodily sensations (leading to panic disorder, health anxiety and social phobia), intrusive thoughts (leading to obsessive compulsive disorder and generalised anxiety disorder) and intrusive memories (leading to PTSD). A key treatment common to all these approaches is normalisation of these physiological or cognitive phenomena.

It is important to remember that this process is not purely restricted to CBT. For example, the medical model is, perhaps surprisingly, not exclusive of a normalising approach. A good example is asthma. It is useful for the person with asthma to know that anyone will wheeze with a severe chest infection. This reduces catastrophic thoughts about the meaning of the bronchospasm, e.g. "I am dying and this is untreatable." Another example is epilepsy; again the person is reassured to hear that seizures are extremely common and that anyone can have one. This can lead to reduced shame and improved compliance with anticonvulsants.

Definition of normalisation

When we describe normalisation the intention is not to say that the experiences are a sign of health or well-being. Rather, normalisation is a process that emphasises that the experiences a person finds upsetting exist within the range of normal functioning and can be experienced in the absence of distress, or disability. Some cognitive models of psychotic symptoms just as in obsessive compulsive disorder (Salkovskis, 1999) would argue that the development of delusional beliefs or hallucinations has its origins in normal experiences. The difference between non-distressing and distressing experiences lies not in the occurrence or even the uncontrollability of these experiences but rather in the interpretation by the person of the experience.

Normalising psychotic symptoms

This view of what normalisation is immediately brings us up against the issue of whether we can normalise psychosis. Most of us would accept that we know what it feels like to be low or anxious. Our own experiences help us develop empathy for those with depression or anxiety problems. However, normalisation is not just about developing empathy. The message given is that these experiences are not in themselves problematic, and that other people can have them without being distressed. However, psychotic experiences (and in particular the label of schizophrenia) have been catastrophised rather than normalised, not just by the patient, but also by society and the media. Psychotic experiences were seen to be discontinuous with normal experience and a sign of a qualitative change in a person, presumably owing to a biological disease process (Bentall, 2003).

This view of psychosis has consequences. The mere act of labelling an individual with psychosis as mentally ill is linked with an increased perception of their unpredictability and dangerousness (Angermeyer and Matschinger, 2005). Clinicians have been known to catastrophise the diagnosis of schizophrenia and so find it hard to communicate the diagnosis to the person directly, thus leaving them to find out by other means. The person may then learn of their diagnosis from a carer or deduce it through recognition of the symptoms from a television programme, the internet, or reading the information accompanying any prescribed medication. This process then leaves the person to draw unhelpful conclusions about why they weren't told directly, again often leading to catastrophisation of the problem such as beliefs that they are "mad", there "is no hope" for their recovery or they will be "locked up" (Bentall, 2003). There has also been a general opinion that discussing psychotic symptoms with a client can lead to an exacerbation of the problem, but a lack of discussion can again lead to the client catastrophising their perceived "untreatability" which in turn leads to greater distress (Kingdon and Turkington, 2005).

However, it has become increasingly evident through research that psychotic experiences exist in the general population on a continuum of severity rather than as categorically different phenomena (van Os et al., 2001). Surveys of the general population have been carried out using questionnaires or interviews to measure psychotic symptoms, and findings show that a range of symptoms, from paranoia to hallucinations, are relatively common in apparently healthy community samples. For example, van Os et al. (ibid.) reported that 25 per cent of people had experienced psychotic symptoms. Freeman et al. (2005) reported that over a third of their sample of 1,200 undergraduates had experienced paranoid thoughts about the intentions of others within the last week. Their survey revealed thoughts that friends, acquaintances, or strangers might be hostile or deliberately watching them. Hence, suspiciousness and paranoid ideation appears to be an everyday occurrence for many people. In fact, 52 per cent endorsed the idea that "I need to be on my guard against others" as occurring on a weekly basis. To a lesser extent people believed that there may be someone plotting against them or an active conspiracy against them (8 per cent in the last week). The prevalence of symptoms in the general public could provide a key element to the normalising process as it indicates the presence of psychotic symptoms and experiences is far greater than the level of identified mental illness.

Johns *et al.* (2004) investigated self-reported psychotic symptoms from the general public. The annual prevalence of psychotic symptoms in the general population was 5.5 per cent. They found that psychotic symptoms were more likely to occur in people with factors such as substance misuse, neurotic symptoms, adverse life events or victimisation in their lives, and each of the different factors has supporting literature that can be used as part of the normalisation process. One of the socio-demographic influences highlighted by Johns *et al.* (ibid.) was urbanisation, and previous research has highlighted that psychotic symptoms in the general community increase in prevalence as the level of urbanisation increases (van Os *et al.*, 2001). People who live in highly urbanised areas may be able to identify with these findings, and it may be helpful for them to discover that the general public are affected in a similar way. Other studies show that victimisation and stressful life events specifically increase levels of paranoid ideation.

Significant life events often precede the onset of psychosis, in a similar way to the onset of depression or post-traumatic stress disorder (Zubin and Spring, 1977). For instance, hallucinations are common in those who have suffered prolonged or brutal sexual abuse (Ensink, 1992). Although many people will not disclose such things even when given the opportunity to do so, when they do it can be useful to highlight the possible connection to help give an understanding of symptom development. Grassian (1983) has also identified that prisoners who were kept for prolonged periods in solitary confinement were prone to develop psychotic symptoms. Excessive bed rest or other sensory deprivations have also been found to induce hallucinations (Slade, 1973). Research has also identified that sleep deprivation can be a trigger for psychotic symptoms, leading to illusions, hallucinations and paranoid ideation (ibid.). Such literature can be presented to people with such experiences so that they can identify with the triggers and feel less alienated by their experiences.

Hence, we have seen that normalisation is a common component of CBT when working with non-psychotic disorders, and also that the assumption psychotic experiences are categorically different from other experiences does not hold up when considering the circumstances in which these develop or the fact that they can be experienced without a person experiencing distress. Therefore, we turn our attention to the process of normalisation within cognitive behavioural therapy for psychosis (CBTp).

Normalising process in CBT for psychosis

The first stage of CBTp is engaging the client and forming a therapeutic alliance that will allow a collaborative approach (see Chapter 5). This first step is crucial, and generally this is encouraged through empathy, warmth, genuineness and unconditional acceptance displayed by the therapist, who would also display a knowledge of typical modalities of psychotic expression (hallucinations, delusional perceptions, systematisation of delusions, etc.). Therapists can often be put off by the large delusional systems, but through the engaging phase you can work towards a formulation of symptom emergence to allow therapy to begin. The therapist can also provide reading material, case examples and personal disclosures about how one has used that particular technique to overcome problems (e.g. anxiety).

The process of normalisation can be used as a therapeutic tool towards forming this alliance through work on non-threatening exploratory areas prior to tackling the person's own symptomatology, reducing the chances of experiencing shame. Normalisation can also help pave the way for collaborative formulation, thus helping the client become an active agent in his or her own treatment. The therapist should also convey accuracy and consistency in their approach to the client, being careful not to invalidate any experiences through verbal or non-verbal cues, for example directly confronting a belief. Care should be taken that normalisation is not used in the extreme, which may be perceived by the person as the therapist minimising the problem. If normalisation is used insensitively the client may perceive that his or her problem is something that other people just cope with (e.g. everyone hears voices), or therapeutic work could miss out important issues such as the person believing that he or she is bad (especially if his or her problem is normalised, e.g. "If this isn't my illness making me think such things then I must be bad"). Therapists must remain aware of how far they are going in saying that psychotic symptoms are normal, and it is also important to identify possible influences from their own personal beliefs (Garrett et al., 2006).

After engaging the client it is useful to provide an explanation of puzzling and distressing symptoms as well as dealing with catastrophic cognitions concerning insanity. The person can be led towards an understanding that there is probably a discernable reason or reasons why the symptoms have occurred and the possibility that anyone stressed in certain ways would develop psychotic symptoms. If there is a family predisposition to respond in this way this can also be fully explored to help the person to feel less different and isolated. At this point literature detailing the prevalence of psychotic symptoms in the general population (Johns et al., 2004) or more specific literature about particular life experiences, such as sexual abuse or solitary confinement, could be discussed with the person.

The Stress Vulnerability Hypothesis (Zubin and Spring, 1977) could also be introduced as this model simply states that vulnerabilities and stresses combine to produce the symptoms characteristic of psychosis. A close examination of the antecedents of psychotic breakdown may be necessary, and it is often useful to itemise the types of stressors that can typically produce psychotic symptoms. The crucial period leading up to a breakdown should be worked through with inductive questioning, imagery and role play. Key cognitions can be detected from this period, pointing to underlying schemas concerning achievement, approval and control that may be addressed in later sessions.

The normalising approach can help the person realise that everyone has upsetting automatic thoughts, intrusive thoughts or even obsessions during times of stress and worry. Generally the experiences of these thoughts can be similar to voice-hearing experiences (e.g. they can be quite violent, sexual or religious), and it can be helpful for the person to discover that others get anxious about their thoughts, too, but most people choose not to act on them. This process of normalisation can pave the way for imagery, role play or schema level work to be undertaken to help deal with beliefs about voices and hence to manage to command hallucinations differently (Morrison et al., 2004).

Is normalisation an important part of treatment?

We know that CBT is an effective treatment for people with persistent symptoms of schizophrenia (Sensky et al., 2000). Whilst its value is proven, there is less evidence as to what are the mechanisms of change. CBT, generally, consists of a number of core components (Beck, 1995) that include a good therapeutic relationship, a style of collaborative empiricism, the use of cognitive and behavioural change techniques, and the use of a disorder-specific model as the basis of the formulation. There has been limited investigation of the active and successful components of treatment in CBT generally. There is evidence that positive therapeutic alliance can potentiate the effectiveness of empirically supported therapies (Raue and Goldfried, 1994), and also evidence that the use of effective therapy approaches leads to a more positive therapy alliance (DeRubeis et al., 2005). However, there is virtually no such research undertaken about the effective components treating psychotic illness. Broadly speaking, there is only emergent empirical evidence that any or all of these components are necessary.

Despite the lack of empirical support the components mentioned above are also incorporated into the CBTp treatment manuals (i.e. Morrison et al., 2004). In these specialised approaches there is often an increased emphasis on engagement and rapport building, normalising unusual psychotic symptoms and decatastrophising distressing appraisals of what it means to have a psychotic illness such as schizophrenia (Kingdon and Turkington, 2005). Hence, it is apparent that CBTp relies on the core components of CBT as well as components more specific to psychotic conditions. However, within CBTp the process and role of formulation is considered to be especially important (Morrison et al., 2004).

Formulation is the process of integrating the person's specific information with the cognitive model and serves to help understand the onset and maintenance of the current difficulties as well as directing the therapist to key points of intervention (Kuyken *et al.*, 2009). Given this function, formulation is considered to be the linchpin of CBT (ibid.). Despite the central prominence given to the role of formulation there is actually an absence of evidence for the value of a formulation in producing a successful outcome (ibid.). Hence, even one of the most important components of CBT has strikingly little evidence for its therapeutic value. Formulation in work with people with psychotic illness helps provide a shared understanding, and this is particularly relevant when working with symptoms that can initially appear "incomprehensible" (ibid.). Formulation in CBTp is heavily reliant on normalisation as together the therapist and client are trying to generate and test a new, less threatening alternative explanation for the person's experiences, and information about the symptoms is vital in this process.

To date, only two studies have investigated formulation in CBTp. The first was undertaken by Chadwick *et al.* (2003) who reported that formulation had no impact on the perceived therapeutic relationship from the client's point of view, psychotic symptoms, or levels of anxiety and depression.

The second study (Dudley *et al.*, 2007) investigated which components of CBTp were used most in working with those people with schizophrenia who respond to CBTp, in comparison with those who did not respond in a randomised controlled treatment trial (Sensky *et al.*, 2000). Following each session of therapy the therapist completed forms indicating components of treatment that were used in that session. Individual techniques that differentiated responders and non-responders included the use of education about schizophrenia as well as the use of personal disclosure. Both would appear to be very normalising processes as they are used to help make sense of the development of psychosis and are the building blocks of a formulation.

Conclusion

Hence, we have some preliminary evidence for the value of formulation in CBTp and within that for the vital role of normalisation. However, it brings us back to how far we can normalise psychotic experiences. We have all experienced memory slips, perhaps forgetting someone's name or the name of an object. However, few of us would say we could use this experience to normalise the experience of amnesia or dementia. The same issue applies to our normalisation of psychotic experiences. How far can we accept that these experiences are normal? We may have experienced feeling suspicious of other people, or heard a voice calling our name when waking from sleep, but does this really map onto the experience of believing that your parents are dead and have been replaced by alien impostors, or a voice shouting that you are evil for hours on end? There may be a point at which the frequency, loudness, and vividness of a voice or its content make the experience different to that experienced by people who are not distressed by these experiences. At present we do not know if it is a difference of degree or of quality. This is a challenge to us as clinicians and researchers, and there is difference within the CBTp models as to how far these experiences can be normalised. However, it is also the case that what makes an experience abnormal is to some extent culturally defined. The apparent improved outcome of people with psychotic experiences in non-Western societies (Bentall, 2003) may in part be attributable to differences in appraisal of these experiences. Moreover, as experiences are culturally defined as normal it is important to remember that these definitions can and do change over time.

While the evidence supporting its value is limited, normalising has been increasingly incorporated into CBT treament manuals for anxiety disorders and depression. It now appears that normalising may be one of the most important components of successful CBT for people with psychosis. It has been incorporated in recent treatment manuals (Kingdon and Turkington, 2005) and self help materials (i.e. Turkington *et al.*, 2009), and it can be effectively taught to psychiatrists in training (Garrett *et al.*, 2006). The challenge now is to disseminate this training more widely and to make formulation-based CBT available for those who need more intensive treatment due to chronicity or co-morbidity.

References

Angermeyer, M. C. and Matschinger, H. (2005). Labeling – stereotype – discrimination: An investigation of the stigma process. *Social Psychiatry and Psychiatric Epidemiology*, 40, 391–395.

Beck, J. S. (1995). *Cognitive Therapy: Basics and Beyond*. London: Guilford Press.

Bentall, R. (2003). *Madness Explained: Psychosis and Human Nature*. Allen Lane: The Penguin Press.

Chadwick, P., Williams, C. and Mackenzie, J. (2003). Impact of case formulation in CBT for psychosis. *Behaviour Research and Therapy*, 40, 671–680.

DeRubeis, R. J., Brotman, M. A. and Gibbons, C. J. (2005). A conceptual and methodological analysis of the nonspecifics argument. *Clinical Psychology: Science and Practice*, 12, 174–183.

Dudley, R., Bryant, C., Hammond, K., Siddle, R., Kingdon, D. and Turkington, D. (2007). Techniques in cognitive behavioural therapy: Using normalising in schizophrenia. *Journal of the Norwegian Psychological Association*, 44, 562–571.

Ensink, B. J. (1992) *Confusing Realities: A Study on Child Sexual Abuse and Psychiatric Symptoms*. Amsterdam: Free University Press.

Freeman, D., Garety, P. A, Bebbington, P. E., Smith, B., Rollinson, R., Fowler, D., Kuipers, E., Ray, K. and Dunn, G. (2005). Psychological investigation of the structure of paranoia in a non-clinical population. *British Journal of Psychiatry*, *186*, 427–435.

Garrett, M., Stone, D. and Turkington, D. (2006). Normalizing psychotic symptoms. *Psychology and Psychotherapy: Theory, Research and Practice*, *79*, 595–610.

Grassian, G. (1983). Psychopathology of solitary confinement. *American Journal of Psychiatry*, *140*, 1450–1454.

Johns, L., Singleton., N., Murray, R. M., Farrell, M., Brugha, T., Bebbington, P., Jenkins, R. and Meltzer, H. (2004). Prevalance and correlates of self-reported psychotic symptoms in the British population. *British Journal of Psychiatry*, *185*, 298–305.

Kingdon, D. G. and Turkington, D. (2005). *Cognitive Therapy of Schizophrenia*. London: Guilford Press.

Kuyken, W., Padesky, C. A. and Dudley, R. (2009). *Collaborative Case Conceptualization: Working Effectively with Clients in Cognitive-Behavioral Therapy*. New York: Guildford Press.

Morrison, A. P., Renton, J. C., Dunn, H., Williams, S. and Bentall, R. P. (2004). *Cognitive Therapy for Psychosis: A Formulation-Based Approach*. New York: Brunner Routledge.

Raue, P. J. and Goldfried, M. R. (1994). The therapeutic alliance in cognitive behavioral therapy. In A. O. Horvath and L. S. Greenberg (Eds.), *The Working Alliance: Theory, Research and Practice* (pp. 131–152). New York: Wiley.

Salkovskis, P. (1999). Understanding and treating obsessive compulsive disorder. *Behaviour Research and Therapy*, *37*, 29–52.

Sensky, T., Turkington, D., Kingdon, D., Scott, J. L., Scott, J., Siddle, R. *et al.* (2000). A randomised controlled trial of cognitive behavioural therapy for persistent symptoms in schizophrenia resistant to medication. *Archives of General Psychiatry*, *57*, 165–172.

Slade, P. D. (1973). The psychological investigation and treatment of auditory hallucinations: A second case report. *British Journal of Medical Psychology*, *46*, 293–296.

Turkington, D., Kingdon, D., Rathod, S., Wilcock, S. K. J., Brabban, A., Cromarty, P. *et al.* (2009). *Back to Life, Back to Normality: Cognitive Therapy, Recovery and Psychosis*. Cambridge: Cambridge University Press.

van Os, J., Hanssen, M., Bijl, R. V. and Vollebergh, W. (2001). Prevalence of psychotic disorder and community level of psychotic symptoms: An urban rural comparison. *Archive of General Psychiatry*, *58*, 663–668.

Zubin, J. and Spring, B. (1977). Vulnerability a new view of schizophrenia. *Journal of Abnormal Psychology*, *86*, 103–126.

Note

1 This chapter is based on the work undertaken by Dudley *et al.* (2007) and we acknowledge the contribution of Caroline Bryant, Katherine Hammond, Ronald Siddle and David Kingdon.

Chapter 7

Cognitive behaviour therapy and early intervention

Jean Addington, Enza Mancuso and Maria Haarmans

Introduction

One of the most important recent developments in schizophrenia research and treatment is the concept of early intervention and prevention. Recent research has targeted either the late pre-onset or early post-onset phases of schizophrenia. Since it has been suggested that delays to treatment impede recovery and may impact outcome, the goal of post-onset studies is to detect and treat schizophrenia close to the onset in order to minimize the duration of untreated psychosis. Pre-onset studies are more controversial because the development of a disorder is only a probability and these studies are dealing with the future risk of schizophrenia. Pre-morbidly, risk may be evident in genetic heritage, but in these genetic high-risk studies the risk of converting to psychosis is relatively low (approximately 10 per cent to 20 per cent). In the putatively prodromal phase of schizophrenia the formation of symptoms and disability has already begun and may actually provide enough predictive power for the disorder to be tested as a new diagnostic threshold.

Subtle pre-illness clinical, psychosocial and cognitive deficits have been reported for many years. But it is only in the past decade that systematic, reliable identification of "prodromal" individuals has become possible, based on the presence of subthreshold psychotic symptoms and/or a family history of schizophrenia with signs of functional deterioration. These individuals who appear to be in a prodromal phase of schizophrenia or other psychotic illnesses have high rates of conversion to psychosis (ranging from 20–50 per cent in most studies) over about two years. In the prodromal phase the formation of symptoms and disability has already begun. Many of these individuals are help-seeking since their symptoms, although attenuated or subthreshold for psychosis, are already debilitating.

Intervention at the first episode

The goals of early intervention are to reduce the delay in accessing treatment and to offer optimal treatment in the early, most critical years following onset. Often treatment is offered in comprehensive programs specifically designed to target a first episode of psychosis in order to reduce relapse and disability and enhance recovery. Many young people experiencing a first episode of psychosis will achieve remission from positive symptoms within the first year, with varying patterns of recovery (Addington, 2008). However, a significant proportion continues to experience disabling positive and negative symptoms, at times making working and self-support difficult (ibid.).

A combination of pharmacotherapy and psychological intervention is considered paramount in achieving optimal recovery in individuals with psychosis. One psychological intervention that has received much attention is cognitive behaviour therapy (CBT) for psychosis. Outcome trials of CBT for psychosis are promising, and several recent reviews and meta-analyses support the effectiveness of CBT for psychosis in individuals experiencing a more chronic course of illness (Tarrier and Wykes, 2004; Turkington *et al.*, 2006). The focus of this chapter is on the use of CBT for individuals in the early stages of psychosis.

Rationale for CBT in first-episode psychosis

Even in the case of "best practice", there are significant limitations to biological interventions that may impact recovery. First, in the first year of treatment, approximately 60 per cent of first-episode individuals are non-adherent to medication and as many as 40 per cent are non-adherent in the first six months of treatment alone. More than 60 per cent have intermittent periods of non-adherence. Even with proper adherence to medication, relapse is often a problem within the first year (Addington, 2008). Second, functional recovery remains a challenge. Significant symptomatic improvement is not matched by improvement in functional recovery (i.e. social, vocational, and school functioning and interpersonal relationships) (ibid.). Third, there is good evidence supporting the effectiveness of CBT in treating depression, anxiety and substance misuse disorders – all of which have a high co-morbidity in first-episode psychosis.

CBT trials for first-episode psychosis

Few studies have evaluated the effectiveness of CBT in the initial phase of psychosis. In an early study, CBT was superior to treatment as usual (TAU) in reducing positive symptoms and in decreasing time to recovery. But in the five-year follow-up, the only significant difference was an increase in perceived "control over illness" in individuals receiving CBT over activities and support (Drury *et al.*, 2000). Study limitations included a small sample size (two thirds had chronic histories and multiple episodes), experimenter bias, the multi-modal CBT treatment, and failure to control for non-specific factors such as therapist contact.

Jackson *et al.* (1998) administered Cognitively Oriented Psychotherapy for Early Psychosis (COPE), aimed at promoting adjustment to psychosis, to a sample of 80 first-episode patients. At one-year follow-up, those who received COPE compared with a historical control and those who had refused to participate in groups differed only on a measure of integration versus sealing over (Jackson *et al.*, 2001). In a subsequent non-randomized COPE intervention study with 91 first-episode subjects, Jackson *et al.* (2005) found no differences between the groups on all outcome measures. Study limitations included alternate subject assignment and poor measurement of non-compliance to medication.

One of the most methodologically rigorous randomized controlled trials was the SoCRATES study in the UK (Lewis *et al.*, 2002). This trial had a large representative sample (*n* = 315; 83 per cent first-episode) and compared a five-week, ten session treatment package of CBT plus routine care (RC) with supportive therapy (ST) plus RC and with RC alone during the acute phase of the psychotic illness (Lewis *et al.*, 2002; Tarrier *et al.*, 2004). At 70 days, there were trends towards faster improvement of positive symptoms in the CBT group compared with ST and RC (Lewis *et al.*, 2002). By 18 months, both the CBT and the ST groups demonstrated significant advantages over RC, but there were no significant differences between the impact of CBT and ST on symptoms, relapse or rehospitalisation (Tarrier *et al.*, 2004). The one exception was that auditory hallucinations responded better to CBT relative to ST. Thus, CBT was more effective than RC, but never significantly better than ST. The major limitation of this study was that there was most likely an insufficient time period for the CBT to have had an impact. A high recovery rate in the acute phase under RC is to be expected, since up to 85 per cent of patients recover from a first episode under a standardized drug regime. In this context, there is limited room for CBT to impact positive symptoms at the acute phase.

A more recent randomized controlled trial by Jackson *et al.* (2008) included 62 individuals in the acute phase of their first psychotic episode, in a single treatment setting. Subjects were randomly assigned to either a 14-week, 20 session cognitive therapy condition (ACE; Active Cognitive Therapy for Early Psychosis) or to a Befriending control condition (BF). Three months into treatment, the ACE group demonstrated marked improvement in functioning, but not in positive or negative symptoms. By the end of treatment both groups improved. ACE continued to demonstrate moderately better functioning but there were no meaningful differences in positive and negative symptoms between the groups. At the one year follow-up there was no real evidence that ACE produced differential outcomes over BF on any of the outcome measures. In fact, the results suggest that the BF group caught up on any differences initially observed at the midpoint and at the end of treatment. This study suggests that functional recovery can occur sooner with a CBT intervention, but gains cannot be sustained relative to a control therapy matching therapist contact and expectations about therapy. It is likely that the average number of therapy sessions received (ACE = 9; BF = 7) was too low to adequately address the needs of this sample, particularly in light of the high proportion of participants diagnosed with at least one co-morbid disorder (47 per cent). There were fewer sessions than planned because the 20 sessions were to be delivered over a 14-week period and the therapist found it too difficult to administer more than one session per week. Furthermore, if patients missed a week then they lost sessions as the therapy had to be completed within 14 weeks. Patients would only come once a week and were not always available every week. Other limitations of this study include the small sample size, and failure to include a routine care control group to determine if observed improvements were not attributable to the high quality of the standard of care itself.

Further research is needed to determine the impact of CBT in first-episode samples. A more detailed evaluation of what works and for whom, and under what conditions CBT may work best, is needed. Uncovering the mechanisms through which treatments work is likely to lead to more evidence-based and effective therapies. The limited evidence nonetheless does suggest that CBT is at least an appropriate intervention at the first episode.

Intervention at the pre-psychotic phase

More recently, the early intervention field has considered the possibilities of intervening with those at high risk of psychosis, that is those who may be putatively prodromal for psychosis. One recent strategy has been the detection of attenuated or subthreshold psychotic symptoms, which are suggestive of imminent psychosis. Criteria have been defined for three groups that identify as at clinical high risk for developing a psychotic disorder in the near future. The criteria are a mix of recent-onset functional decline plus genetic risk, or recent-onset-subthreshold or brief-threshold psychotic symptoms. Using these new criteria, the risk of converting to psychosis increases from approximately 10 per cent in the genetic high-risk group to approximately 25 per cent to 40 per cent by one year, as reported in several studies as described below. The reliability of these criteria has been excellent, and studies using these criteria support the view that prodromal persons are symptomatic and at high and imminent risk for psychosis.

There are few published studies to date addressing intervention in a clinical high-risk group. The first study, completed by McGorry et al. in Melbourne, randomized 59 "ultra-high-risk" subjects to six months of active treatment (risperidone 1-3 mg/day plus a modified CBT) or to a needs-based intervention (McGorry et al., 2002). By treatment end, significantly fewer individuals in the active treatment group had progressed to a first episode of psychosis (9.7 per cent vs 36 per cent). No significant differences were noted six months post-treatment, as more of the active treatment group converted to psychosis (19 per cent vs 36 per cent). Limitations of this study included the non-blinding of subjects and raters to group assignment, the uncertainty of the relative contribution of medication over CBT, and the failure to control for medication adherence. Despite these limitations, the McGorry trial was undoubtedly a landmark study.

The second trial was a more rigorous randomized double-blind, parallel study of 60 help-seeking prodromal subjects, comparing the efficacy of a low-dose antipsychotic (olanzapine) vs placebo in preventing or delaying the onset of psychosis (Miller *et al.*, 2003). At one-year follow-up, 16 per cent of olanzapine-treated subjects converted to psychosis compared with 35 per cent of placebo-treated subjects, plus olanzapine was associated with significantly greater symptomatic improvement in prodromal symptoms than the placebo (McGlashan *et al.*, 2006). Although not statistically significant, interpretation of the findings is likely limited by the small sample size.

The third published trial was the Early Detection and Intervention Evaluation (EDIE), a single-blind, randomized trial of CBT with individuals at high risk for psychosis (Morrison *et al.*, 2004). Fifty-eight participants were randomized to either CBT for the first six months, or to monitoring. All received monthly monitoring for 12 months. CBT significantly reduced the likelihood of progression to psychosis as defined on the Positive and Negative Syndrome Scale (PANSS) over 12 months, the likelihood of antipsychotic medication use and of meeting criteria for a DSM-IV diagnosis of a psychotic disorder. CBT also improved positive symptoms in the sample. It is noteworthy that 95 per cent of subjects consented to participate in this trial, suggesting an interest in and willingness to engage in a psychological therapy.

Rationale for CBT for those at clinical high risk

These reports of trials attempting to prevent or delay onset, with one exception, have involved medications – mainly antipsychotics. Medication seems to alleviate the early symptoms in those who may be prodromal for schizophrenic psychosis and possibly even delay the onset. Subjects entering medication trials (McGorry *et al.*, 2002; Miller *et al.*, 2003) are usually in the late pre-onset period as reflected by their high rate of attenuated psychotic symptoms, poor level of functioning and high rates of conversion to psychosis. The feasibility, safety, and ethics of early intervention research need to be seriously considered. Clinical trials using medication with prodromal subjects have generated a great deal of controversy and debate (Bentall and Morrison, 2002). Despite offering substantial advantages over the traditional first-generation medications, there are medical risks associated with the newer antipsychotics, such as weight gain. This is of particular concern with the false positive cases.

These issues have led to a logical case for considering the application of psychological treatment approaches for psychotic symptoms in the emergent phase of psychotic disorders. Bentall and Morrison (2002) suggest that the evaluation of psychological treatment approaches in this early phase of psychotic disorders would be a more acceptable and much safer first step in the development of preventive interventions, which might in itself reduce or avoid the need for drug treatment. Furthermore, since these subjects are help-seeking they may benefit from a psychological intervention even if they are false positives (i.e. not at risk of psychosis).

There are different phases to the prodromal period of schizophrenic psychosis. Different treatments, including *both* pharmacotherapy and psychological interventions, may be appropriate and effective at different times during this period. Antipsychotics might be expected to be important in the later phases of the prodrome when attenuated psychotic symptoms are clearly evident and the individual is potentially on the cusp of a conversion. Psychological interventions might be expected to be most promising at earlier and less symptomatic stages of the prodrome. In fact, in the early stages of the prodromal period the presenting symptoms are not only less severe but also less specific. These individuals present with a wider constellation of concerns. They need and want to understand their perceptual difficulties, to manage the stress, depression, anxiety, sleep disturbance and decline in functioning, and to be supported through this difficult period of their lives. These symptoms and concerns may be more modifiable with a psychological intervention than with medication.

There are several arguments to support why CBT may be a beneficial psychological intervention for this clinical high-risk group (French and Morrison, 2004). First, CBT is likely to help with both the attenuated and the brief intermittent psychotic symptoms. CBT has demonstrated effectiveness in helping those with schizophrenia to cope with psychotic symptoms and to reduce associated distress (Tarrier and Wykes, 2004) and risk of relapse. Second, a CBT approach is a valuable intervention for depression, anxiety and the non-specific emotional problems that are often observed during the prodromal period. Increased problems with metacognitions and self-schemas, which are psychological processes typically targeted during CBT, have been observed in those at clinical high risk (French and Morrison, 2004). CBT approaches have also been useful in addressing substance use, which is believed to be a common and important contributing factor in the development of psychosis in those at risk. Third, CBT interventions fit very well in a stress-vulnerability model and may be an invaluable therapy to teach subjects the types of coping strategies that may offer protection against environmental stressors that risk conversion.

Thus, CBT is the model of psychological intervention that holds the greatest promise for being effective in: (i) addressing the range of symptoms and concerns present in this putatively prodromal period, and (ii) teaching potentially effective strategies to protect against the impact of environmental stressors that may contribute to the emergence of psychosis.

The use of CBT in early psychosis

CBT for those at clinical high risk tends to occur in research settings. Current models of CBT for this group have been well described in the excellent text by French and Morrison (2004) and in a recent handbook of psychological interventions for those at high risk of psychosis by Addington *et al.* (2005).

For those experiencing a first episode of psychosis, comprehensive early intervention programs are being developed throughout the world. Typically, services include ongoing optimum pharmacotherapy and psychiatric and case management, plus a range of psychosocial treatments that encompass psychoeducation, individual CBT, phase-of-illness specific groups, vocational services and a family component.

The focus of CBT for psychosis is the subjective experience of the psychosis and the collaborative attempt at understanding that experience. Hallucinations and delusions are placed on a continuum with normal beliefs, and perceptions are explored and understood in the context of the individual's social, cultural and psychological world (French and Morrison, 2004). Psychotic symptoms can be seen to mirror everyday concerns such as fear of being excluded, unworthy, ridiculed or harmed. Psychoeducation and normalization are used to help facilitate adjustment, particularly in young individuals.

CBT for early psychosis must accommodate critical developmental tasks that are unique to the young individual. Understanding overwhelming and disorganized psychotic phenomena – while facilitating individuation and self-identity, and minimizing disruption to psychological, vocational and social trajectories – is central to the process of recovery in young adults with a first episode of psychosis. The social impact of the onset of a first episode of psychosis is substantial, particularly for the young adult who has newly formed and critical peer, work and intimate relationships. Individual therapy with a young person in the early phase of the disorder should facilitate these developmental tasks.

Goals of CBT in early psychosis

The goals of CBT include addressing not only the symptoms of the illness and the anomalous experiences, but also the impact of the illness on an individual. For both first-episode patients and, at times, clinical high-risk individuals this may include isolation from families and friends, damage to social and working relationships, depression and demoralization, and an increased risk of self-harm, aggression and substance abuse. Pertinent goals of CBT, for both first episode of psychosis patients and clinical high-risk groups include: reducing distress and disability associated with psychotic and subclinical psychotic phenomena; increasing insight into the psychotic disorder and the anomalous experiences; improving mood and self-esteem; and assisting in improving social, vocational and community functioning.

A modular approach to CBT for early psychosis

To address the needs of those individuals experiencing a first episode of psychosis, Addington and Gleeson present a modular approach (2005). These modules include engagement, education, addressing adaptation, treating coexisting anxiety or depression, coping strategies, relapse prevention, and treating positive and negative symptoms. These approaches are guided by a wide range of texts and manuals of empirically supported treatment models that offer both unique and complementary perspectives of CBT for psychosis (e.g. Chadwick *et al.*, 1996; Fowler *et al.*, 1995; Kingdon and Turkington, 2005; Morrison, 2002). A manual drawn from the work of several of the above texts, *STOPP: Systematic Treatment of Persistent Psychosis: A Psychological Approach to Facilitating Recovery in Young People with First-Episode Psychosis* (Herrmann-Doig *et al.*, 2003), is the only manual that has a specific focus on CBT for first-episode psychosis.

One advantage of this modular approach is that there is a range of interventions to meet the wide range of problems and needs of first-episode clients. Although it may be possible for CBT to be effective at the different phases of illness – acute inpatient, acute outpatient, in recovery, in remission and in prolonged recovery – it is recommended that CBT be introduced to first-episode patients once medication, stabilization and symptom remission has begun in order to enhance the goal and expectation of optimum recovery. Typically, the length of treatment is approximately 20 sessions over six months. We provide a more detailed overview of these modules elsewhere (Addington and Gleeson, 2005).

Engagement, assessment and formulation phase

In this phase the formation of the therapeutic alliance, assessments, and the development of a formulation of the presenting problems occur. Engagement occurs not only between therapist and client, but also between client and therapy by socializing the client to the cognitive model. Development of an individualized formulation starts from the first session. This allows the therapist and the client to develop a shared understanding of the key elements that contributed to the development and maintenance of the psychotic symptoms as well as other presenting problems. This process occurs in conjunction with any assessment and is ongoing throughout the course of the therapy. Assessment of the background to the psychotic illness places the psychotic episode in a specific biological, psychological and social context which is integral to the formulation and helps the client make sense of the links among these components. This formulation guides the direction of the therapy, such as the selection of interventions and length and frequency of sessions.

Psychoeducation

In the early stage of CBT therapy it is important that the young person has some understanding of the concept of psychosis and what it means for him or her. This includes symptoms, diagnoses, theories of psychosis, individual explanatory models of psychosis, impact of substance use, medications, warning signs, nature of recovery, and agencies and personnel involved in treatment. Such knowledge helps with the process of normalization, which in turn may help decatastrophize various fears.

Adaptation to psychosis

Changed perceptions of well-being and one's sense of self, combined with the potentially enduring traumatic nature of a psychotic episode itself, may play a significant role in the individual's capacity to recover. Thus, in this module the focus is on the individual and addresses his or her understanding of the psychosis, the impact of psychosis on the self, and adaptation to the psychosis. Taking stock of strengths and limitations, expanding coping skills, and making realistic future plans assists these young people in realizing their potential, despite psychosis. Self-esteem is enhanced by having them distance themselves from the negative aspects of their environment and focus on strengths and accomplishments. Examples of interventions in this module may include challenging social fears, increasing competence and improving self-esteem. With these newfound strengths and skills, these young people can then begin to implement change to improve their functioning. The hope is that these changes will also be self-reinforcing.

Treatment of secondary morbidity

Secondary morbidity results from a failure to adapt and typically may include depression, anxiety and substance abuse. In this phase individuals learn about the nature of the secondary condition. Typical interventions include cognitive restructuring where underlying beliefs and assumptions are examined, challenged and replaced with more appropriate and rational beliefs and assumptions. This can be supplemented by group-based interventions for anxiety management or substance use.

Coping strategies

Coping strategies are designed to help with positive and negative symptoms and with the functional and emotional problems that arise from the symptoms. First, the positive symptoms that will be targeted need to be identified. Available strategies include enhancing coping strategies, assertiveness training and diary recording of mastery and pleasure. Specific behavioural and cognitive strategies are available to help patients work towards improved functional outcome, despite symptoms.

CBT can be used to help clients who may require a more structured behavioural approach, for example those presenting negative symptoms and poor social functioning. Interventions for negative symptoms typically include behavioural tasks such as behavioural self-monitoring, paced activity scheduling, assertiveness training, diary recording of mastery and pleasure, and graded task assignments. Young people experiencing negative symptoms often engage in very few pleasurable activities, which may serve to maintain negative affective states and thus contribute to the persistence of negative symptoms. Cognitive targets include personal interactions and perceptions of others and the self (i.e. if others are perceived as "too demanding" and if the self is perceived as "a failure") that may contribute to low self-efficacy and hopelessness.

Relapse prevention

A range of interventions and general principles derived from CBT have been described to address relapse prevention. These include monitoring for early warning signs of relapse, and cognitive restructuring of enduring self-schema that may be associated with elevated risk of relapse (for further details on relapse prevention, see Chapter 10).

Techniques to address delusions and beliefs about voices

Specific techniques for addressing positive symptoms have been well described in the literature (see also Chapters 1, 2, 3 and 8). For example, when working with auditory hallucinations, one technique is to conduct a collaborative critical analysis of beliefs about the origin and nature of the voice(s), which can then be followed by the use of voice diaries, reattribution of the cause of the voices, and generation of possible coping strategies.

Interventions for delusions can include identifying precipitating and maintenance factors, modifying distressing appraisal of the symptoms and generating alternative hypotheses for abnormal beliefs (Turkington *et al.*,

2006). It is possible to engage young people with psychosis in a colla-borative fashion and to systematically explore the logical and empirical bases for their delusions. When helping clients with delusional beliefs, it is better to avoid direct confrontation since confrontation can strengthen rather than weaken the conviction of beliefs. Clients should be encouraged to use behavioural experiments to help discover disconfirming evidence. In this way, alternative hypotheses are generated and schemas analyzed to attain a collaborative understanding of the development of the distorted beliefs. Peripheral evidence and beliefs are addressed before more central beliefs, in order to minimize psychological reactance (Chadwick *et al.*, 1996). In this way, disabling emotional disturbances can be reduced.

Summary

This chapter has reviewed the use of CBT for early intervention for both those experiencing a first episode of psychosis and for those at clinical high risk of psychosis. Although there are several studies supporting the effec-tiveness of CBT for psychosis, there are very few published outcome studies of CBT for first-episode patients. Some of those that have been published have some methodological problems. Results from studies of the use of CBT for those at clinical high risk are promising. Replications of larger studies are now under way in the UK, Canada and Australia. Since CBT appears to be an appropriate therapy to meet some of the diverse needs of these young people, it is important to do further research to determine what aspects of CBT work, for whom, and under what conditions this therapy may work best. It is only by uncovering the mechanisms through which CBT works that we will obtain more evidence-based and effective therapies.

References

Addington, J. (2008). The promise of early intervention. *Early Intervention in Psychiatry*, *1*, 294–307.

Addington, J. and Gleeson, J. (2005). Implementing cognitive behavioural therapy for first-episode psychosis. *British Journal of Psychiatry*, *187* (Suppl. 48), 72–76.

Addington, J., Francey, S. M. and Morrison, A. P. (Eds.). (2005). *Working with People at High Risk of Developing Psychosis: A Treatment Handbook*. Chichester, UK: Wiley.

Bentall, R. P. and Morrison, A. P. (2002). More harm than good: The case against using anti-psychotic drugs to prevent severe mental illness. *Journal of Mental Health*, *11*, 351–356.

Chadwick, P., Birchwood, M. and Trower, P. (1996). *Cognitive Therapy for Delu-sions, Voices and Paranoia*. New York, NY: John Wiley & Sons Ltd.

Drury, V., Birchwood, M. and Cochrane, R. (2000). Cognitive therapy and recovery from acute psychosis: A controlled trial. *British Journal of Psychiatry*, *177*, 8–14.

Fowler, D., Garety, P. and Kuipers, E. (1995). *Cognitive Behavior Therapy for Psychosis*. Chichester, UK: John Wiley & Sons.

French, P. and Morrison, A. P. (2004). *Early Detection and Cognitive Therapy for People at High Risk of Psychosis: A Treatment Approach*. Chichester, UK: John Wiley & Sons.

Herrmann-Doig, T., Maude, D. and Edwards J. (2003). *STOPP: Systematic Treatment of Persistent Psychosis: A Psychological Approach to Facilitating Recovery in Young People with First-Episode Psychosis*. London, UK: Martin Dunitz.

Jackson, H., McGorry, P., Edwards, J., Hulbert, C., Henry, L., Francey, S., Maude, D., Cocks, J., Power, P., Harrigan, S. and Dudgeon, P. (1998). Cognitively oriented psychotherapy for early psychosis (COPE): Preliminary results. *British Journal of Psychiatry*, *172*, 93–100.

Jackson, H., McGorry, P., Henry, L., Edwards, J., Hulbert, C., Harrigan, S., Dudgeon P., Francey, S., Maude, D., Cocks, J. and Power, P. (2001). Cognitively oriented psychotherapy for early psychosis (COPE): A 1-year follow-up. *British Journal of Clinical Psychology*, *40*, 57–70.

Jackson, H., McGorry, P., Edwards, J., Hulbert, C., Henry, L., Harrigan, S., Dudgeon, P., Francey, S., Maude, D., Cocks, J., Killackey, E. and Power, P. (2005). A controlled trial of cognitively oriented psychotherapy for early psychosis (COPE) with four-year follow-up readmission data. *Psychological Medicine*, *35*, 1295–1306.

Jackson, H., McGorry, P., Killackey, E., Bendall, K., Allot, P., Dudgeon, J., Gleeson, J., Johnson, T. and Harrigan, S. (2008). Acute-phase and 1-year follow-up results of a randomized controlled trial of CBT versus befriending for first-episode psychosis: The ACE project. *Psychological Medicine*, *38*, 725–735.

Kingdon, D. G. and Turkington, D. (2002). *The Case Study Guide to Cognitive Behavior Therapy of Psychosis*. Chicester, UK: John Wiley & Sons.

Kingdon, D. G. and Turkington, D. (2005). *Cognitive Therapy of Schizophrenia*. London, UK: The Guilford Press.

Lewis, S., Tarrier, N., Haddock, G., Bentall, R., Kinderman, P., Kingdon, D., Siddle, R., Drake, R., Everitt, J., Leadley, K., Benn, A., Grazebrook, K., Haley, C., Akhtar, S., Davies, L., Palmer, S., Faraqher, B. and Dunn, G. (2002). Randomised controlled trial of cognitive behavioral therapy in early schizophrenia: Acute-phase outcomes. *British Journal of Psychiatry*, *181* (Suppl.), 91–97.

McGlashan, T. H., Zipursky, R. B., Perkins, D., Addington, J., Miller, T., Woods, S. W., Hawkins, K. A., Hoffman, R. E., Preda, A., Epstein, I., Addington, D., Lindborg, S., Trzaskoma, Q., Tohen, M. and Breier, A. (2006). Randomized double-blind trial of olanzapine versus placebo in patients prodromally symptomatic for psychosis. *American Journal of Psychiatry*, *163*, 790–799.

McGorry, P. D., Yung, A. R., Phillips, L. J., Yuen, H. P., Francey, S., Cosgrave, E. M., Germano, D., Bravin, J., McDonald, T., Blair, A., Adlard, S. and Jackson, H. (2002). A randomized controlled trial of interventions designed to reduce the risk of progression to first-episode psychosis in a clinical sample with subthreshold symptoms. *Archives of General Psychiatry*, *59*, 921–928.

Miller, T. J., Zipursky, R. B., Perkins, D., Addington, J., Woods, S. W., Hawkins, K. A., Hoffman, R., Preda, A., Epstein, I., Addington, D., Lindborg, S., Marquez, E., Tohen, M., Breier, A. and McGlashan, T. H. (2003). A randomized double-blind clinical trial of olanzapine versus placebo in patients at risk of being prodromally symptomatic for psychosis II: Baseline characteristics of the "prodromal" sample. *Schizophrenia Research*, *61*, 19–30.

Morrison, A. P. (Ed.). (2002). *A Casebook of Cognitive Therapy for Psychosis*. New York, NY: Taylor and Francis.

Morrison, A. P., French, P., Walford, L., Lewis, S. W., Kilcommons, A., Green, J., Parker, S. and Bentall, R. P. (2004). Cognitive therapy for the prevention of psychosis in people at ultra-high risk: A randomised controlled trial. *British Journal of Psychiatry*, *185*, 291–297.

Tarrier, N. and Wykes, T. (2004). Is there evidence that cognitive behaviour therapy is an effective treatment for schizophrenia? A cautious or cautionary tale? *Behaviour Research and Therapy*, *42*, 1377–1401.

Tarrier, N., Lewis, S., Haddock, G., Bentall, R., Drake, R., Kinderman, P., Kingdon, D., Siddle, R., Everitt, J., Leadley, K., Benn, A., Grazebrook, K., Haley, C., Akhtar, S., Davies, L., Palmer, S. and Dunn, G. (2004). Cognitive behavioral therapy in first-episode and early schizophrenia. *British Journal of Psychiatry*, *184*, 231–239.

Turkington, D., Kingdon, D. and Weiden, P. J. (2006). Cognitive behavioral therapy for schizophrenia. *American Journal of Psychiatry*, *163*, 365–373.

Chapter 8

Command hallucinations

Theory and psychological interventions

Maria Michail and Max Birchwood

Introduction

Schizophrenia affects 0.8 per cent of the UK population, usually starts in early adult life and leads to persistent disability in most cases (Birchwood and Jackson, 2001). It carries a high risk of suicide (10 per cent) and deliberate self harm (Harris and Barrowclough, 2001) and, on a population basis, people with schizophrenia are more likely to perpetrate acts of aggression than their peers (Brennan *et al.*, 2000). While drug treatment has improved, approaching 50 per cent will continue to experience treatment-resistant symptoms (Kane, 1996) or symptoms arising from refusal to adhere with drug regimes (Nose *et al.*, 2003).

Among the most prominent of the treatment-resistant symptoms – and the most distressing – are command hallucinations (Shawyer *et al.*, 2003). Yet little is known about the phenomenology and the processes that underlie the development and maintenance of these symptoms and apart from high levels of containment and high doses of medication there are no other therapeutic interventions available (Shawyer *et al.*, 2003; Trower *et al.*, 2004). A recent review of command hallucinations (CHs) by Shawyer *et al.* (2003, p. 104) concluded that "CHs are one of the more disturbing symptoms of psychosis. Standard treatment has proved to be of limited value; there is indisputable need for improved treatment in this area."

Prevalence and phenomenology of command hallucinations

Command hallucinations are very prevalent in people who experience schizophrenia. A recent review of eight studies by Shawyer *et al.* (2003) reported a median prevalence rate of 53 per cent with a wide range (from 18 per cent to 89 per cent) in a sample of adult psychiatric patients. Furthermore, it was reported that 48 per cent of command hallucinations stipulate harmful or dangerous actions (Shawyer *et al.*, 2003) rising to 69 per cent among patients in medium secure units (Rogers *et al.*, 2002). This rate was significantly higher in the forensic population with 83 per cent of voice hearers experiencing command hallucinations with *criminal* content (Shawyer *et al.*, 2003). In a recent study by Trower *et al.* (2004) the most commonly reported commands experienced by individuals were commands to kill self (25 out of 38 patients), kill others (13 out of 38), harm self (12 out of 38) and harm others (14 out of 38). Some of these individuals also experienced innocuous commands (e.g. make a cup of tea, wash your hands) and commands that led to minor social transgressions (e.g. shout in public, break the window). Therefore, the severity of the commands may vary; however, the majority of them are associated with high levels of distress and depression (Shawyer *et al.*, 2003; Trower *et al.*, 2004).

Command hallucinations and harmful compliance

The link between command hallucinations and harm to self or others is not straightforward. Population studies have shown that patients with psychosis are more likely to perpetrate acts of violence and aggression (Brennan *et al.*, 2000). A review by Walsh *et al.* (2002) of the literature on the epidemiology of violence and schizophrenia showed that approximately 20 per cent of patients admitted to hospital for the first time had exhibited aggressive or violent behaviour prior to their admission.

However, what has proved difficult to ascertain is the association between individual symptoms of schizophrenia and the risk of acting or responding to these symptoms. In the MacArthur study (Appelbaum *et al.*, 2000; Monahan *et al.*, 2001) no link was found between the presence of delusions or command hallucinations and violence (GBH, assault and threats with a weapon). However, *thoughts* about violence were a strong predictor of violence six months later. A recent secondary analysis of the MacArthur study by Rogers (2004, 2005) found that an additional significant predictor of aggression is an individual's beliefs about having to "obey" the voice. Thus, it appears to be the content of the individual's thinking and how this reflects the dynamics of the individual's relationship with their supposed persecutor, who is commanding them, that is what we have found to be predictive of harm to both self and others in command hallucinations (Beck-Sander *et al.*, 1997; Trower *et al.*, 2004). In Shawyer *et al.*'s study (2003), 48 per cent of CHs were instructing the individual to perform harmful or dangerous actions and over 30 per cent of individuals experiencing CHs directly complied with their voices (usually by self-harming or harming others). A further 30 per cent have attempted to resist the voice. Trower *et al.* (2004) have identified a significant number of people who "*appease*" the voices. Appeasement behaviour refers to actions an individual takes as a result of hearing a voice which may be harmful and may function as a safety behaviour to minimise the perceived threat from

Table 8.1 Types of command hallucinations and associated compliance and appeasement behaviour in a sample of 38 individuals with command hallucination[1]

Type of commands	Example	Compliance	Appeasement
Command to kill self	Take an overdose Hang yourself Stab yourself	Nine patients had attempted suicide. One patient committed suicide during the trial	Collecting tablets and planning to take them Putting a scarf of a belt around the neck Carrying a knife with them all the time
Command to kill others	Go and kill someone Cut his throat Kill your husband	Four patients attempted to kill someone by suffocation, poisoning or physical assault with a weapon	Carrying a weapon with them (e.g. a knife, an axe)
Command to harm self	Burn yourself Cut your arms Walk in the middle of the road	Nine patients harmed themselves in direct response to voices by cutting themselves, swallowing small objects or jumping in front of cars	Picking at previous wounds (as a way of showing to the voice that they are harming themselves) Standing on the kerb (but not going into the road)
Command to harm others	Hit them Touch your children Rape your neighbour	Seven patients harmed others in direct response to voices by hitting them, scolding them or attacking them	Hitting others with minimal force Verbally threatening others (instead of physically attacking them)

the voice. One type of appeasement is to comply with innocuous commands but ignore the severe commands. Nonetheless, people who appease the voice are still placing themselves at risk of later compliance. Some examples of compliance and appeasement from a study we conducted recently with people who experienced command hallucinations (Trower *et al.*, 2004) are shown in Table 8.1.

Nevertheless, predicting *who* will act on their voices, and *when* they will do this, has proved difficult in spite of these epidemiological data. *Why* people respond to their voices in the above varying ways (e.g. complying, appeasing) is also something that warrants exploring.

Command hallucinations: A cognitive model

As mentioned previously, the relationship between command hallucinations and compliance is very complex. It is often assumed that the presence of such symptoms will inevitably trigger emotional and behavioural responses (e.g. compliance). However, previous studies (Trower *et al.*, 2004) have shown that there is considerable variation in how people with command hallucinations respond to their voices. A review of the literature on command hallucinations and compliance by Braham *et al.* (2004) showed that the mere presence of CHs is not sufficient to produce compliance; rather, this relationship is mediated by factors such as beliefs about the *power* and the authority of voice; the *identity* of the voice (e.g. it is the Devil); beliefs about the *malevolence* or *benevolence* of the voice and also its *meaning* and purpose (e.g. it is punishing for past sins). Therefore, it is important to examine the role of beliefs about voices in order to gain a better understanding of the relationship between command hallucinations and compliance.

A cognitive model of voices and its application to command hallucinations

According to the cognitive model of auditory hallucinations by Chadwick and Birchwood (1994) and Birchwood and Chadwick (1997), the emotional (e.g. distress, anger, depression) and behavioural (compliance, appeasement) responses to voices are not triggered merely as a result of the content or topography of the voice. Rather, the individual's beliefs about the meaning and the purpose of the voice are fundamental. Figure 8.1 illustrates how a voice, as an activating event (A), following the basic principles of the rational emotive behaviour therapy, gives rise to different beliefs and appraisals by the individual according to their belief system (B). It is these beliefs that then trigger emotional and behavioural consequences (C). With regards to CHs and compliance, the voice is perceived as the trigger of the core beliefs of power, authority and subordination which subsequently elicit emotional responses in terms of fear, depression, sometimes elation and behavioural responses such as compliance or appeasement. These types of behaviours can also be perceived as *safety behaviours* as they appear to "save" the person (e.g. "If I did not do as the voice told me I would die") but on the contrary, they serve the purpose of maintaining their unfounded beliefs.

Another important aspect of the cognitive model of voices is the nature of the individual's perceived relationship with their voices and its role in triggering distress, fear and behavioural responses to voices. Chadwick and Birchwood (1994) found evidence demonstrating that differences in the way individuals engage with their voices – fear, reassurance, engagement and resistance – reflect vital differences in beliefs about the voices. These beliefs

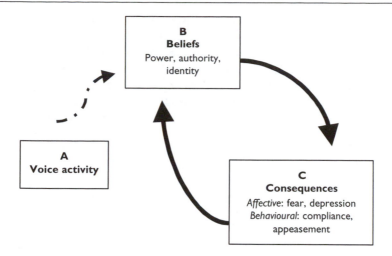

Figure 8.1 Cognitive model of command hallucinations[2]

refer primarily to the power and omnipotence, identity and meaning of the voice. Power in particular refers to the individual's beliefs about how much they can control the voice and whether they believe they have to comply. Identity refers to beliefs about "who" the voice is. Most commonly the voice is ascribed a supernatural identity, e.g. a spirit, a ghost, God or the Devil. Beliefs about the meaning and purpose of the voice can be understood as an attempt to explain the voices and where they are coming from. Chadwick and Birchwood (1994) have found that such beliefs about the voices' identity and meaning led to voices being construed as either "benevolent" or "malevolent". For example, if the individual believes the voice is punishing them for something wrong they did in the past, the voice will most likely be perceived as malevolent (intent to harm); whereas, if the individual believes that the voice has given them a special mission in life (e.g. to save the world) the voice will be perceived as benevolent (intent to help and protect). Most importantly, beliefs about voices were not always linked to voice content; in 31 per cent of cases beliefs were incongruous with content, which suggests that it is the meaning attached to the voice rather than the voice itself that led to the maintenance of the appraisals (Chadwick and Birchwood, 1994).

Research has provided empirical support for the relationship between power beliefs and affective and behavioural responses to voices. Birchwood *et al.* (2000; 2004) have demonstrated the power differential that exists between the voice and the voice hearer; the voice is usually appraised as dominant, omnipotent and shaming, whereas the individual is seen as subordinate, shamed and inferior. This degree of powerlessness in relation to the dominant voice is closely linked to distress and depression.

Furthermore, the powerlessness and inferiority that voice hearers experience in their relationships with others in general is strongly linked to the power of voices. This suggests that the interpersonal relationships an individual has with others (for example, powerlessness/subordination, being down-ranked) are mirrored in the inner experiences with voices – an individual who feels inferior to their voices will also feel inferior to others in their social environment (ibid.). In relation to compliance, research by Beck-Sander *et al.* (1997) has shown that it is the individual's appraisals of the power and omnipotence of the voice, and not so much the content, that predicts their response to voice. Therefore, the more powerful and controlling a voice is perceived to be, the more likely it is that the person will comply. This relationship is moderated by appraisals of the voice's intent (malevolent or benevolent) and consequences of resisting the voice. Thus, a voice perceived as "benevolent" is usually complied with, irrespective of the content, whereas a "malevolent" voice might be initially resisted but then inevitably submitted to or appeased (Beck-Sander *et al.*, 1997; Birchwood and Chadwick, 1997).

To summarise, the cognitive model of voices suggests that it is the appraisals of the voices (power, identity, meaning) rather than the voices per se that elicit distress and compliance. This model provides a thorough understanding of the processes involved in maintaining those dysfunctional appraisals. It is important to now explore how and why these appraisals are generated in the first place.

Social rank theory

Birchwood *et al.* (2000; 2004) have shown that the relationship between a voice and a voice hearer can operate in the same way as an external social relationship. So, if a person is feeling inferior in comparison to their voices then they will feel down-ranked and inferior in their social environment, too. The mechanisms that underlie this relationship can be explained on the basis of the Social Rank Theory, which provides a comprehensive account of social comparison or conflicts in interpersonal situations in an attempt to understand human behaviour. This theory has also been used to examine psychopathology from an evolutionary adaptationist point of view.

According to Price (cited in Gilbert and Allan, 1998), the Social Rank Theory suggests that access to resources such as food and territories triggers the emergence of conflicts between pursuers, during which some will win while others will lose. In such circumstances of defeat, it is important for losers to have an internal inhibitory mechanism, which will force some of them to cease competing and so reduce challenging behaviour. There are two basic processes: a) escalation (threaten others, keep competing, etc.); and b) de-escalation (back off, retreat). De-escalation comes into operation when an individual is in a disadvantaged position as it inhibits competing behaviour and promotes accommodation to the fact that one has lost (Gilbert and Allan, 1998). Furthermore, it sends signals of submission to the attacker so as to disengage them from inflicting further harm.

In human studies the ranking theory proposes that social life is organized in terms of hierarchies, with those in higher hierarchies being more dominant and those in lower hierarchies having less power and control (Trower and Gilbert, 1989). The desired goal in the dominat heirarchies is the achievement of a higher status in terms of dominance hierarchies or the maintenance of the already achieved social status. Social attractiveness plays a significant role in ensuring someone's status in the social hierarchy and, moreover, establishing group relationships (Gilbert, 1997). Experiences of being devalued and perceived as socially unattractive could pose a threat not only to someone's social identity but also to the social bonds he/she has already established. In order to avoid such a possibility, individuals engage in various strategies aimed at reducing the perceived threat and its consequences. Trower and Gilbert (1989) have proposed two kinds of systems which are activated in cases of unfavourable social comparisons. The "defense system" involves behavioural strategies characterized by attempts to inhibit attacks and signal submission, attempts to renegotiate the relationship with dominant others, a state of alertness, and what is called "braced readiness" – where people are alert to withdraw or send submissive signals so as to deter further attacks from those who are more dominant. The process of appeasing the voices serves a similar function. The "safety system", on the other hand, adopts a more positive approach in social hierarchies; others are not seen as a source of constant threat, but rather as a source of safety and support. The signals sent between the members of the social group aim at inducing contact and positive reinforcement. These social ranks, according to Gilbert (1989), will be represented in the mind as dominant-subordinate cognitive schemas or "mentalities" and will be used as a guide in the social relationships of individuals. Very relevant to this is also Beck's theory about dysfunctional schemata and how they remain dormant until current events that bear similarities to the original cause them to resurface (Beck et al., 1979).

Taking into consideration a) the basic tenets of Social Rank Theory and b) evidence that shows how the relationship with the voice is reflected in the everyday relationships with social others (Birchwood et al., 2000; 2004), it now becomes clear how appraisals about the power and identity of the voice are generated. As stated by Byrne et al. (2006), the perceived dominant-subordinate relationship between the voice and the individual could be driven by the individual's core interpersonal schemata. Based on the above, Byrne et al. (ibid.), in their manual of CBT for command hallucinations, propose that harmful actions by people who experience CHs are a result of their beliefs about the voices in terms of power and control and their conviction that they have to comply or appease the voices other-wise consequences for the self and others will follow.

Cognitive behavioural therapy for command hallucinations (CTCH)

The CBT model for CHs, as outlined in the casebook by Byrne *et al.* (2006), has been developed based on the cognitive model of voices and Social Rank Theory. The CTCH aims to reduce motivation to comply or appease the voice by:

- Undermining the power of the voice and its perceived ability to harm and shame
- Increasing the power of the voice hearer
- Improving interpersonal effectiveness.

Here we will briefly outline the different stages of the intervention based on Byrne *et al.*'s casebook (ibid.) and provide a case example taken from the above manual with the permission of the authors.

CTCH Level 1: Assessment, engagement and formulation

The main aim of this stage is to assess and evaluate psychotic symptoms, in particular CHs and associated cognitive, behavioural and emotional responses. Assessment is an ongoing process and is expected to continue throughout the therapy in order to be able to evaluate the outcome of the intervention. Engagement is extremely important and can be quite chal-lenging due to the distressing and distracting nature of the voices. Therefore, the following key principles are fundamental in the development and maintenance of a therapeutic relationship:

- Establishing good rapport and a trusting relationship through empathic listening
- Encouraging the individual to give a detailed account of their experiences and their beliefs
- Anticipating difficulties with engagement and work towards weakening beliefs that could challenge or threaten engagement (e.g. voices may comment adversely on the therapist)
- The use of a symbolic "panic button" (e.g. tapping three times) to give the individual control during the therapy.

It is also important at this stage to begin the process of helping the individual to distinguish between *facts* and *beliefs*. For example, experiencing a voice is seen as a fact, whereas the perceived power and control over the voice hearer is a belief. During the process of assessment and formulation, the key beliefs related to the commanding voice are identified and formulated; this process is ongoing and likely to be modified during therapy. These key beliefs refer to:

- Power and control
- Compliance, resistance and appeasement
- Identity
- Purpose and meaning.

Having developed a formulation based on the model above, the next step is to communicate this to the individual, tentatively proposing it to them with the aim of achieving a shared understanding. Following this, the psychological origins of this power relationship between the voice and the individual can be explored at a later stage.

CTCH Level 2: Promoting control

The aim of this stage is to emphasize the person's strengths in coping with their voices, and to start to build evidence against their powerlessness; to highlight the person's ability to have some control over their voices, and thereby to build evidence against the voice's power; and to develop an understanding of factors that increase/decrease the presence of voices and to bring some immediate relief.

The process of promoting control involves developing or reinforcing a coping repertoire for reducing the distress and compliance behaviour associated with the voices. Common strategies suggested in order to control the voices are: watching TV, listening to the radio, wearing ear plugs, following lyrics to favourite songs in one's head, or assertively addressing the voice. Learning to develop boundaries between the voice and the voice hearer is also a useful strategy to help the individual gain control over their voices (e.g. by turning the voice off).

CTCH Level 3: Disputing power beliefs

The overall aim of this phase of CTCH is to address the perceived power imbalance which underlies compliance and distress. Specifically, to:

- Reduce the perceived power of the voice and increase the perceived power of the voice hearer
- Reduce compliance, appeasement and other safety behaviours, and increase resistance

- Weaken the conviction that the client is being and will be punished or harmed
- Weaken the conviction about the identity of the voice.

Challenging power beliefs includes techniques such as questioning the evidence for the beliefs, following a line of logical reasoning that exposes inconsistencies in the client's beliefs, reality testing in a bid to disconfirm the beliefs, 'normalizing' the voice qualities, and encourage the individual to respond more assertively to the voice.

CTCH Levels 4 and 4a: Reducing safety behaviours and compliance

Safety behaviours have an important psychological function for the individual in that they appear to prevent harm (e.g. "If I did not do as the voices asked something terrible might have happened to me".) They are natural coping strategies, albeit dysfunctional ones, and it is likely that people will be resistant to reducing their safety behaviours as this may increase their anxiety and make them feel that they have less ability to resist harmful commands.

Behavioural experiments can be used to test the validity of a belief. For example, carrying out or withholding a behaviour in order to test a prediction that something catastrophic will happen. This is particularly useful for testing beliefs that the voice will punish the client if they do not comply. The individual is encouraged to reduce the degree of appeasement (e.g. resisting more serious commands by acting on innocuous commands) and note that the feared outcome does not occur, hence weakening the belief. Questioning the voice's command is the next step towards shifting the power differential between the voice and the voice hearer. The voice may now be challenged more assertively, for example, in response to a voice command, the individual may ask, "Why should I do that?" or "Why don't you do it yourself?" Such behavioural responses are designed to get the client to act against the dysfunctional power beliefs and in line with the new functional beliefs, thus further weakening the former and strengthening the latter. Therefore, the individual is now ready to identify evidence of their own mastery and control.

CTCH Level 5: Addressing broader interpersonal power issues – Preventing relapse

The aim of this stage is to change the individual's broader interpersonal behaviour in order to increase their social rank and at the same time reduce likely subordination to powerful voices. The intervention here also serves to reduce events which may trigger or exacerbate voices or act as maintenance factors (relapse prevention).

CTCH Level 6: Working with personal meaning

At this stage it is possible to work on and offer an alternative explanation for the voices based on a developmental perspective. The presence of traumatic and stressful events could provide an insight into the life context in which the voices, and the beliefs about them, arose. The aim is to identify the psychological origins of the voice and even its identity. Having achieved a shared reformulation, it may be possible to proceed in addressing and challenging negative self-evaluative beliefs. This is particularly relevant as for some people such negative self-beliefs or low self-esteem may underpin and drive their delusional thinking (inferential thinking).

A case example: Ralph[3]

Background

Ralph is a 33-year-old man who began hearing voices at the age of 16. He reported being sexually abused at nine years of age. He was bullied by some of his peers, both physically and emotionally, and was tormented by them over the abuse. He became increasingly disruptive and difficult to manage, and was put into care at 14 years as his mother was unable to cope. At 16 he received a youth custody sentence for stealing; it was during this time that he began to hear voices. From 22–25 years he experienced remission from the voices but, since then, he has reported hearing them almost daily.

Stage 1: Assessment

During the initial assessment, Ralph reported hearing three hostile dominant male voices to which he felt extremely subordinated. The content of these voices was always in the nature of put downs, including personal threats to self (e.g. "we are going to stab you"), personal verbal abuse relating to his self-concept (e.g. "you are a pervert"; "you are evil") and commands to self harm and harm others (e.g. "kill yourself, you deserve to die"; "go and get a hammer: kill X [Ralph's abuser]"; "kill your Dad"). As a result, Ralph described feeling extremely frightened, inferior and weak. Ralph said that he heard the voices at least once a day, particularly at night, often lasting for hours at a time. He felt that he had no choice but to listen to them. He coped by shouting and swearing at the voices, listening to the TV or radio, and drinking alcohol.

The Voice Power Scale (Birchwood *et al.*, 2000) showed that Ralph believed the voices were much more powerful, strong, confident, knowledgeable and superior to him, and much more able to harm him than he was of defending himself. He believed that the voices were very powerful because:

- he had no control over them
- of their frequency
- they said things in a loud, persistent way
- if they told him something, it must be true
- they had taken over his mind.

Beliefs about identity

Ralph reported being 100 per cent certain that one of the voices was that of his abuser, and that the other two were from the devil, because "they sounded like them".

Beliefs about meaning

Ralph believed that he was being persecuted by people for bad things in his past: he had committed burglary and theft as a young adult; he felt responsible for his mother's death; and he believed the voices were a punishment because he was sexually abused, for which, he believed, he bore responsibility.

Beliefs about compliance/resistance

Ralph had a past history of taking two overdoses in response to the voices, and he had previously cut his wrists superficially in order to appease the voices. He reported feeling compelled to obey the voices but had resisted commands to kill others for fear of being put in prison, although he feared acting on the commands if they continued to be so distressing. He acted on commands to get out of bed on the majority of occasions.

Beliefs about control

Ralph believed that he had some control over the voices, but only occasionally.

Target behaviours

The main compliance behaviour targeted for intervention was acting on commands to harm himself or others, including wrist cutting (appeasement behaviour).

Stage 2: Intervention

Challenging beliefs about control over the voices

Supported by the therapist, Ralph developed a range of coping strategies which helped him to have more control over the voices: he found talking to someone he trusted helped when the voices were distressing. Other helpful strategies included: telling the voices to stop or go away in a firm voice (out loud when alone or to himself when in company); listening to the radio or watching football on TV; keeping active by meeting with friends; taking regular medication. These strategies were reinforced and it was suggested that these offered him some control.

Exploring the evidence for and against the power of the voices

Using the above coping strategies, Ralph began to believe that he had more control over the voices and was not a helpless victim. He used the evidence that he could cope as evidence to support an emerging belief that he had as much power and rank as the voices.

Gradually, Ralph became aware that his voices often worsened (i.e. became louder, more frequent) when he was depressed or anxious. Learning strategies for coping with anxiety and depression also made him feel more empowered. In addition, the belief that the voices were powerful because if they said something, it must be true was explored:

- The voices said "you killed your mother". The circumstances of his mother's death were explored. Ralph had believed that he should have done something to stop his mother's cancer. However, he accepted that he and his family had done all they could to help their mother through her illness. Ralph concluded that she had died of an illness (cancer) and that he was in no way responsible for her death.
- The voices called Ralph a pervert. However, there was no evidence to support this claim. Ralph had never taken advantage sexually of another person; moreover, he had been the victim of abuse as a child, not the perpetrator.
- The voices called Ralph evil. Ralph defined an evil person as someone who would not feel guilty about, but would enjoy, physically or emotionally hurting someone and would not help other people in anyway. There was no evidence that Ralph was evil but there was much evidence that Ralph was kind and caring and disliked upsetting people.

Such evidence helped Ralph change his belief that the voices were powerful dominants. The evidence cast doubt on the truth of what the voices said, leading Ralph to conclude that the voices were liars and not to be trusted.

Consequently, he concluded that he did not have to believe the voices when they threatened or said unpleasant things about him or others.

The following belief was also explored: that because the voices said things frequently, sometimes getting louder, this meant they should be obeyed. This was challenged by asking him to consider whether saying "you are a pink giraffe" to someone over and over again would make this statement true. Ralph concluded that just because something is said repeatedly does not automatically mean it is true or that he should act on it. Gradually, Ralph began to believe that he could choose whether or not to believe what the voices said, and he could choose whether or not to act on their commands.

Reducing appeasement

Ralph chose to resist more serious commands to harm himself or others. But he did respond to commands to "get out of bed" which, though obviously totally innocuous, was viewed as an appeasement in social rank terms, and therefore as a safety/defensive behaviour that stopped him behaviourally testing the social rank beliefs. Having reframed things in this way, Ralph agreed he would resist even these minor commands to see if the supposed consequences ensued. They did not. We should note that often the best way of helping the client to re-evaluate commands is by starting the process with innocuous commands of this type.

Exploring beliefs about meaning and identity

Ralph believed he was being persecuted for past misdemeanours. An alternative explanation was proposed, namely the notion that stressful events in childhood and adolescence had triggered the development of Ralph's mental health problems. As found by Birchwood *et al.* (2000), the relationship between a person and their voice(s) is often mirrored in dominant–subordinate relationships they have, or have had, with people in their lives. Working on these relationships can be important. Links were made between Ralph's relationship with the voices and his relationship with his abuser. As a child, Ralph had felt powerless to act against the abuser; similarly, he had perceived himself to be subordinate to the voices, just like with the abuser. Ralph was able to use this social rank account of the early dominant–subordinate victimisation to understand the later voice relationship. This in turn enabled him to become more assertive with the voices and with significant others; for example, Ralph was learning that he could make choices about his behaviour which may contradict the voices' commands. Ralph began to describe various situations with friends, family and staff in which he had been able to assert himself: for example, he initiated a move from a flat into supported housing because he felt that this would be beneficial for his mental health; he began to actively seek support from trusted others whenever he felt distressed by the voices or other events; and he started to talk more openly about his experiences with trusted others, no longer feeling ashamed to do so.

Outcome:

The Voice Power Differential (VPD) Scale (Birchwood *et al.*, 2000) and the control and distress scales of the Psychotic Symptom Rating Scales (PSYRATS; Haddock *et al.*, 1999) were administered before and after the intervention. The VPD measures the power differential between voice and voice hearer on five-point scales, with regard to overall power and a number of related characteristics. The PSYRATS measures the severity of a number of dimensions of auditory hallucinations and delusions, including amount and intensity of distress associated with these symptoms. A major reduction in distress was observed accompanied by a shift in the power balance favouring Ralph. The results indicate that the majority of targeted beliefs about the voices had significantly changed by the end of therapy. Ralph believed that he had more control over the voices and was equally as powerful as them. He had not felt compelled to act on serious commands to harm himself or others and he no longer believed that he was being persecuted. In addition, the findings indicate that Ralph was somewhat less distressed by the voices post-therapy, although he was still upset by the fact that he continued to hear malevolent voices. With regard to the voices' identity, some doubt had been cast on Ralph's belief that one of the voices was that of his abuser, although he remained partially convinced. Ralph felt that he had benefited from having the opportunity to talk about the voices, in terms of learning how to cope with them and learning that he was able to question what they said and stand up to them.

Conclusion

Command hallucinations are among the most high-risk and distressing symptoms of schizophrenia. They are associated with high levels of distress and depression and they are medication resistant. In this chapter we provided a comprehensive account of a cognitive model for command hallucinations in order to understand the processes that underlie their development and maintenance in people with schizophrenia. An innovative intervention primarily targeting beliefs about voices has been presented based on the manual of our colleagues, Byrne *et al.* (2006). Preliminary findings (Trower *et al.*, 2004) point towards its reasonable effectiveness but a large-scale trial which is underway will provide more definitive results about the efficacy of the intervention and the durability of its effects.

References

Appelbaum, P. S., Robbins, P., Monahan, J. (2000). Violence and delusions: Data from the MacArthur Violence Risk Assessment. *American Journal of Psychiatry*, *157*, 566–572.

Beck, A. T., Rush, A. J., Shaw, B. F. and Emery, G. (1979). *Cognitive Therapy of Depression*. New York: Guilford.

Beck-Sander, A., Birchwood, M. and Chadwick, P. (1997). Acting on command hallucinations: A cognitive approach. *British Journal of Clinical Psychology*, *36*, 139–148.

Birchwood, M. and Chadwick, P. (1997). The omnipotence of voices: Testing the validity of a cognitive model. *Psychological Medicine*, *27*, 1345–1353.

Birchwood, M. and Jackson, C. (2001). *Schizophrenia*. Hove: Psychology Press.

Birchwood, M., Meaden, A., Trower, P., Gilbert, P. and Plaistow, J. (2000). The power and omnipotence of voices: Subordination and entrapment by voices and significant others. *Psychological Medicine*, *30*, 337–344.

Birchwood, M., Gilbert, P., Gilbert, J., Trower, P., Meaden, A., Murray, E. and Miles, J. (2004). Interpersonal and role-related schema influence the relationship with the dominant "voice" in schizophrenia: A comparison of three models. *Psychological Medicine*, *34*, 1571–1580.

Braham, L., Trower, P. and Birchwood, M. (2004). Acting on command hallucinations and dangerous behaviour: A critique of the major findings in the last decade. *Clinical Psychology Review*, *24*, 529–555.

Brennan, P., Mednick, S. and Hodgkin, S. (2000). Major mental disorders and criminal violence in a Danish birth cohort. *Archives of General Psychiatry*, *57*, 494–500.

Byrne, S., Birchwood, M., Trower, P. and Meaden, A. (2006). *A Casebook of Cognitive Behaviour Therapy for Command Hallucinations. A Social Rank Theory Approach*. London and New York: Routledge.

Chadwick, P. and Birchwood, M. (1994). The omnipotence of voices: A cognitive approach to command hallucinations. *British Journal of Psychiatry*, *164*, 190–201.

Gilbert, P. (1989). *Human Nature and Suffering*. Hove, UK: Lawrence Erlbaum Associates.

Gilbert, P. (1997). The evolution of social attractiveness and its role in shame, humiliation and guilt and therapy. *British Journal of Medical Psychology*, *70*(2), 113–147.

Gilbert, P. and Allan, S. (1998). The role of defeat and entrapment (arrested flight) in depression: An exploration of an evolutionary view. *Psychological Medicine*, *28*, 585–598.

Haddock, G., McCarron, J., Tarrier, N. and Faragher, E. B. (1999). Scales to measure dimensions of hallucinations and delusions: The psychotic symptom rating scales (PSYRATS). *Psychological Medicine*, *29*, 879–889.

Harris, E. and Barraclough, B. (2001). Suicide as an outcome for mental disorders. *British Journal of Psychiatry*, *170*, 205–228.

Kane, J. M. (1996). Treatment-resistant schizophrenic patients. *Journal of Clinical Psychiatry*, *57*, 35–40.

Monahan, J., Steadman, H., Silver, E., Appelbaum, P. S., Robbins, P. C., Mulvey,

E. P. *et al.* (2001). *Rethinking Risk Assessment: The MacArthur Study of Mental Disorder and Violence*. Oxford: Oxford University Press.

Nose, M., Barbui, C. and Tansella, M. (2003). How often do patients with psychosis fail to adhere to treatment programmes? A systematic review. *Psychological Medicine*, *33*, 1149–1160.

Rogers, P. (2004). *Command Hallucinations and Violence: Secondary Analysis of the MacArthur Violence Risk Assessment Data* (PhD Dissertation). Institute of Psychiatry, King's College, London.

Rogers, P. (2005, January). *The Association Between Command Hallucinations and Prospective Violence: Secondary Analysis of the MacArthur Violence Risk Assessment Study*. Conference presentation at the Institute of Psychiatry Medium Secure Unit Conference, London.

Rogers, R., Watt, A., Gray, N. S., MacCulloch, M. and Gournay, K. (2002). Content of command hallucinations predicts self harm but not violence in a medium secure unit. *Journal of Forensic Psychiatry*, *13*, 251–262.

Shawyer, F., Mackinnon, A. and Farhall, J. (2003). Command hallucinations and violence: Implications for detention and treatment. *Psychiatry, Psychology and Law*, *10*, 97–107.

Trower, P. and Gilbert, P. (1989). New theoretical conceptions of social anxiety and social phobia. *Clinical Psychology, Review*, *9*(1), 19–35.

Trower, P., Birchwood, M. and Meaden, A. (2004). Cognitive therapy for command hallucinations: A randomised controlled trial. *British Journal of Psychiatry*, *184*, 312–320.

Walsh, E., Buchanan, A. and Fahy, T. (2002). Violence and schizophrenia: Examining the evidence. *British Journal of Psychiatry*, *180*, 490–495.

Notes

1 Reproduced with the permission of Trower *et al.*, 2004.
2 Reproduced with the permission of Byrne *et al.*, 2006.
3 Reproduced with the permission of Byrne *et al.*, 2006.

Chapter 9

Cognitive characterization and therapy of negative symptoms and formal thought disorder

Neal Stolar and Paul Grant

"Cognitive-free" symptoms of schizophrenia

Factor analytic studies of the symptoms of schizophrenia conducted in several cultures across the world (Andreasen *et al.*, 2005) all converge on, at minimum, a three-factor solution: (i) psychotic symptoms (hallucinations and delusions); (ii) disorganized symptoms (bizarre behavior and positive formal thought disorder); and (iii) negative symptoms (flat affect, alogia, avolition, anhedonia and asociality). Such studies are a part of an emerging database that corrects the overly narrow definition of schizophrenia that has enjoyed prominence in psychiatry over the past 40 years – that of being predominantly a psychotic disorder (Carpenter, 2006). While the three-dimensional solution returns the field to the richer and more accurate accounts of its pioneers (Bleuler, 1911; Kraepelin, 1913), the cornerstone of schizophrenia treatment continues to be a pharmacotherapy that is largely an antipsychotic enterprise. That the negative and disorganized dimensions are not the focus of treatment may go a long way toward explaining why these dimensions are associated with poorer outcome in schizophrenia (Kirkpatrick *et al.*, 2006).

Over the past 15 years, cognitive therapy has emerged as an innovative and effective treatment for individuals diagnosed with schizophrenia and schizo-affective disorder (Wykes *et al.*, 2008). However, this therapeutic effort has been, like pharmacotherapy, primarily focused upon the psychotic symptoms. One explanation for this emphasis is that the symptoms of psychosis are cognitive in nature: hallucinations often occur in the form of "voices" with reportable verbal content, potentially reflecting automatic or "hot" cognition (Beck *et al.*, 2009); delusions, by definition, are reported beliefs (APA, 2000). The other two clusters of symptoms, by contrast, are typically devoid of meaningful verbal content: patients with negative symptoms are characterized by a reduction in verbal and non-verbal communication (Kirkpatrick *et al.*, 2006), while the disturbance of formal thought disorder (FTD) often renders verbal content difficult, if not impossible, to comprehend (Andreasen, 1979). Another factor is the widely held perception that patients who are significantly disorganized or emotionally non-responsive or unengaged in their lives might be difficult, if not impossible, to engage in the efficacious collaborative therapeutic process entailed by cognitive therapy (Kingdon and Kirschen, 2006). Indeed, we note that researchers in the UK have recently advocated the adoption of the term CBTp (Wykes et al., 2008), which serves, among other things, to emphasize the idea that cognitive therapy predominantly addresses the psychotic dimension within schizophrenia.

Although negative symptoms and thought disorder have limited cognitive content of a meaningful nature, we propose that specific active psychological processes contribute to what on the surface might seem to be more behavioral, linguistic and emotional deficiencies. Our formulation is similar to, and owes much to, the framework employed by Beck in the early 1960s, in which he showed that cognitive aspects of depression, far from being epiphenomena, were fundamental participants that precede emotional and behavioral aspects. We hypothesize that those with negative symptoms or thought disorder have low expectations of success and/or pleasure in the activities of daily living such as education, employment, and social interaction. We further hypothesize that these attitudes are key cognitive participants in both dimensions of symptoms: when success or pleasure is not anticipated from an activity, desire to engage in that activity is, often completely, reduced (negative symptoms); when the activity is engaged, more stress results, and, in the case of acts of communication, disorganization can result. While keeping this integrative hypothesis in mind, we will initially present the cognitive conceptualization of these classes of symptoms separately, and then discuss a cognitive therapy approach that is tailored to negative symptoms and formal thought disorder.

Cognitive conceptualization of negative symptoms

The negative symptoms include reduced verbal (alogia) and non-verbal (affective flattening) expressivity, as well as limited engagement in constructive (avolition), pleasurable (anhedonia), and social (asociality) activity (Kirkpatrick et al., 2006). The consistency with which these symptoms cluster in factor analyses has been taken as evidence of the validity of the negative symptom construct in schizophrenia. Further validation comes from the temporal profile: negative symptoms, relative to psychotic or disorganized symptoms, tend to appear earlier and tend to be more stable across the chronic course of schizophrenia. Furthermore, negative symptoms are associated with poorer outcomes, compared with the other symptom dimensions, over 5- and 10-year follow-up periods. Antipsychotic medications have demonstrated minimal efficacy with regard to negative symptoms, making treatment innovation in this domain a priority of schizophrenia treatment research (ibid.).

Explanatory models of negative symptoms have, since the seminal writings of Hughlings Jackson (1931), appealed to degenerative neurobiology. One proposal is that loss of brain tissue causes the loss of capacity characteristic of negative symptomatology, as indicated by studies that find enlarged cerebral ventricles associated with prominent negative symptoms in schizophrenia. Another theoretical approach, using frontal lobe patients as analogy, proposes that pathology in the frontal lobes produces reduced activation levels which, in turn, causes loss of motivation, reduced emotionality, and minimal willful behavior. Yet a third approach attributes the cause of negative symptoms to the cognitive impairment – deficits of memory, attention and executive function – characteristic of the vast majority of individuals diagnosed with schizophrenia. While the evidence supporting these neurobiological models is mixed (Stolar, 2004), the formulations all characterize negative symptoms as biological deficits: the prominent negative-symptom patient is represented as limited by his neurobiology such that he cannot engage in constructive activity, generate expressive responses, etc. The recently published NIMH-MATRICS consensus statement on negative symptoms (Kirkpatrick et al., 2006) continues this trend, clarifying conceptual, measurement and research design issues so that the basic neuropathology of negative symptoms might be more effectively characterized and, importantly, made amenable to treatment by bioactive agents or devices.

We share Tarrier's (2006) concern that the consensus achieved by the NIMH-MATRICS group is too narrowly focused upon the biological aspects of negative symptoms and places far too much emphasis on pharmacotherapy. Moreover, there is an emerging literature that is beginning to chart the psychological aspects of negative symptoms in schizophrenia. Anhedonic patients diagnosed with schizophrenia, for example, have been shown to experience pleasure to an equivalent degree to normal control subjects (Gard et al., 2007), a result that contradicts the notion that these patients have a neurobiological deficit that hinders their ability to experience pleasures. Rather, a cognitive factor, expectation, distinguishes the two groups: the patients erroneously expect not to enjoy themselves and, thereby, engage in pleasurable activities to a lesser extent than the controls. In a similar vein, Rector (2004) has found that elevated negative symptoms are associated with attitude endorsements such as "If I don't do something well, there is no point in doing it at all." Significantly, the correlation between the attitudes and negative symptoms holds when severity of depression is controlled. This set of beliefs, endorsed by patients with negative symptoms, has subsequently been labeled *defeatist performance attitudes* (Grant and Beck, 2009a), because the attitudes are over-generalized, inaccurate and feed into a vicious cycle of avoidance, apathy, passivity, and isolation which may protect the patient from the pain of rejection, but lead to unhappiness and an empty life.

Integrating findings on the psychology of negative symptoms, Beck *et al.* (2009) have hypothesized that dysfunctional, negativistic beliefs contribute to the avoidance of constructive activity seen in individuals with schizophrenia. The relevant factors contributing to loss of motivation and avoidance are low expectancies for pleasure (e.g. "I won't enjoy it"), low expectancies for success at social and non-social tasks (e.g. "I am not going to be good enough"), low expectancies for social acceptance (e.g. "What do you expect? I am mentally ill"), and defeatist beliefs regarding performance (e.g. "If I am not sure I will succeed at a task, there's no point in trying"). The negativistic and overly general beliefs stymie the initiation of action (including speech and emotional expression). These cognitive causes (including demoralization and fear of rejection) may not be obvious, depending on the insight of the person afflicted, and thus negative symptoms deemed as primary might arise from these negative attitudes as well.

Ultimately, we propose a stress-diathesis framework in which defeatist beliefs are mediators in the causal chains that link cognitive impairment, negative symptoms and poor functioning in schizophrenia. Abnormal pruning, ventricular enlarging and other physiological disruptions may produce alterations in neuro-connectivity, causing poor integrative functioning of the brain and, hence, limited processing resources and poor neurocognitive performance. Cognitive deficits combined with limited availability of processing resources will likely provoke those with vulnerability for negative symptoms, producing adverse developmental stressors, such as social and academic failures. There can even be a vicious cycle in which physiologically caused negative symptoms lead to negative attitudes that perpetuate and exacerbate the symptoms of avolition and apathy.

Cognitive conceptualization of formal thought disorder

Formal thought disorder, along with inappropriate affect and bizarre behavior, comprise the disorganization dimension in schizophrenia (Andreasen *et al.*, 2005). It is associated with poor educational, occupational and social functioning. Thought disorder is considered a subset of the language disorder found in individuals with schizophrenia. McKenna and Oh (2005) have summarized four theoretical approaches: thought disorder as (i) dysphasia; (ii) communicative incompetence; (iii) a dysexecutive phenomenon; and (iv) a dyssemantic phenomenon.

As defined by Andreasen (1979), positive forms of thought disorder include loosening of associations (various forms of getting off the track of the flow of a conversation, as well as tangential replies to questions) and idiosyncratic use of language, such as neologisms (creating new words) and word approximations (using existing words in a new way). At its most extreme, positive formal thought disorder manifests as incoherence or word salad (random use of words). Negative thought disorder symptoms include blocking (interruption in the flow of thought) and poverty of content of speech, which itself includes concreteness, perseveration, clanging and echolalia.

The following sample of formal thought disorder in the context of an interview contains a few of these types of thought-disordered speech:

Interviewer: Do you have any family members around here that you're in contact with?

Patient: Well, it's just my fiancé. That's, that's Carrie. That's really not a relative. We just met. She's 47. I'm 45. We just met. And, uh, it was a program. We met accidentally, uh, actually, it was at the nurses' station. We said hi. And, uh, I'm 45. She's 47. She has a daughter. She has a granddaughter. She has a daughter. And she has a granddaughter. I've seen her daughter in person. [perseveration]

I haven't seen her in a while only because that, by accidentally, I told her about who really my fiancé is, is, uh, Jill. It's not just one lady. She . . . they lets me think that's okay. Cos, uh, sometimes, maybe that it could be it. I didn't . . . It's. Other. She has in-laws. [incoherence]

There's a messy forest, or a Macy's at her house. [Loosening of association (slight). The word "messy" is what is unusual here. There may be a forest and/or a Macy's near her house. The sentence is likely based on the similar sound of "messy" and "Macy". Clanging is a possibility here, but it would more often involve words in a row, e.g. "She has a messy, Macy, mousy at her house".]

Interviewer: So you told me you haven't seen your fiancé in a while, but is having a romantic relationship important to you?

Patient: [After an extended pause] Hm?

Interviewer: You told me you haven't seen your fiancé in about a year or so, but is that relationship important to you? Is having a romantic relationship important to you?

Patient: It's ok. I'm sorry. I have a little mental block. I'm sorry. [Possibly blocking – with insight into and labeling of the event as a mental block. Usually blocking occurs in the midst of a person's speech as opposed to at the start of a response, as in this example. The latter could often result from a lack of attention or difficulty in comprehending the question and thus is harder to clearly label specifically as blocking.]

That's the questions, right? I'm sorry, Janice. I just like to say another name only cos I don't like to get into my grand pop or dad name, their name. I don't mean any harm. Like you can call me "corny" or "nell", "cornflakes' sister". It's not a problem. [loosening of association]

Formal thought disorder symptoms have been shown to worsen when the topic of conversation is emotionally salient or when the person is criticized by family members (Rosenfarb *et al.*, 1995). This research accords with our clinical experience that the client with thought disorder is often quite lucid when discussing neutral topics (e.g. "How did you get here?") or positive topics (e.g. sports), but becomes very thought disordered when discussing topics related to their treatment. Accordingly, we propose that situational and psychological aspects play a key role in the day-to-day experience of thought disorder. Specifically, formal thought disorder is, in part, a stress response to "hot" topics and situations. In this regard, thought disorder is analogous to stuttering, where particular thoughts (e.g. "They won't understand me?"; "I am stupid") elicited by certain situations lead to an increase in communicative difficulty. A vicious cycle, again, can be triggered by social feedback, as the people in the patient's environment struggle to comprehend his speech and become increasingly frustrated and impatient, while, at the same time, the patient's level of tension goes up and he experiences increased intrusive ideation regarding failure – the end result being even more disorganized speech. Repeated experiences of this sort could well lead to a preference, on the part of the patient, to avoid social interactions, which might partially explain the association between thought disorder and poor social functioning.

As in depression and anxiety disorders, specific types of automatic thoughts (ATs) and distorted beliefs will lead to the occurrence of the thought disorder symptoms. Our research indicates that patients with thought disorder have a heightened fear of negative evaluation; moreover, this fear of being judged was found to moderate the relationship between cognitive impairment and thought disorder, even when psychotic, negative and depressive symptoms are statistically controlled (Grant and Beck, 2009b). While this sort of research is in its infancy, we believe that the understanding of thought disorder will be greatly advanced by studies exploring psychological aspects such as beliefs and expectations.

Cognitive therapy for the treatment of negative symptoms and thought disorder

While there is a tradition of psychosocial treatment of negative symptoms that has focused upon behavioral methods, such as skills training, token economies and psychiatric rehabilitation, we are unaware of any such efforts targeting formal thought disorder. Cognitive therapy, despite its historical emphasis upon psychotic symptoms in schizophrenia, has, nonetheless, begun to establish a promising track record with regard to negative symptoms (Beck *et al.*, 2009). Sensky *et al.* (2000), for example, in a study targeting treatment-resistant positive symptoms in outpatients, found that cognitive therapy produced a significant reduction in negative symptoms across a nine-month follow-up period as compared with patients in an informal support control group. This reduction in negative symptoms has proved impressively durable, as the cognitive therapy patients continued to show fewer negative symptoms five years after treatment subsided (Turkington *et al.*, 2008). Similarly, in a trial that is notable for explicitly targeting negative symptoms, Rector *et al.* (2003) found cognitive therapy, compared with enriched treatment as usual, to have reduced negative symptomatology over the nine-month follow-up period.

While we are encouraged by these results, it is our belief that more assertive tactics will, ultimately, add considerable efficacy to the treatment of both negative symptoms and thought disorder. Goal-directed cognitive therapy has been developed by Aaron T. Beck at the University of Pennsylvania with difficult to treat cases in mind. The general framework of this approach is to establish plausible long-term goals with the patient, followed by a series of short-term goals. As therapy proceeds, the therapist works collaboratively with the patient to move through the goals step by step. Thought disorder, low motivation and other symptoms, such as hallucinations and delusions, are addressed as they become obstacles to the patient reaching his goals.

Negative symptoms

A protracted period of engagement with specific, direct questioning may be needed to access the goals of someone with negative symptoms. There is often a need to involve family and/or mental health staff to determine a patient's current needs as well as their improvement as therapy progresses. Some modifications may be necessary when engaging in therapy with someone with negative symptoms. Patience is required in that responses may be slow and devoid of significant detail. Open-ended questions may need to be followed by direct or even forced-choice questions. The cognitive impairment that often accompanies negative symptoms may necessitate the use of slow, repetitive speech on the part of the therapist. The patient may need to be asked to repeat key items to check for understanding. Agenda-setting may be limited by the patient's apathy. A therapist can follow the step-wise approach of allowing more than the usual amount of time to respond, asking about recent events and concerns about them, addressing common long-term goals (relationships, work, hobbies), and providing a choice of possible agenda items. As therapy progresses, the patient may be better able to formulate goals and agendas.

Given that bio-behavioral models of negative symptoms postulate diminished activity in the systems responsible for motivated behavior (Stolar, 2004), external stimulation may energize the patient. In this regard, the therapist is a primary catalyst to help the patient identify goals and begin to ratchet up motivation and the successful execution of goal-directed behavior. The primary therapeutic tools of this activating process are activity scheduling with mastery and pleasure ratings and graded task assignments (Beck *et al.*, 2009). The more concrete the plan, and the more immediate the outcome, the better. Accordingly, rewards, including frequent reminders of any incremental progress, should be immediate, and steps to achieve certain activities need to be specified and even written down as cues.

Cognitively, eliciting and addressing the patient's negative attitudes about their abilities can help reverse the cycle of resignation and disappointment. Rather than the presence of thoughts about negative consequences of actions, there may be a lack of positive cognition in the sense that activities (including speech and facial expressions) may not be viewed as having any value. Helping a client think of positive consequences of certain actions may help produce motivating thoughts. Cost-benefit analyses can aid in examining the advantages and disadvantages of doing some activity or doing nothing. Chronic patients' underlying assumptions and beliefs may be long-standing and not necessarily associated with recent situations. These assumptions may be reflected behaviorally in over-cautiousness, passivity, and distancing the self from risks. These beliefs can be addressed as they interfere with the patient's new set of goals, which involve more engagement with life and a better quality of life. Similarly, hallucinations and delusions that cause, via secondary psychological process, negative symptoms can become obstacles to the patient's ongoing goals. They can, as such, be addressed with appropriate cognitive and behavioral techniques (Beck *et al.*, 2009).

Formal thought disorder

Treatment begins, as in all types of therapy, with establishing rapport. If FTD is due to negative automatic thoughts related to social performance, including conversation, it may be reduced merely by establishment of the therapeutic alliance, as trust and confidence builds. One of the authors sees someone with schizophrenia who presented in the first session with severe thought disorder. However, it was virtually absent by the second session. The person admitted that she had been apprehensive about changing therapist. She may have been most anxious in the initial session but less so in subsequent ones, leading to a dramatic reduction in FTD.

Cognitive assessment of FTD can be initiated as soon as its presence is detected. One component of this assessment concerns the content of disordered speech, as this content may have pertinent psychological meaning. Therefore, efforts should be made to discern as much as possible the ideas the patient is attempting to communicate, keeping an eye, particularly, on the emergence of themes. Being able to pose relevant questions to the patient serves a double purpose: the problem-solving activity of goal-directed therapy can be advanced at the same time that the patient appreciates that he is being understood. The latter aspect can then help reduce stress and potentially reduce the FTD itself.

Intermittent FTD, or fluctuations in its severity in a session, calls for employment of a second cognitive assessment component – guided discovery for antecedent automatic thoughts that lead to the stress response manifested as disorganized speech. The therapist may be able to note what topics or situations (such as the presence of family members in certain sessions) lead to worsening of FTD in session. This can generate appropriate questions leading to the discovery of ATs preceding the exacerbation of FTD.

Given that people with schizophrenia exhibit more thought-disordered speech when discussing personal, emotion-laden items, a useful strategy for reducing thought disorder symptoms would be to utilize therapeutic methods aimed at emotion regulation and stress reduction. Standard cognitive therapy techniques for managing depressive, anxiety and anger difficulties, as well as for ameliorating the emotional effects of hallucinations and delusions, can indirectly help to improve organization of speech.

Kingdon and Turkington (1994) suggest, additionally, using role plays to help the patients understand how their communication might not be comprehended by others and how to use clearer language by taking the position of the listener. This method has support from studies showing that patients are able to explain previously expressed thought-disordered discourse, provide meanings of neologisms, and improve communication after listening to audiotapes of prior conversation.

Ultimately, therapist and patient work to improve communication, in part to facilitate the goals of therapy itself. Nelson (2005) recommends questioning patients directly when units of speech are not understood. In addition, Pinninti et al. (2005) recommend: (i) the five-sentence rule in which therapist and patient limit speech to five sentences at a time so that disorganization has less chance of worsening with length of conversation; (ii) taking two-minute relaxation breaks using deep breathing, or switching to a neutral topic when emotionally laden material elicits thought disorder symptoms; and (iii) asking about communication difficulties with others.

It is best to use reflective listening for those passages that are clearly understood so that the patient gets positive feedback for precise communication (and correction by the patient can be made if those passages are actually not understood correctly). Focus can then be directed at the incoherent items. More general questions ("What do you mean by. . .?") can be followed, if necessary, by suggested meanings based on the context and tone of the item in question. Clearly divergent, irrelevant material (such as clanging) may be ignored for the most part, but care should be taken to not throw out the baby with the bath water by mistaking emotionally relevant material for impertinent minutiae. For instance, the first word in a series of rhyming words may be important (e.g. "I'm depressed, oppressed, confessed, undressed").

Since the use of cognitive therapy for the treatment of schizophrenia has not yet focused on formal thought disorder, much work remains to be done to test the usefulness of these focused approaches. Improving the flow of speech can enable many people with schizophrenia and thought disorder to then engage in the approaches for hallucinations, delusions, and negative symptoms that previously would have been hampered by the thought disorder itself.

By determining what negative thoughts a person may be thinking prior to the moment of disorganized speech, strategies for cognitive therapy may be developed for that person and perhaps applied to other patients as well. This latter application is important since it may be very difficult to access the automatic thoughts of more severe cases of FTD. General automatic thoughts revealed in less severe cases (e.g. "I won't know what to say") may have to be applied in the treatment of more severe cases until FTD is diminished in these latter cases to the point that formal cognitive therapy can be initiated and idiosyncratic ATs accessed.

In addition to determining initial cognitive precipitants of FTD, it would also be useful to explore cognitive reactions to the social effects of FTD (which may lead to worsening, or at least perpetuation of FTD). The possibility that disorganized thought, elicited by anxiety, may lead to a freezing of planning and behavior indicates that stress reduction methods, including relaxation techniques as well as cognitive treatment of depression, anxiety, anger and positive symptoms, may help reduce the negative symptoms. The basic cognitive technique of slowing one's thoughts and examining them may help more directly in counteracting disorganized thinking to allow for meaningful behavioral output.

Summary

Although, on the surface, negative symptoms and formal thought disorder appear to be devoid of meaningful cognitive content and therefore inaccessible by cognitive therapeutic methods, we hypothesize that these symptoms emerge in part as a result of dysfunctional negative attitudes related to low expectations of success and/or pleasure. These beliefs result in either limited activity (including minimal speech and affect) in the case of the negative symptoms, or in disorganization (including disorganized speech) that is secondary to the stress of attempting to engage in activities despite these negative expectations. Data supporting this view have been obtained in the case of negative symptoms, and preliminary findings suggest that this hypothesis applies to thought disorder as well. The standard cognitive therapy approach of eliciting negative automatic thoughts and examining the evidence can be applied to these symptoms, modifications being introduced when these symptoms directly impede the communicative aspects of therapy. Since patients can also have low expectations for success in the therapy sessions, engagement processes can be critical to achieving therapeutic gains. With further refinement of the use of cognitive therapy for negative symptoms and formal thought disorder, many more patients previously considered out of the reach of psychotherapy can start on the road to a more enriched life.

References

Andreasen, N. C. (1979). Thought, language, and communication disorders: II. Diagnostic significance. *Archives of General Psychiatry, 36*(12), 1325–1330.

Andreasen, N. C., Carpenter, W. T., Kane, J. M., Lasser, R. A., Marder, S. R. and Weinberger, D. R. (2005). Remission in schizophrenia: Proposed criteria and rationale for consensus. *American Journal of Psychiatry, 162*, 441–449.

APA (2000). *Diagnostic and Statistical Manual of Mental Disorders (DSM-IV)* (4th edn, text revision). Washington, DC: American Psychiatric Association.

Beck, A. T., Rector, N. A., Stolar, N. M. and Grant, P. M. (2009). *Schizophrenia: Cognitive Theory, Research and Therapy*. New York, NY: Guilford Press.

Bleuler, E. (1911). *Dementia Praecox or the Group of Schizophrenias* (J. Zinkin, Trans., published in 1950). New York, NY: International Universities Press, Inc.

Carpenter, W. T., Jr. (2006). The schizophrenia paradigm: A hundred-year challenge. *Journal of Nervous and Mental Disease, 194*(9), 639–643.

Gard, D. E., Kring, A. M., Gard, M. G., Horan, W. P. and Green, M. F. (2007). Anhedonia in schizophrenia: Distinctions between anticipatory and consummatory pleasure. *Schizophrenia Research, 93*(1–3), 253–260.

Grant, P. M. and Beck, A. T. (2009a). Defeatist beliefs as mediators of cognitive impairment, negative symptoms and functioning in schizophrenia. *Schizophrenia Bulletin, 35*(4), 798–806.

Grant, P. M. and Beck, A. T. (2009b). Evaluation sensitivity as a moderator of communication disorder in schizophrenia. *Psychological Medicine, 39*(7), 1211–1219.

Hughlings Jackson, J. (1931). *Selected Writings*. London: Hodder & Stoughton.

Kingdon, D. G. and Turkington, D. (1994). *Cognitive Behavioral Therapy of Schizophrenia*. New York, NY: Guilford.

Kingdon, D. G. and Kirschen, H. (2006). Who does not get cognitive behavioral therapy for schizophrenia when therapy is readily available? *Psychiatric Services, 57*, 1792–1794.

Kirkpatrick, B., Fenton, W., Carpenter, W. T. J. and Marder, S. R. (2006). The NIMH-MATRICS Consensus Statement on Negative Symptoms. *Schizophrenia Bulletin, 32*(2), 214–219.

Kraepelin, E. (1913). *Dementia Praecox and Paraphrenia* (R. M. Barclay, Trans., published in 1971). Huntington, NY: Robert E. Krieger Publishing.

McKenna, P. J. and Oh, T. M. (2005). *Schizophrenic Speech: Making sense of Bathroots and Ponds that Fall in Doorways*. New York, NY: Cambridge University Press.

Nelson, H. (2005). *Cognitive Behavioral Therapy with Schizophrenia: A Practice Manual*. Cheltenham: Stanley Thornes Ltd.

Pinninti, N. R., Stolar, N. and Temple, S. (2005). 5-minute first aid for psychosis.

Defuse crises; help patients solve problems with brief cognitive therapy. *Current Psychiatry*, *4*, 36–48.

Rector, N. A. (2004). Dysfunctional attitudes and symptom expression in schizophrenia: Differential associations with paranoid delusions and negative symptoms. *Journal of Cognitive Psychotherapy: An International Quarterly*, *18*, 163–173.

Rector, N. A., Seeman, M. V. and Segal, Z. V. (2003). Cognitive therapy of schizophrenia: A preliminary randomized controlled trial. *Schizophrenia Research*, *63*, 1–11.

Rosenfarb, I. S., Goldstein, M. J., Mintz, J. and Nuechterlein, K. H. (1995). Expressed emotion and subclinical psychopathology observable within the transactions between schizophrenic patients and their family members. *Journal of Abnormal Psychology*, *104*(2), 259–267.

Sensky, T., Turkington, D., Kingdon, D., Scott, J. L., Scott, J., Siddle, R. *et al.* (2000). A randomized controlled trial of cognitive behavioral therapy for persistent symptoms in schizophrenia resistant to medication. *Archives of General Psychiatry*, *57*(2), 165–172.

Stolar, N. (2004). Cognitive conceptualization of negative symptoms in schizophrenia. *Journal of Cognitive Psychotherapy: An International Quarterly*, *18*, 237–253.

Tarrier, N. (2006). Negative symptoms in schizophrenia: Comments from a clinical psychology perspective. *Schizophrenia Bulletin*, *32*, 231–233.

Turkington, D., Sensky, T., Scott, J., Barnes, T. R. E., Nur, U., Siddle, R. *et al.* (2008). A randomized controlled trial of cognitive behavior therapy for persistent symptoms in schizophrenia: A five-year follow-up. *Schizophrenia Research*, *98*(1–3), 1–7.

Wykes, T., Steel, C., Everitt, B. and Tarrier, N. (2008). Cognitive behavior therapy for schizophrenia: Effect sizes, clinical models, and methodological rigor. *Schizophrenia Bulletin*, *34*(3), 523–537.

Chapter 10

Staying well after psychosis

A cognitive interpersonal approach to emotional recovery and relapse prevention

Andrew Gumley

Introduction

At the heart of recovery for individuals with a diagnosis of schizophrenia is the core of emotional recovery. Garfield (1995) has argued that unbearable affect lies at the core of psychosis and that repair following psychosis involves the processes of acknowledging, bearing and putting in perspective the intolerable emotions which often have their origins in early development. This chapter builds on these early psychoanalytic perspectives by drawing upon key developmental and interpersonal processes that provide a context for understanding, formulating and responding to painful affect and its (dys)regulation among individuals recovering from psychosis.

Maintaining a sustained recovery in early psychosis is a challenge for individuals, their families and loved ones, and for service providers. The five years after the first episode of psychosis is regarded as the critical period that determines long-term outcome. Relapse is a crucial factor in the evolving long-term course of the illness. Relapse occurs in 20–35 per cent at one year, 50–65 per cent at two years and 80 per cent at five years (Robinson *et al.*, 1999). Recovery from subsequent episodes of psychosis is less satisfactory than the first, with individuals being more likely to experience persistent and distressing psychotic experiences (Wiersma *et al.*, 1998). The recurrence of psychosis provides the basis for development of feelings of demoralisation and entrapment, and has been linked to compromised emotional adaptation following psychosis (Birchwood *et al.*, 2000). Service users who feel unable to prevent relapse are more likely to develop depression and anxiety (Gumley *et al.*, 2004). Such negative feelings about psychosis and the loss of personal agency are grounded in the reality of individuals' experiences of their psychosis. These feelings are associated with persisting distressing psychotic experiences, more involuntary admissions, heightened awareness of the negative consequences of psychosis, greater awareness of the stigma of psychosis, being out of work, and loss of social status and friendships (Rooke and Birchwood, 1998). In addition, individuals in the early phase of psychosis are more likely to develop depression and suicidal thinking (Birchwood *et al.*, 2000).

Despite the growing evidence over the last decade for the effectiveness of cognitive behavioural therapy for psychosis (CBTp) in alleviating persistent and distressing psychotic experiences, the evidence concerning the prevention of relapse has been disappointing (Wykes *et al.*, 2008). In one of the most significant CBTp trials to date, Garety *et al.* (2008) appear to have confirmed this lack of evidence concerning the effectiveness of CBTp for relapse prevention. In their methodologically robust randomised controlled trial they did not find that CBTp reduced rates of relapse or improved rates of remission at 12 or 24 months (although for those individuals living with the support of a carer there was improvement in distress related to delusions and social functioning). Two possible reasons for these largely negative findings have been put forward: sampling and therapy. In terms of sampling, those randomised were all persons in hospital following an acute relapse or exacerbation. Many of them were responsive but non-adherent to medication and thus showed a rapid response to reinstituting treatment. In addition, many did not particularly wish for psychological therapy and may have had a tendency to "seal-over" (Tait *et al.*, 2004) their experiences. Furthermore, this was a trial of generic CBTp based on a general psychological model of psychotic symptoms and the trial therapists reported that it was sometimes difficult, in the absence of symptoms or of distress, to maintain a clear focus on the positive psychotic symptoms. Indeed, Garety *et al.* (2008) found that the therapy did not influence the predicted mediators of change, such as specific core beliefs or reasoning biases.

In this chapter I will argue that the focus on positive symptoms and their underlying mechanisms (e.g. core beliefs and reasoning biases) are not the correct target for effective relapse prevention. The paradox that I will outline is that the problem of relapse is not a problem of psychotic experiences; that is, psychosis is merely the output of other core underlying processes. Therefore, having a therapeutic focus on psychotic experiences focuses attention on the end stage of the relapse process, which is often too late. Furthermore, there may well be systemic and organisational responses that will impede successful relapse prevention based on a model with positive symptoms as the main focus. Gumley and Park (2010) have recently made reference to the *"relapse dance"* to describe the cycle of unsuccessful, thwarted or aborted help-seeking and relapse. Given the traumatic and distressing nature of psychosis, help-seeking itself may produce fearful expectations. For instance, individuals with psychosis may fear increased medication, re-hospitalisation, and involuntary procedures. Individuals might also experience feelings of shame, guilt, and embarrassment in relation to disappointing or letting down their case worker. Furthermore, many individuals find help-seeking a challenge and may have experienced their relationships and previous interactions with others (including clinicians) as unhelpful, aversive, or rejecting. Thus, by focusing on detection and prevention of psychotic experiences, clinicians may inadvertently create the expectation in individuals that they should seek help in the context of high levels of distress, a context that for some individuals can outstrip their internal and external resources. This is particularly relevant for those individuals who are experiencing a more protracted, difficult, and complex recovery. This may result in a defensive but understandable delay in help-seeking. Delayed help-seeking may unintentionally result in service providers adopting more crisis-driven and coercive responses to the threat of relapse, thus confirming the person's negative expectations of help-seeking and increasing feelings of lack of control and entrapment in illness.

Psychotic relapse as an outcome of affect regulation

Phenomenological evidence shows that feelings of fear, depression, helplessness, hopelessness, embarrassment and shame are common emotional experiences prior to relapse, and that these emotional responses arise in the context of the emergence of low-level psychotic-like experiences including cognitive perceptual anomalies, hearing voices, suspiciousness and interpersonal sensitivity. The combinations of these experiences are sensitive but not specific to relapse. This means that while most relapses are preceded by these experiences, the occurrence of low-level psychotic experiences in combination with affective distress does not necessarily lead to a relapse. Therefore it is more appropriate to consider early signs of relapse as indicating an "at risk mental state".

A person's cognitive, behavioural and interpersonal coping reactions and resources probably moderate the intensity of emotional distress. For example, maintaining a reflective awareness characterised by a non-catastrophic reaction combined with productive coping and recruitment of productive help and support from others is likely to decelerate and abort relapse. However, for many individuals the threat of relapse is likely to lead to catastrophic expectations and a disorganisation of the person's coping responses.

It is now established that the experience of psychosis is traumatic and is often associated with the development of psychosis-related post traumatic stress disorder, which is characterised by intrusive memories linked to the experience of psychosis, hypervigilance and fear, and sealing-off and avoidance. The threat of recurrence of psychosis is therefore likely to generate competing and disorganised reactions such as catastrophic appraisals of relapse, fear, vigilance, and interpersonal threat sensitivity on the one hand, and cognitive, emotional and behavioural avoidance and delayed help-seeking on the other (Gumley and Macbeth, 2006). Fear of relapse has been previously identified in retrospective studies of the phenomenology of early relapse (e.g. Herz and Melville, 1980).

Furthermore, although delayed help-seeking can be conceptualised as a defensive response to the threat of relapse, there is an accompanying probability that this unintentionally increases the likelihood of increased severity of psychotic experiences, admission to hospital and use of involuntary procedures, thus fulfilling catastrophic expectations. Therefore, relapse detection and prevention relies heavily on the presence of a productive and secure working relationship between service users and care providers including health professionals. This fact is not lost on service users who value services as a secure base for exploration and proximity seeking (Goodwin et al., 2003). This provides us with an important link to the developmental and interpersonal roots of affect regulation (or dysregulation) based on the organisation (or disorganisation) of attachment representations, which in turn are likely to inform us about the nature and vulnerability to problematic recovery from psychosis.

Developmental and interpersonal roots of recovery from psychosis

It is well established that good pre-morbid child and adolescent academic and emotional adjustment is a predictor of better outcome after first-episode psychosis and that this predictor is independent of duration of untreated psychosis (Marshall et al., 2005). Conversely, poor pre-morbid adjustment predicts poor outcome. Such data can, however, be understood from a developmentally based attachment perspective.

There is now evidence to suggest that attachment security may be compromised or even disorganised in infants who are later diagnosed with schizophrenia. It has been shown that the mothers of persons who go on to be diagnosed with schizophrenia are more likely to have experienced loss or trauma in the two years prior to or after childbirth (Pasquini et al., 2002). In addition, there is also evidence that being an unwanted child increases risk of becoming psychotic in later life. Both of these types of events are highly significant risk factors for infant attachment disorganisation. Maintenance of attachment insecurity and transition from attachment security is predicted by stressful life events. The AESOP study (Aetiology and Ethnicity in Schizophrenia and Other Psychoses; Morgan et al., 2007) has found that separation from, and death of, a parent before the age of 16 were both strongly associated with a two- to threefold increased risk of psychosis irrespective of ethnicity. Life events such as sexual abuse, homelessness, assault and being in care (Bebbington et al., 2004) predict risk of developing psychosis, even after controlling for mood, substance use and interdependence of life events. These life events are also known to lead to the collapse and disorganisation of attachment, characterised by impaired mentalisation and theory of mind; fragmentation, dissociation and segmentation of episodic memories; and use of competing and inconsistent coping responses (Liotti and Gumley, 2008).

Most recent evidence shows that attachment insecurity is associated with the use of avoidant coping strategies which correlate with problematic service engagement including lack of help-seeking (Tait *et al.*, 2004). Using the Adult Attachment Interview, Dozier (1990; Dozier *et al.*, 2001) have shown that psychosis is associated with an insecure avoidant attachment organisation which is associated with a closing off of affect and episodic memories associated with affect. This attachment organisation is also associated with minimisation of symptoms, reduced help-seeking and greater caseworker and family anxiety. It is noteworthy that most of these attachment transcripts are also classified as unresolved with respect to loss or trauma. Such a sealed-off/avoidant style of affect regulation is likely to locate greater anxiety in busy case workers and may produce greater use of more catastrophic or coercive strategies in community-based teams thus maintaining a sense of relational insecurity and entrenched non-engagement.

Emotional recovery and relapse prevention: Two sides of the same coin

Birchwood *et al.* (2000) found that, in a sample of 105 individuals, 36 per cent developed Post Psychotic Depression (PPD) without concomitant changes in positive and negative symptoms. Participants who developed PPD were more likely than their non-PPD counterparts to attribute the cause of psychosis to themselves (self-blame), perceive greater loss of autonomy and valued role, and perceive themselves as entrapped and humiliated by their illness. In addition, individuals with and without PPD aspired to similar social and vocational roles. However, consistent with the predictions of social ranking theory, those who developed PPD saw their future status as lower. These participants also had greater insight into having a psychotic illness. Therefore, psychosis can be conceptualised as a life event that triggers depression via awareness of its social, interpersonal and affiliative implications. Individuals who develop depression following psychosis appraise this life event as representing a humiliating threat to their future status, leading to the loss of valued social roles, from which escape is blocked due to actual or feared relapse, or indeed persistent symptoms. When we compared relapsers (n = 24) versus non-relapsers (n = 42) over the period of one year we found that individuals who relapsed experienced higher levels of psychological distress. In addition, we have found that relapsers have significantly greater feelings of self-blame, loss and low self-esteem (Gumley *et al.*, 2006). These data attest to the psychological toxicity of relapse and thus show how relapse prevention and emotional recovery are interlinked dual outcomes.

In our study of cognitive behavioural therapy for relapse prevention (Gumley *et al.*, 2003) we randomised 144 persons with a diagnosis of schizophrenia to CBT (n = 72) or treatment as usual (TAU; n = 72). CBT was delivered in two phases. The initial engagement phase focused on the development of an individualised formulation of relapse risk, which was then used to devise an idiosyncratic early signs monitoring measure. This measure was then sent to participants on a fortnightly basis by post and returned by participants in a sealed envelope. Individuals were eligible for the second phase of CBT (Targeted CBT) if they had an increase in early signs or did not return their early signs for two or more occasions. Of those randomised to CBT (n = 72), 66 (92 per cent) engaged in the treatment. Of those who either relapsed or were deemed at risk of relapse (n = 34), 28 (82 per cent) engaged in targeted CBT. The study found a significant reduction in relapse, and a significant improvement in psychotic symptoms, negative symptoms and social functioning. In addition, those participants receiving CBT showed greater improvement in feelings of loss and self-esteem (Gumley *et al.*, 2006). Since this study we have further extended and manualised this intervention and incorporated a developmentally based understanding of affect regulation. Our approach is distinct from other CBTp approaches because we target affect regulation and not psychotic symptoms per se. Affect regulation is targeted via (a) threat-based appraisals linked to both arrested emotional recovery and relapse; (b) development of more helpful (non-avoidant) coping strategies; and (c) implementation of these strategies are provided in the context of early signs of relapse.

Cognitive interpersonal therapy

Cognitive interpersonal therapy (CIT) is a formulation-based psychological therapy, which has as its primary focus an emphasis on affect and affect regulation (Gumley and Schwannauer, 2006). Based on client problem lists, priorities and goals, the therapist systematically identifies barriers to emotional recovery, relapse detection and relapse prevention. The therapist works with the client to develop productive interpersonal coping and intrapersonal coping, and helpful affect regulation strategies are identified, developed and strengthened.

Overview

Cognitive interpersonal therapy for staying well is designed as a 25 to 30-session intervention, which is conducted over nine months. It is divided into three distinct but overlapping phases: engagement and formulation; transforming beliefs and problematic interpersonal strategies; end phase and closure. Over these phases the frequency of therapy is variable with frequent sessions (once per week) at the beginning of therapy when the therapist is focused on the development of a shared formulation, alliance and mutuality of goals and tasks. Sessions are less frequent in the middle phase (once per fortnight), allowing for greater reflection and exploration of predominant cognitive themes and interpersonal strategies. In the end phase, sessions are more frequent to enable issues such as loss, separation and dependency to be addressed.

For some individuals who engage well in psychotherapeutic work and who might focus on particular areas of interpersonal functioning, it can be important to keep the therapeutic frame stable and to keep the regularity of weekly sessions throughout the treatment. Contracting such a long period of therapy can be difficult for many individuals. Therefore, therapy may be contracted in blocks of sessions determined by agreement between client and therapist. For example, initial sessions may be contracted to explore whether therapist and client get on with each other and whether goals can be formulated which are suitable for psychotherapeutic work, whereas later sessions may contract work on specific problems. Just as the frequency of therapy is variable, so is the pacing of sessions. Therapists need to be mindful when exploring experiences and cognitive themes that are associated with strong affect. High levels of affect can overwhelm clients' ability to reflect on their experiences and to mentalise the beliefs and intentions of others. It is important at this juncture that a therapeutic relationship is established that allows clients to clarify and explore difficult emotional content or particular experiences within a containing and safe interpersonal context. In working with this client group, therapists often need to model the expression of tensions and uncertainties in the room and allow for these anxieties to be verbalised as they can often become roadblocks in the interpersonal context of therapy and therefore prevent an open exploration of emotions attached to psychotic experiences.

Case formulation

Case formulation is tailored according to the function of case formulation within the therapeutic progression, the client's interpersonal and recovery style, and the timing or phase in therapy. Case formulation evolves throughout therapy and is seen as a live, creative and ongoing process. It is not an event that is delivered to the patient by the therapist in a static or one-dimensional manner. Case formulation during the engagement phase is designed to capture the client's valued goals and important emotional meanings, and facilitate the development of therapeutic working alliance. The process of formulation and therapy planning can be facilitated by the use of the interpersonal inventory, which provides a careful review of the client's current and past social relationships, current sources of emotional, instrumental, motivational and social support, the reciprocity and mutuality of these supports, and their patterns and mutual expectations. Changes in relationships preceding, during or consequent to the psychosis are elicited, for example, the death of a loved one (potential complex grief), leaving home for University (role transition), deterioration of family relationships (a role dispute). The development of the interpersonal inventory provides a context to understand how the client's interpersonal situation impacts on formulation and the relevance of interpersonal problem areas including (a) grief and loss; (b) role transitions; (c) role disputes; and (d) interpersonal deficits and their implications for impoverished social networks. The interpersonal context of current adaptation demands placed on the individual to reorganise provide an opportunity to develop a sense of how affects are experienced, attended to, reflected on, and clarified and communicated to others. In so doing the therapist is mindful of the developmental and attachment-based origins of affect regulation and control.

Therapeutic relationship

The therapeutic relationship is central to cognitive interpersonal therapy, wherein the development of a collaborative working alliance is central to achieving client goals (see Chapter 5). In the context of staying-well therapy, the therapeutic relationship becomes an important scaffold to facilitate the development of the client's understandings of their own experience and their understanding of the beliefs and intentions of others. Process factors within therapy such as those expressed in concepts derived from psychodynamic therapies (e.g. transference and countertransference) are embraced within therapy. These are important constructs, functioning to allow the therapist to mentalise how their own affective, cognitive, and interpersonal responses within therapy may facilitate or interfere with recovery. The establishment of a containing and reflective therapeutic relationship will enable therapeutic change to take place within an interpersonal context that can in itself provide an essential corrective emotional experience. Within the structure of a stable and consistent therapeutic relationship interpersonal problems and ruptures can be detected and explored that might not otherwise be volunteered or raised by the client. This is important when considering that the client may be highly avoidant and unaware of possible problems. Alternatively, for some clients there is a lack of emotionally close or confiding relationships, thus underlying interpersonal problems never become overtly expressed.

Narrative style

Cognitive Interpersonal Therapy is concerned with how therapists encourage clients to engage in therapeutic dialogues which foster and heighten their ability to reflect on their construction of meaning in relation to their sense of agency and self. This process encourages attending to affects, clarifying their nature and experience, and communicating their meaning in context – a process that is active and participatory rather than passive and observed. This is the essence of personal recovery and staying well. In addition, Greenberg and Pascual-Leone (1997) have suggested that a pivotal task of therapy is, in the context of a safe therapy relationship, to increase awareness of emotion by focusing attention on emotional experiences, and the development of a narrative enabling symbolic self-reflection on the fundamental experiential meanings embedded in personal experience. In their process-experiential approach to psychotherapy, Greenberg and Pascual-Leone have emphasised therapeutic tasks as facilitating experiential rather than conceptual processing of events. The therapeutic narrative gives an indication of the levels of processing and understanding achieved by the client and can be used to focus therapeutic discourse. For example, when discussing trauma it is not unusual for narrative to become fragmented, difficult to follow and impoverished. This acts to signal to the therapist the presence of problematic or unresolved experiences.

Basic elements of the therapeutic stance

Siegel (1999) proposes five basic elements of how caregivers can foster a secure attachment in the children under their care. These elements also form the basic elements of any therapeutic discourse.

Collaboration

Secure relationships are based on collaborative and carefully attuned communication. Collaboration is developed though the careful negotiation of the client's problems and goals within therapy, and the therapist's encouragement for the client to develop an active, enquiring and explorative approach to understanding and resolving emotional distress.

Reflective dialogue

There is a focus on the person's internal experience, where the therapist attempts to make sense of client communications in their own mind and then communicate their understanding in such a way that helps the client create new meanings and perspectives on their emotions, perceptions, thoughts, intentions, memories, ideas, beliefs and attitudes.

Repair

When attuned communication is disrupted, there is a focus on collaborative repair, allowing the client to reflect upon misunderstandings and disconnections in their interpersonal experiences.

Coherent narratives

The connection of past, present and future is central to the development of a person's autobiographical self-awareness. The development of coherent narratives within therapy aims to help foster the flexible capacity to integrate both internal and external experiences over time.

Emotional communication

The therapist maintains close awareness not only of the contents of narrative but also the client's emotional communications. In focusing on negative or painful emotions within sessions the therapist communicates and encourages self reflection, understanding, acceptance and soothing.

General outline of therapy sessions

Psychosis is a powerful event characterised by severe and distressing changes in thinking and experiences that are unified by a pervasive sense of serious interpersonal threat, dominance and paranoia combined with a sense of personal vulnerability. While psychosis, as a disorder, signifies stigmatising negative life trajectories generating feelings of hopelessness or triggering defensive denial and sealing-over, the symptoms themselves have the potential to undermine basic assumptions of safety, interpersonal security, intimacy and attachment.

The therapist's orientation throughout therapy is the collaborative development of a coherent client narrative that optimises the evolution of their self-reflectiveness, the crafting of alternative helpful beliefs and appraisals, and the development of adaptive coping and interpersonal behaviours. Through the discourse of psychotherapy, the focus on narrative, and the use of cognitive and interpersonal techniques the therapist supports the client in meshing behavioural and cognitive change. Underpinning this process, the therapist carefully nurtures the therapeutic alliance and provides the client with a secure base from which to explore difficult issues.

Engagement and formulation

The initial sessions over the first three months (sessions 1–10) focus on developing therapeutic alliance and bond, and mutual tasks and goals. During this phase the therapist and client collaboratively develop and prioritise a problem list from the client's perspective. The therapist needs to listen carefully and feedback their understanding of the client's experiences, interpretations and problems in their own words. During the early engagement sessions (sessions 1–4) the focus tends to be on the client's immediate problem list and goals before exploring more difficult and affect-laden experiences. Where relevant, negative experiences of treatment are explored sensitively and the therapist encourages the client to reflect on the implications of these experiences for the therapeutic relationship. In this way the therapist can begin to develop an understanding of the synchrony between the client's specific autobiographical memories and their beliefs, attitudes and expectations of treatment.

Negative experiences of psychosis are also explored. Again the therapist attempts to maintain a fresh and open dialogue by attending to specific examples of the client's descriptions. This process allows the therapist to develop further hypotheses about the nature of the client's idiosyncratic appraisals of psychotic experiences and how these are likely to shape recovery and determine emotional and behavioural responses to the threat of relapse should early signs of relapse occur in the future. During narratives exploring experiences of treatment and psychosis the therapist needs to maintain sensitivity to the client's trauma by being aware of changes in voice tone, eye contact and body posture. These changes often signal changes in affect and the occurrence of intrusive thoughts or images.

Such changes are thus important opportunities to help develop the client's own self-reflectiveness and their awareness of the importance of their experiences and interpretations in mediating their adaptation and adjustment to the experience of psychosis. However, in doing this, the therapist needs to be careful to support clients in regulating the affect within sessions by carefully timing exploration of these sensitive areas. The therapist can calibrate their timing by reflecting on the strength of the therapeutic alliance, and the client's resilience and/or access to coping skills and interpersonal resources. In addition, the therapist can structure sessions in a way that enable exploration of more difficult issues during the middle phase of sessions, thus allowing the session to shift focus onto other matters towards the end. The use of agenda setting and item prioritisation can support this process. Formulation during this phase is tailored to the person's recovery style, the level of alliance and the nature of goals and tasks, which have been agreed. Therapists often make errors in using formulation to explain clients' problems at a level that is important to the therapist (in terms of guiding treatment, looking for barriers etc.) but have less relevance for the client. For example, it is often important for the therapist to understand how beliefs have evolved from very early childhood experiences. However, the client may see such an approach to formulation as a stereotypical attribution of adult problems to childhood experiences (e.g. "you mean it's all to do with my childhood!"). The client may connect problems to experiences in a way that activates strong negative (and potentially overwhelming) negative affect, or the client may be attempting to seal-over and isolate their psychotic experiences from other aspects of their life history. This can be avoided through working with a person's interpersonal context, which facilitates this process of exploration in terms of changes in the nature and structure of the client's relationships, the availability of different kinds of support, and the experience of trust, mutuality, reciprocity, closeness and intimacy. Availability of support structures also incorporates the client's experiences of helping relationships and their mutuality and expectations. This provides an understanding of the interpersonal context of recovery, interpersonal problem domains that may limit recovery, and the developmental and attachment basis to the client's ability to attend to, reflect on and clarify painful and complex affects.

The engagement phase determines that the function of formulation at this stage is to support the development of alliance, client self-reflectiveness, and accurate mentalisation of the therapist's beliefs and intentions.

Transforming beliefs and problematic interpersonal strategies

This middle phase of therapy tends to be conducted over sessions 11 to 20 and focuses upon the development of a more careful understanding of how the client's experiences have led to the development of their negative beliefs about the self, others, the world, and the future. Within a compassionate framework (Gilbert, 2005) the therapist explores with the client how helpful (and unhelpful) their specific beliefs and appraisals are in terms of achieving their specific goals. For example, a client may describe feeling lonely and isolated and want to develop more meaningful relationships with others. However, based on their experiences prior to their first episode of psychosis they believe other people are intrinsically untrustworthy. Often individuals also have an extremely limited experience of confiding and trusting peer relationships. Furthermore, in many cases they might not have had a chance to develop these as their first episode of psychosis interrupted the development of appropriate interpersonal skills and social integration. Therefore, in order to reduce their sense of vulnerability they often avoid contact with others. In this scenario, the functional significance of avoidance can be validated, and the negative consequences for the person explored.

In addition, the therapist maintains a mindful awareness of a number of key dimensions or themes relevant to staying well after psychosis, including (a) emotional distress; (b) interpersonal trust and intimacy (encompassing the ability to interpret and predict the responses of others); (c) feelings of entrapment, shame or humiliation in psychosis; (d) the client's sense of hope and optimism for recovery; and (e) help-seeking in the context of distress and self-experienced vulnerability to relapse. The therapist helps the client mesh their negative beliefs with functional aspects of their coping and interpersonal behaviours in order to create opportunities for the client to consider developing new or underdeveloped interpersonal strategies. For example, a client may describe his parents as critical and intrusive and feel angry when they complain about his behaviour at home. In response to this the client shouts at his parents, leaves the room, and avoids speaking to them. While it is important for this client to maintain his sense of autonomy and independence and to avoid been treated in a childlike manner, the costs of this strategy for the client are increased distress, rumination, negative reactions from parents, and an increase in feelings of suspiciousness and paranoia. The therapist might work with the client to develop alternative strategies including assertiveness and anger regulation combined with developing a compassionate mentalisation of his parents' anxieties, worries and concerns for his well-being. This latter strategy allows him to develop a reassuring communicative style with his parents.

The development of new or underdeveloped interpersonal strategies provides an important opportunity for the therapist and client to craft alternative accounts of the client's experiences, enabling the development of alternative beliefs. For example, on reflecting on his parents' behaviour this client considered how their anxiety and worry reflected their parental feelings towards him, and how they had valued his development. This was particularly so given their harsh upbringing in the shipbuilding areas of Glasgow. Their expectations had been devastated by his first psychotic episode, and they had thought that he would never work again. This client valued his independence and autonomy, and saw an important aspect of this transition as reducing their anxiety about his well-being.

The therapist further fosters the client's recognition of the presence of existing strengths and skills that enable them to survive and endure traumatic and distressing experiences and adverse life circumstances. We feel it important that a formulation at this stage incorporates both negative and positive aspects of existing strategies in order to develop meaning-making that incorporates positive life experiences without minimisation of negative life events. In this sense the therapist encourages a model of complex affect, encouraging integration of both positive and painful emotions. In this way the therapist helps the client not to disregard or avoid negative emotions in association with their psychotic experiences.

End phase and closure

The end phase of therapy, from sessions 21 to 30, focuses on the continued meshing of interpersonal and cognitive changes, issues arising from closure and ending of therapy, and the rehearsal of a formulation-driven approach to detection and response to at risk mental states for relapse. In order to address issues of separation and dependency that may have arisen during therapy, the frequency of sessions is increased during this phase to once per week. This enables an increased focus on the tasks required for preparing for the end of therapy and allows expression of feelings arising from therapy closure. Therapist and client collaborate on the development of both a narrative-based and a diagrammatical formulation of relapse. This formulation lays down the basis for planned interventions in the event of *an at risk mental state* for relapse. These interventions may involve targeted cognitive behavioural therapy (Gumley *et al.*, 2003), key worker interventions or changes in prescribed medication (depending on the client's choice). It is vitally important that the end phase of treatment acknowledges the ending of the therapeutic relationship and the negative emotions associated with this. Often individuals in this client group are socially isolated and have had a number of negative interpersonal experiences. They therefore can be particularly vulnerable to feelings of loss and perceived rejection. It is essential therefore for the feelings and attributions associated with this loss to be recognised and dealt with within the therapeutic discourse.

Conclusions

There remains a major challenge to researchers and clinicians alike. The evidence for CBT in the prevention of relapse is limited unless CBT is dedicated to relapse prevention. There is therefore an urgent need to develop psychological therapies that can specifically target relapse. Relapse following first episode is high and acceptance of routine treatment is low, indicated by high rates of non-adherence in the first two years of psychosis (Robinson *et al.*, 1999). Recent evidence suggests that unplanned discontinuation of antipsychotic medication due to treatment side effects is a major contributor to relapse following a first episode of schizophrenia or schizoaffective disorder (Robinson *et al.*, 2002). Cognitive interpersonal relapse prevention is a psychological treatment approach that is dedicated to relapse prevention. It builds on our earlier experience (Gumley *et al.*, 2003), which explicitly aims to enhance service engagement and help-seeking, reduce relapse vulnerability, and facilitate emotional recovery and personal re-organisation in early psychosis (Gumley and Schwannauer, 2006). Therefore, this approach is explicitly concerned with a primary focus on affect, drawing upon an interpersonally based developmental understanding of affect regulation as a means of promoting emotional recovery and relapse prevention.

References

Bebbington, P. E., Bhugra, D., Brugha, T., Singleton, N., Farrell, M., Jenkins, G. and Meltzer, H. (2004). Psychosis, victimisation and childhood disadvantage: Evidence from the second British National Survey of psychiatric morbidity. *British Journal of Psychiatry*, *185*, 220–226.

Birchwood, M., Iqbal, Z., Chadwick, P. and Trower, P. (2000). Cognitive approach to depression and suicidal thinking in psychosis: 1. Ontogeny of post-psychotic depression. *British Journal of Psychiatry*, *177*, 516–521.

Dozier, M. (1990). Attachment organization and the treatment use for adults with serious psychopathological disorders. *Development and Psychopathology*, *2*(1), 47–60.

Dozier, M., Lomax, L., Lee, C. L. and Spring, W. (2001). The challenge of treatment for clients with dismissing states of mind. *Attachment and Human Development*, *3*(1), 62–76.

Garety, P. A., Fowler, D., Freeman, D., Bebbington, P., Dunn, G. and Kuipers, E. (2008). Cognitive behavioural therapy and family intervention for relapse prevention and symptom reduction in psychosis: A randomized controlled trial. *The British Journal of Psychiatry*, *192*, 412–423.

Garfield, D. A. S. (1995). *Unbearable Affect: A guide to the Psychotherapy of Psychosis*. New York: John Wiley & Sons.

Gilbert, P. (Ed.). (2005). *Compassion: Conceptualizations, Research, and Use in Psychotherapy*. London: Brunner-Routledge.

Goodwin, I., Holmes, G., Cochrane, R. and Mason, O. (2003). The ability of adult mental health services to meet clients' attachment needs: The development and implementation of the service attachment questionnaire. *Psychology and Psychotherapy: Theory, Research and Practice*, *76*, 145–161.

Greenberg, L. S. and Pascual-Leone, J. (1997). Emotion in the creation of personal meaning. In M. Power and C. R. Brewin (Eds.), *The Transformation of Meaning in Psychological Therapies*. Chichester: John Wiley & Sons Ltd.

Gumley, A. I. and Macbeth, A. (2006). A trauma-based model of relapse in psychosis. In W. Larkin and A. T. Morrison (Eds.), *Trauma and Psychosis*. Hove, East Sussex: John Wiley & Sons.

Gumley, A. I. and Schwannauer, M. (2006). *Staying Well After Psychosis: A Cognitive Interpersonal Approach to Recovery and Relapse Prevention*. Chichester: John Wiley & Sons.

Gumley, A. I. and Park, C. (2010). Relapse prevention in early psychosis. In. P. French, M. Reed, J. Smith, M. Rayne and D. Shiers (Eds.), *Promoting Recovery in Early Psychosis: A Practice Manual*. Chichester: Wiley-Blackwell (pp. 157–167).

Gumley, A. I., O'Grady, M., McNay, L., Reilly, J., Power, K. G. and Norrie, J. (2003). Early intervention for relapse in schizophrenia: Results of a 12-month randomised controlled trial of cognitive behavioural therapy. *Psychological Medicine*, *33*, 419–431.

Gumley, A. I., O'Grady, M., Power, K. G. and Schwannauer, M. (2004). Negative beliefs about illness and self-esteem: A comparison of socially anxious and non-socially anxious individuals with psychosis. *New Zealand and Australia Journal of Psychiatry*, *35*(11–12), 960–964.

Gumley, A. I., Karatzias, A., Power, K. G., Reilly, J., McNay, L. and O'Grady, M. (2006). Early intervention for relapse in schizophrenia: Impact of cognitive behavioural therapy on negative beliefs about psychosis and self-esteem. *British Journal of Clinical Psychology*, *45*, 247–260.

Herz, M. I. and Melville, C. (1980). Relapse in schizophrenia. *American Journal of Psychiatry*, *137*(7), 801–805.

Liotti, G. and Gumley, A. I. (2008). An attachment perspective on schizophrenia: Disorganized attachment, dissociative processes, and compromised mentalisation. In A. Moskowitz, M. Dorahy and I. Schaefer (Eds.), *Dissociation and Psychosis:*

Converging Perspectives on a Complex Relationship. Chichester: John Wiley & Sons Ltd.

Marshall, M., Lewis, S., Lockwood, A., Drake, R., Jones P. and Croudace, T. (2005). Association between duration of untreated psychosis and outcome in cohorts of first-episode patients: A systematic review. *Archives of General Psychiatry*, *62*(9), 975–983.

Morgan, C., Kirkbride, J., Leff, J., Craig, T., Hutchinson, G., McKenzie, K. *et al.* (2007). Parental separation, loss and psychosis in different ethnic groups: A case-control study. *Psychological Medicine*, *37*, 495–503.

Pasquini, P., Liotti, G., Mazzotti, E., Fassone, G., Picardi, A. and The Italian Group for the Study of Dissociation (2002). Risk factors in the early family life of patients suffering from dissociative disorders. *Acta Psychiatrica Scandinavica*, *105*, 110–116.

Robinson, D., Woerner, M. G., Alvir, J., Geisler, S., Koreen, A., Sheitman, B. *et al.* (1999). Predictors of relapse following response from a first episode of schizophrenia or schizoaffective disorder. *Archives of General Psychiatry*, *56*, 241–246.

Robinson, D., Woerner, M. G., Alvir, J., Bilder, R. M., Hinrichsen, G. A. and Lieberman, J. A. (2002). Predictors of medication discontinuation by patients with first-episode schizophrenia and schizoaffective disorder. *Schizophrenia Research*, *57*, 209–219.

Rooke, O. and Birchwood, M. (1988). Loss, humiliation and entrapment as appraisals of schizophrenic illness: A prospective study of depressed and non-depressed patients. *British Journal of Clinical Psychology*, *37*, 259–268.

Siegel, D. J. (1999). *The Developing Mind: Toward a Neurobiology of Interpersonal Experience*. New York: Guilford Press.

Tait, L., Birchwood, M. and Trower, P. (2004). Adapting to the challenge of psychosis: Personal resilience and the use of sealing-over (avoidant) coping strategies. *British Journal of Psychiatry*, *185*(5), 410–415.

Wiersma, D., Nienhuls, F. J., Slooff, C. J. and Giel, R. (1998). Natural course of schizophrenic disorders: A 15-year follow-up of a Dutch incidence cohort. *Schizophrenia Bulletin*, *24*, 75–85.

Wykes, T., Steel, C., Everitt, B. and Tarrier, N. (2008). Cognitive behavior therapy for schizophrenia: Effect sizes, clinical models, and methodological rigor. *Schizophrenia Bulletin*, *34*, 523–537.

Chapter 11

Implementing cognitive behaviour therapy for psychosis

Issues and solutions

Tania Lecomte and Claude Leclerc

Introduction

Many countries, notably the UK, are offering cognitive behaviour therapy (CBT) as an evidence-based therapy for symptoms of psychosis. The literature on CBT for psychosis is showing enough strong results, notably the diminution of distress and reduction of delusions and hallucinations, to recommend it to be widely offered to persons living with psychosis (Tarrier and Wykes, 2004). But many reasons make it quite difficult to implement CBT in Canada, as well as in other countries. In Canada, these reasons are linked principally to the mental health system's organization and the universities' curriculum for mental health professionals. In the first part of this chapter, we will discuss organizational barriers to implementing CBT for psychosis and problems with the training of skilled CBT for psychosis therapists, using Canada as an example of barriers also found in other countries. The second part will present two opposing solutions to these barriers. The first solution is to suspend the implementation of CBT for psychosis until there are enough competent clinicians trained and there are enough funds to train them. The second solution is to modify and adapt current practices in CBT for psychosis in order to make them applicable by existing mental health clinicians with very little training. The second solution will be discussed extensively since it has been developed and empirically tested by our team in a randomized controlled trial.

Organizational barriers to implementing CBT

In Canada, health and social services delivery stem from the provincial jurisdiction and offer services to all residents. Public resources finance most of these services (78 per cent) with important support for the private sector. Only nine per cent of the health budget of the Province of Quebec is allocated to mental health services. The mental health services continuum of care is organized according to a traditional model including a few psychiatric hospitals, psychiatric and mental health units in general hospitals, and outpatient clinics in hospital settings or in different parts of the cities. During the last ten years, case management has been introduced to complement the service continuum, but this is not in place everywhere. As far as we know, there are no case management services that specifically offer CBT for psychosis in Canada.

Limited human resources and high case loads

In some parts of Canada, as in other countries, the waiting list for mental health evaluations or treatment is very long. Some people with a first episode of psychosis have a long wait; this goes against evidenced-based recommendations. These delays could be explained by limited human resources or by the mental health system's organization. While some individuals might need more intensive levels of services, demand exceeds availability in the present health organizational system. When it exists, case management is offered individually with often excessive case loads (35 to 75 clients per case manager).

Though individual interventions are the common way of delivering services, few structured or evidenced-based therapies are being offered. Only specialized clinics, such as mood disorder clinics or first-episode clinics, offer group interventions or specific therapies such as CBT for psychosis. Medication is widely available and covered by government insurance. Therapy, however, is not always offered by community teams, and when it is offered, it mostly consists of supportive therapy.

Insufficiently trained staff

In Canada, none of the mental health disciplines (psychiatry, psychology, nursing, social work, occupational therapy) offering services and therapy to persons living with psychosis receive specific training in CBT for psychosis. Some psychologists can choose to be trained in CBT during their graduate studies, but the training focuses on people with anxiety or mood disorders, but not with severe mental illness. Other disciplines are trained to work with individuals with psychosis, but they are trained in a conceptual framework inspired by humanistic therapy (Rogers) and mostly offer supportive therapy either individually or in a family context. In the late 1980s, many mental health workers were trained in social skills training, and have therefore learned some principles of behaviour therapy, though few settings still offer these interventions. Contrary to the UK situation, in Canada there are very few psychologists hired within mental health teams working with individuals with psychosis. It is, however, possible to find some psychologists in front-line intervention teams and in psychiatric departments. Still, their number is small and insufficient to offer CBT for psychosis to most of the clients who need it. The situation is quite similar in the US, with a recent compilation revealing CBT for psychosis being offered in a total of 12 settings in the country, many of those being private office settings.[1] The vast majority of psychologists in Canada can be found in private practice, and their services are covered only for clients with specific insurances. Individuals with severe mental illness rarely benefit from such employer-related insurances, and few can afford to seek therapy with a psychologist in private practice.

Furthermore, specific restrictions are now in place regarding who can deliver psychotherapy. In the Province of Quebec, for instance, a new definition of psychotherapy was determined by the *Office of Professions* in 2006. It demands that psychotherapeutic training be introduced at graduate levels, not before, for all mental health disciplines in years to come. Actually, mental health clinicians receive very little continuing education following their degree. While some mental health professionals continue to graduate levels of training, most do not pursue any specialization or get any specific therapy training. The proximity of a university is, however, linked to staff specialization, with the three biggest cities in Canada (Montreal, Toronto and Vancouver) having the highest percentage of clinicians from nursing, social work and occupational therapy trained at graduate levels.

Extensive training and resources

With few training opportunities offered by employers, extensive therapy training for clinicians is seen as almost impossible. High case loads and minimal human resources have to be taken into account whenever a workshop or training is planned, since managers need to pay the clinicians attending the training, pay for their replacement in order to insure continuity of care, and pay the instructors or the institute offering the training. Every training day is costly, and managers are constantly dealing with cuts in their budgets, limiting possibilities of offering expensive trainings to mental health workers.

Another reality is that though work is being done at the organizational level to improve services, human resources are currently suffering from the retirement of experienced clinicians (from the baby boomers generation). The new clinicians, fresh from universities, are not yet trained to intervene therapeutically with persons living with psychosis. At this point the various stakeholders consider it almost impossible to increase the intensity of mental health services offered – by offering CBT for psychosis, for instance – due to limited human resources and insufficient number of trained clinicians in CBT for psychosis. Given the current situation, how can one comply with the best practices guidelines and offer CBT for psychosis to all those needing it?

Implementing CBT for psychosis: Two solutions

Given this situation (also found in many North American and European settings), two potential solutions emerge. *The first solution* is to suspend the implementation of CBT for psychosis until there are enough competent clinicians trained and there are enough funds to train them. This implies putting pressure on government, particularly the health ministry, in order to assure the appropriate financing of clinicians able to deliver CBT for psychosis. If the clinicians targeted are psychologists, practicums and courses in psychology departments for psychology graduates need to be developed and offered. Such courses and training curriculums have been in place in the UK for many years, but only exist in a handful of places in North America. Of the places offering any type of training for psychologists interested in working with the severely mentally ill, few have specific CBT components and those that do have only recently started to offer it. To date in North America, most psychologists trained in CBT for psychosis are self-trained, i.e. they took the initiative themselves to seek training with experts in the field or had previous training in CBT with other types of pathologies and learned how to translate their knowledge to individuals with psychosis. The strategy of training future psychologists in CBT for psychosis is worthy, but implies many years before having enough trained individuals, particularly given the number of years necessary to become a certified psychologist and the limited number of students accepted in graduate clinical psychology programs.

An alternative strategy involves training clinicians already working with individuals with psychosis, particularly psychiatric nurses, to deliver individual CBT for psychosis. This has been done in the UK with positive results (Durham *et al.*, 2003): selected nurses completed either one day a week for one year (such as the Oxford course), with added supervision; a part-time course for two years (Southampton's MSc program); or a full-time one-year program (Institute of Psychiatry, King's College, London) in CBT for psychosis. The problem of funds arises here again, since sending nurses away for training for many days is impossible in most settings. In the US, the Beck Institute offers a similar concept of intensive short-term CBT training with long-term supervision (by sending tapes) for people other than psychologists, but the workshop covers multiple pathologies, not just psychosis, and is again very costly both in terms of covering for the absentees and for sending the person to the workshop.

In terms of pushing the government to improve funds in order to pay for training more clinicians in evidenced-based practices such as CBT, such initiatives have been ongoing for years with little or fluctuating success (Mueser *et al.*, 2003). Associations made up of parents and friends of people with schizophrenia can have some power, mostly in community mental health resources, by pressuring them into spending part of their continuing education funds on education pertaining to CBT for psychosis, for instance, rather than only on new medication updates. However, successes on a larger scale are few and widely dispersed. They are vulnerable to changes in the elected political party with new initiatives being easily shut down when a more conservative government takes power.

The second solution is to modify and adapt current practices in CBT for psychosis in order to make them applicable to existing mental health clinicians and needing very little training. The idea here is to ensure that as many people as possible that could benefit from receiving CBT for psychosis actually have access to it, rather than simply treating the select few who can be seen by experts or waiting for more experts or more funds. This solution implies modifying the typical CBT for psychosis approach in order for it to be better adapted to the reality of the community mental health clinicians. Our team has developed several strategies in this regard, with the most important ones being: 1) offering a structured manual; 2) delivering CBT for psychosis in a group format; 3) training clinicians in an active and brief workshop; and 4) encouraging colleague-to-colleague supervision.

Offering a structured manual

Many CBT therapists oppose the use of a structured manual, stating that the best way of delivering CBT is with an individualized formulation of the client's problems (Fowler *et al.*, 1995; Morrison *et al.*, 2004). Though a manual does not offer the same flexibility as an individual formulation-based CBT intervention, it does not necessarily mean that the treatment can not also be individualized and include most elements of the formulation. In fact, a manualized CBT intervention is nothing like the more traditional manuals for skills training where each sentence and each clinician intervention were dictated. In fact, the purpose of the manual is to serve as a guide to the clinician, making sure that a certain pace is respected (i.e. so that clinicians don't go too fast) and that specific themes, judged to be relevant for many individuals struggling with psychosis, are addressed.

For instance, most CBT for psychosis therapists agree that the first phase of the treatment involves assessments and non-threatening interactions in order to develop a therapeutic alliance, without which no treatment is possible (Kingdon and Turkington, 2005; Lecomte and Lecomte, 2002). During this phase the therapist inquires about the person's difficulties, gathers as much information as possible, and tries to understand the individual's explanation of these difficulties. Only after this phase is the formulation developed and presented to the client. With the manual we developed (Lecomte *et al.*, 2001), the same phases are used but are broken down in specific sessions. For instance, the first session aims simply to introduce each other and ask where the clients are from, what they like

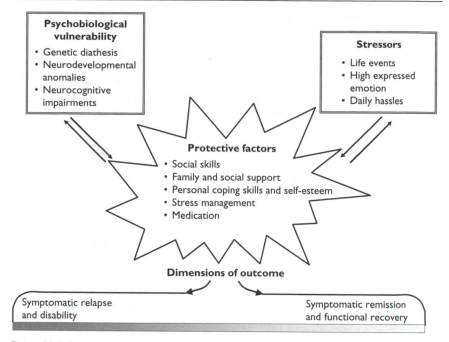

Figure 11.1 Stress–vulnerability–competence model (Ventura *et al.*, 2002)

to do, and what they are good at (therapists also actively participate and share their answers). The second session introduces the concept of stress, and clients are asked to rate their emotional, physical and behavioural reactions to stress. The third session addresses events, people, places and situations that might induce a stress reaction, and clients need to determine what stressors they are particularly sensitive to. By the fourth session, the clients are asked to describe their first hospitalization or their first encounter with a psychiatrist, and explain what they experienced and how they understand what happened. By the fifth session, the stress–vulnerability–competence model (see Figure 11.1) is introduced and personalized. This is considered the first part of the formulation since clients are ready to consider another model than their own to explain their difficulties. By writing down their specific vulnerabilities, their stressors and the emotional and behavioural consequences of the interaction between the stressors and the vulnerability, the clients make the model their own. The model also involves the "competence" part clarifying the person's protective factors, which can act as a shield against fluctuations in stress levels. The concept of protective factors gives a sense of power and control. The clients discover that they can actively work on building more and better protective factors, whereas they can not easily control their vulnerability or the stress in their lives. Many of the protective factors are addressed in the CBT manual, and

Table 11.1 ABCs of CBT exercise

A Antecedent situation?	B Belief thought?	C Consequence behavior? Emotion?
Bus driver is staring at me	He knows things about me	I try to hide from him I'm scared
	I might look like someone . . .	Go on with my day No particular emotion
	He finds me attractive	I smile I feel good!

the clients are informed that they will be working on these during the following sessions.

The individual formulation can also be found at other moments in the manual, particularly at session seven, when the ABCs of CBT are explained. By understanding these links, the clients learn how to apply them to their own beliefs and how changes can be made to reactions to situations. Various exercises are used in order to reflect this link; some involving watching a movie excerpt, generating multiple explanations for given situations and eventually applying this to their own lives. An example of one of the exercises is given in Table 11.1. A detailed description of the 24 sessions covered in the manual has been published elsewhere (Lecomte *et al.*, 2003).

One of the biggest advantages of using a manual is to develop a good pace. Eager and briefly trained clinicians might be tempted to "jump right in" and try to modify dysfunctional beliefs from the start, without really taking the time to build the alliance and really understanding the issues at stake. By getting an optimum pace, such as just one theme per session, with specific, open-ended questions suggested to engage the clients, therapists see the effects of incremental learning while not addressing difficult issues too quickly.

Pace is not only related to speed but also to content. Some issues, such as distressing beliefs, suicidal thoughts, or substance use or abuse, can be difficult to address and might deter clients from continuing the therapy if they feel that the sessions are emotionally too difficult. One way to avoid such an outcome is to alternate more difficult sessions with positive, uplifting sessions on self-esteem. These self-esteem sessions are not perceived as "out of the blue" since self-esteem is considered an important protective factor (see Figure 11.1) and clients truly enjoy those sessions. Apart from its hedonistic properties, working on improving self-esteem is essential for individuals with psychosis for many reasons. Not only is poor self-esteem often linked to the core beliefs, studies have also linked low or unstable self-esteem to psychotic symptoms (Garety *et al.*, 2001), namely to paranoia (Bentall *et al.*, 2001) and poor social functioning (Brekke *et al.*, 1993). Furthermore, studies have shown that CBT-type interventions addressing self-esteem can have positive impacts with this clientele (Lecomte *et al.*, 1999). In the CBT manual, self-esteem is tackled in various ways: by setting weekly personal goals, determining positive qualities and values, modifying attributions to become more optimistic in life, and discovering one's competence in coping with various thoughts, voices or stressors. The manual also allows the clinician to introduce various CBT techniques at the appropriate time.

A lot has been written on the CBT techniques, how to use them, their efficacy, etc. A negative consequence of this is that many clinicians might see them as effective ingredients that can be used at random, or at any given moment of the therapy (Lecomte and Lecomte, 2002). A manual-based intervention can in fact help the less-knowledgeable clinician in using appropriate techniques at appropriate moments. For instance, normalization is introduced earlier on whereas seeking alternatives or checking the facts come later, and exploring coping strategies and developing a staying well plan (i.e. relapse prevention) are discussed toward the end of the therapy (see Chapter 10). Even though earlier CBT techniques can be used at later sessions, the clinician is informed not to use a technique that has not yet been introduced in the manual.

An undeniable clinical advantage of using a manual, especially with clients presenting with paranoia, is the safety it procures. Our manual is meant to be used by the clinician as well as the clients. The theme of each session being predetermined, the clients can see what is coming and they can feel reassured that they won't be tricked into discussing issues they would rather not address. Along with the stable structure of the sessions (fixed day, time, etc.), the manual becomes something clients can rely on, and is theirs to keep and bring home either to complete their homework assignments or to refer back to once the therapy is over. In the study that we recently completed with individuals with a first episode of psychosis, the use of the manual was mentioned by many as one of the preferred aspects of the intervention, along with learning from the other group members (Spidel *et al.*, 2006).

Delivering CBT for psychosis in a group format

More and more researchers and clinicians see the value of a group format for delivering CBT for psychosis. Though to date no large-scale study has compared the results of individual CBT and group CBT, those who have undertaken CBT for psychosis group interventions all describe positive effects. In San Diego, Granholm *et al.* (2005) developed a skills training/

CBT approach for older individuals with psychosis and obtained a decrease in negative symptoms and an increase in functioning. In the UK, Wykes *et al.* (1999) obtained improvements in coping with voices as well as increased self-esteem, and Landa's study in New York (Landa *et al.*, 2006) demonstrated a specific impact on paranoid delusions for those attending her group. Our group has recently terminated a randomized controlled trial comparing a CBT group with group skills training for first episodes and has found positive results in terms of symptom reduction, self-esteem and social support (Lecomte *et al.*, 2008). Though the group CBT for psychosis intervention was initially designed for individuals with a first episode of psychosis, clinicians in the community believed that individuals with a longer course of the illness could also benefit. Indeed, many CBT groups, using the proposed manual, have been conducted outside of our study with older clients and have also obtained positive results. To implement CBT for psychosis in a group format is also more feasible in many settings than the one-to-one model found in most UK CBT studies. One of the main reasons is that fewer therapists are needed to offer CBT to more individuals. Typically, a group includes between four and eight participants for two clinicians for a period of five to twelve weeks. Individual therapy length varies from case to case, but often aims at lasting close to nine months and, in order to treat many clients, necessitates much more clinician time. Group therapy, on the other hand, can have beneficial effects from as little as three months when, for instance, offered twice a week.

Another big advantage of group interventions is the normalization aspect (see Chapter 6). One of the important steps in conducting CBT for psychosis is to help clients feel less alienated by normalizing their experience, i.e. making them realize that other people have had similar experiences (Kingdon and Turkington, 2005). Though examples of grief, lack of sleep, and sensory deprivation can be used in CBT to illustrate this concept, the sharing of others' experience in group therapy is a much stronger tool to increase normalization. The group format also allows us to work on one of the most prevalent consequences of psychosis: social isolation. Social isolation, either being linked to social anxiety (Lysaker and Hammersley, 2006), paranoia (Huppert and Smith, 2005), feelings of social incompetence (Couture *et al.*, 2006), or to stigma linked to having a mental illness (Birchwood *et al.*, 2006), has severe consequences on the individual's integration in society. A group intervention offers the opportunity to interact with others in a safe and non-judgemental setting, and therefore to practice social skills and even create friendships. Group cohesion typically takes around six to eight sessions to build, and translates into feelings of belonging, sympathy and empathy for each other, as well as invitations between clients for recreational activities outside of group times (Spidel *et al.*, 2006). In a CBT context, the group participants can also help each other by suggesting alternatives to other members' beliefs, or by trying each other's coping strategies. In fact, the group approach is much less demanding on therapists because the participants are active therapeutic agents, somewhat like co-therapists, who suggest and use CBT techniques for the other participants to use during the sessions. Therefore, the training involved for clinicians wishing to conduct group CBT, in comparison to individual CBT for psychosis, can be much briefer, especially when the group intervention follows a manual.

Training clinicians in an active and brief workshop

The format a workshop takes can greatly influence the retention and actual practice of the information. According to studies in education, most people have an attention span of a maximum of 15–20 minutes and typically retain only 30 per cent of information given in a traditional classroom format. This is mostly true when the material presented is predominantly didactic, rather than interactive, and when the teaching does not involve any actual "in vivo" practice. Our team has developed an active, brief and intensive training program in group CBT for psychosis that has demonstrated positive results in terms of actual application of the skills learned. The training was developed with two goals in mind: being brief enough that most mental health workers could attend, and offering a canvas that closely resembles what running a group looks like.

The first goal was in response to demands from psychiatric hospital clinical directors and regional health authorities asking for CBT for psychosis workshops lasting no more than three days. This constraint was financial and managerial, since freeing up clinician time to attend workshops involved rescheduling clients, work accumulating during the person's absence, and hiring temporary staff to fill in for the absentees. Three days, and at times even two days, was the most that settings could manage. The three-day format involves one day of theoretical information, made interactive with small group discussions, case examples, and questions to the group throughout the day, and two days of role plays with direct supervision. The content covers principles of recovery, principles and rules of group therapy, the basics of CBT for psychosis, and concrete applications of the most common CBT for psychosis techniques in a group setting. Some research results as well as guidelines for supervision (explained later) are also covered. The two-day format is more challenging since we ask the attendees to familiarize themselves with the CBT for psychosis model by reading selected book chapters, and to have previously read the group manual before coming to the workshop. Without this preparation phase, the attendees would not be able to actively participate in a two-day version of the workshop. Though we also recommend the same readings for the three-day version, more time is reserved to review concepts and answer conceptual, theoretical, clinical, and empirical questions.

The second goal stems from the first one, in that for a brief workshop to be effective, learning on multiple levels is targeted, and more than one teaching method needs to be used. Three levels of knowledge need to be targeted in order to promote real change: Know (i.e. the actual content or conceptual information given), Know-How (learning and applying specific skills) and Know-How-To-Be (implies adopting the values and philosophy of the approach) (Lecomte, 2006). The Know is the focus of most traditional workshops and is easily offered through visual presentations (such as Powerpoint) and recommended readings. The main strategy that we have developed for the Know-How is to offer the workshop in a manner that resembles an actual CBT group, allowing participants an experience that they can model. The co-trainers work together in the same way that the co-therapists would interact within the therapy group and the attendees are asked to participate throughout the workshop in a way that is similar to how they would conduct a CBT group. The group format was developed to be delivered by two co-therapists working together, alternating between being the leading therapist and the assisting therapist. In fact, we strongly recommend that therapists chose co-therapists with complementary strengths and qualities and of different gender, in order to build an alliance with as many participants as possible. The group is also designed to be pleasurable, even if the topics addressed can at times be difficult, and therefore the workshop is also an enjoyable learning experience. Each attendee is asked to participate in multiple role plays, either as a co-therapist or a group participant, in order to learn how to concretely apply the skills being learned. Attendees working in pairs are asked to prepare a session, by reading through the manual and using the information presented to them, and to perform part of the session in front of the entire group of attendees, with a small group of them role playing clients.

Attendees are supervised during their preparation for the session, during their session (when needed and if they seem to be diverging from the content or goal) and after their role play. Positive and constructive feedback is offered immediately and, at times, the practicing co-therapists are asked to start over if an element was missed or off-target. All of the attendees get to role play being a co-therapist at least once. The sessions chosen to be role played are the ones judged to be the most challenging or difficult, in order to ensure that things go as well as possible in real-world settings. As much as this might appear stress-inducing for the workshop attendees before doing their first role play, they actually really appreciate this learning strategy not only because it allows them to apply the skills, but also because it is done in a respectful and competence-inducing manner.

Throughout the workshop, a strong emphasis is placed on the Know-How-To-Be aspect of knowledge. The role of the therapist as a collaborator and facilitator rather than an expert, and the importance of trying to understand the clients rather than trying to change them, reflects the importance of a certain set of values and philosophy underlying CBT for psychosis. This shift of philosophy is often discussed energetically, especially by nursing staff (as well as others) who have been previously trained to avoid addressing psychotic symptoms directly, or were taught to help by "doing for them" or finding solutions for the clients as quickly as possible instead of respecting their pace and helping them find their own answers. Know-How-To-Be is also developed by encouraging workshop attendees to practice what they preach, i.e. to learn to identify stress in their own lives and their own vulnerabilities, to use coping strategies, to be authentic (i.e. act the same "in and out" of the therapy), to recognize their strengths as therapists in order to build on them, and to realize the areas they need to further develop. All of these aspects, along with the feedback received following the role plays, help the therapists develop a sense of competence that will enable them to conduct CBT groups following the workshop. Specific strategies to help further develop competence, such as supervision, are also discussed.

Colleague-to-colleague supervision

In order to maintain and further develop competence as a CBT group therapist for psychosis, practice as well as supervision is necessary. There are not enough competent, available and affordable therapists able to offer CBT for psychosis supervision to all who would need it. The solution we recommend is to encourage colleague-to-colleague supervision. The intention is that most mental health workers in a given setting will have participated in the workshop and will therefore have retained specific information from that workshop as well as practiced conducting a specific session and gained particular capacities. Each mental health worker should therefore be able to bring constructive feedback to those running the CBT groups. We recommend that CBT group sessions be videotaped and shown (at least in part) for instance at a weekly lunch meeting. The level of stress involved in being exposed as a therapist in front of colleagues is diminished by the fact that everyone has already had to role play a session in front of colleagues during the workshop, and therefore everyone understands the stress involved and the importance of giving positive as well as constructive feedback. We have found that this formula works very well, particularly when paired with occasional refresher workshops or sporadic external supervision. For instance, some clinical settings asked for a one-day workshop on specific questions that arise during the groups, one year after the initial workshop, whereas others have asked for a two-hour consultation to be reassured in their supervision and group processes, though everything was going great. We realized that people are more accustomed to being supervised by "experts" and to supervise each other can be unsettling, partly because we suggest that they have the necessary competence. With the group therapy, mental health workers are taught to "jump in" with a clear structure, basic knowledge, and previous preparation, but also to learn that true competence only develops with experience, self-reflection, integrating feedback and learning from successes and mistakes. The same guidelines apply for supervision, with the added point that it is important to accept that running CBT groups for psychosis might not be for everyone. Following the workshop, mental health clinicians are typically able to recognize if they have the necessary Know, Know-How, and Know-How-To-Be in order to run CBT for psychosis groups. In some cases, clinical directors have asked us to give them the names of those most likely to succeed immediately in running a group, i.e. to become team "champions" and get the ball rolling. Once the first groups are done, the "champion" therapists with one group under their belt often start groups with other therapists, who will then go on to run groups with others, and so on.

Conclusion

CBT for psychosis has demonstrated its effects in multiple studies and needs to be made accessible to the clients wishing for this intervention. However, the political reality in North American settings is that few funds are reserved for health, and even fewer are geared toward mental health, with direct consequences on the delivery of new interventions needing specific training, such as CBT. Two solutions are discussed: 1) to wait for more funds and for more people trained within academic settings before implementing CBT for psychosis in the community; or 2) to modify the approach, while still respecting its philosophy, in order for CBT to be made accessible quickly to those needing it. In this chapter we have tried to describe the importance of working on the first solution, i.e. to encourage training in academic settings and to push for more governmental funds, while also applying the second solution and offering a CBT for psychosis structure, format, and workshop applicable to the current clinical reality in North America. In the latter context group CBT for psychosis approach does not replace individual CBT given by an expert therapist, but could be considered a good compromise or an adjunct to individual therapy. The group CBT approach has many advantages, including increased socialization, a structured manual that clients can keep, and briefer training for therapists. Furthermore, we anticipate the eventual training and inclusion of "graduates" from CBT groups as future co-therapists. Peer co-therapists could help clients in their recovery by being a role model, as well as from having shared similar experiences and having a thorough understanding of many issues raised by clients.

The proposed group CBT for psychosis can also be used as a platform for other interventions. For instance, after having completed the 24 sessions proposed, some participants wished to work on specific issues linked to intimacy and received a further eight sessions, using the CBT techniques they were already familiar with (Leclerc *et al.*, 2006). Other issues that might need more attention than what is offered in the manual could include dealing with substance abuse problems, low self-esteem, or difficulties in stress management – all of which could be offered as extra sessions using similar CBT techniques and concepts. The group CBT for psychosis format has also been modified to be offered in a brief inpatient setting and will be adapted for forensic settings shortly. Another project is to modify it to be offered within supported employment services. Though more studies are warranted in order to determine the effectiveness and efficacy of group CBT in various settings, we believe that the proposed CBT intervention can easily and successfully be implemented in existing mental health services in North America and perhaps in other countries as well.

References

Bentall, R., Corcoran, R., Howard, R., Blackwood, R. and Kinderman, P. (2001). Persecutory delusions: A review and theoretical integration. *Clinical Psychology Review*, *21*, 1143–1192.

Birchwood, M., Trower, P., Brunet, K., Gilbert, P., Iqbal, Z. and Jackson, C. (2006). Social anxiety and the shame of psychosis: A study in first-episode psychosis. *Behaviour Research and Therapy*, *45*, 1025–1037.

Brekke, J., Levin, S., Wolkon, G., Sobel, E. and Slade, E. (1993). Psychosocial functioning and subjective experience in schizophrenia. *Schizophrenia Bulletin*, *19*, 599–608.

Couture, S. M., Penn, D. L. and Roberts, D. L. (2006). The functional significance of social cognition in schizophrenia: A review. *Schizophrenia Bulletin*, *32*, S44–S63.

Durham, R. C., Guthrie, M., Morton, R. V., Reid, D. A., Treliving, L. R., Fowler, D. and MacDonald, R. R. (2003). Tayside-Fife clinical trial of cognitive behavioural therapy for medication-resistant psychotic symptoms. Results to 3-month follow-up. *British Journal of Psychiatry*, *182*, 303–311.

Fowler, D., Garety, P. and Kuipers, E. (1995). *Cognitive Behavior Therapy for Psychosis: Theory and Practice* London: John Wiley.

Garety, P. A., Kuipers, E., Fowler, D., Freeman, D. and Bebbington, P. E. (2001). A cognitive model of the positive symptoms of psychosis. *Psychological Medicine*, *31*(2), 189–195.

Granholm, E., McQuaid, J. R., McClure, F. S., Auslander, L. A., Perivoliotis, D., Pedrelli, P., Patterson, T., Jeste, D. V. (2005). A randomized controlled trial of cognitive behavioral social skills training for middle-aged and older outpatients with chronic schizophrenia. *American Journal of Psychiatry*, *162*, 520–529.

Huppert, J. D. and Smith, T. E. (2005). Anxiety and schizophrenia: The interaction of subtypes of anxiety and psychotic symptoms. *CNS spectrums*, *9*, 721–731.

Kingdon, D. G. and Turkington, D. (2005). *Cognitive Therapy of Schizophrenia*. New York: Guilford Press.

Landa, Y., Silverstein, S. M., Schwartz, F. and Savitz, A. (2006). Group cognitive behavioural therapy for delusions: Helping patients improve reality testing. *Journal of Contemporary Psychotherapy, 36*(1), 9–17.

Leclerc, C., Gauvin, D. and Lecomte, T. (2006). CBT group to maintain and improve relationships and intimacy abilities of young adults with a first psychotic episode: A pilot study. *Schizophrenia Research, 81*(Suppl.1), S138.

Lecomte, C. (2006). Clinical supervision: A process of self-reflexivity in the development of therapeutic competence. In R. Raubolt (Ed.), *Power Games: Influence, Persuasion, and Indoctrination in Psychotherapy Training*. New York: Other Press.

Lecomte, T. and Lecomte, C. (2002). Towards uncovering robust principles of change inherent to CBT for psychosis. *American Journal of Orthopsychiatry, 72*, 50–57.

Lecomte, T., Cyr, M., Lesage, A. D., Wilde, J. B., Leclerc, C. and Ricard, N. (1999). Efficacy of a self-esteem module in the empowerment of individuals with chronic schizophrenia. *Journal of Nervous and Mental Diseases, 187*, 406–413.

Lecomte, T., Leclerc, C. and Wykes, T. (2001). *CBT* (Participant's workbook: 103 pages; clinician's supplement: 135 pages). Centre de Recherche Fernand Séguin.

Lecomte, T., Leclerc, C., Wykes, T. and Lecomte, J. (2003). Group CBT for clients with a first episode of psychosis. *Journal of Cognitive Psychotherapy: An International Quaterly, 17*, 375–384.

Lecomte, T., Leclerc, C., Corbière, C., Wykes, T., Wallace, C. J. and Spidel, A. (2008). Group cognitive behaviour therapy or social skills training for individuals with a first episode of psychosis? Results of a randomized controlled trial. *Journal of Nervous and Mental Disease, 196*, 866–875.

Lysaker, P. H. and Hammersley, J. (2006). Association of delusions and lack of cognitive flexibility with social anxiety in schizophrenia spectrum disorders. *Schizophrenia Research, 86*, 147–153.

Morrison, A. P., Renton, J. C., Dunn, H., Williams, S. and Bentall, R. (2004). *Cognitive Therapy for Psychosis: A Formulation-Based Approach*. Hove: Brunner-Routledge.

Mueser, K. T., Torrey, W. C., Lynde, D., Singer, P. and Drake, R. E. (2003). Implementing evidence-based practices for people with severe mental illness. *Behaviour Modification, 27*, 387–411.

Spidel, A., Lecomte, T. and Leclerc, C. (2006). Community implementation successes and challenges of a cognitive behavior therapy group for individuals with a first episode of psychosis. *Journal of Contemporary Psychotherapy, 36*, 51–58.

Tarrier, N. and Wykes, T. (2004). Is there evidence that cognitive behaviour therapy is an effective treatment for schizophrenia? A cautious or cautionary tale? *Behaviour Research and Therapy, 42*, 1377–1401.

Ventura, J., Nuechterlein, K., Subotnik, K. and Hwang, S. (2002). Factors influencing coping behavior during ealy schizophrenia. *Acta Psychiatrica Scandinavica, 106*(suppl.), 41.

Wykes, T., Parr, A.-M. and Landau, S. (1999). Group treatment of auditory hallucinations. *British Journal of Psychiatry, 175*, 180–185.

Note

1 Compilation by Jennifer Gottlieb, Boston, MA.

Part III

CBT and co-occurring problems

Chapter 12

The treatment of substance misuse in people with serious mental disorders

David J. Kavanagh and Kim T. Mueser

Introduction

Over the past two decades, extensive research has shown that individuals with serious mental illness such as schizophrenia, bipolar disorder, or treatment-refractory major depression are at substantially increased risk for co-occurring drug and alcohol use disorders. For example, most population surveys indicate lifetime rates of alcohol or drug misuse in the general population in the US, Europe and Australia of approximately 15 per cent, compared with 40–50 per cent for people with serious mental illness (e.g. Regier *et al.*, 1990). Rates of current or recent substance misuse in people with serious mental illness are also high, typically falling between 25 and 40 per cent (ibid.).

Vulnerability to substance misuse in people with serious mental illness is associated with many of the same factors as in the general population. Male gender, younger age, single marital status and lower education have all been related to a higher likelihood of substance use disorder in people with serious mental illness, as in the general population (Kavanagh *et al.*, 2004). Also consistent with general population correlates are observations that a family history of substance misuse, a history of conduct disorder during childhood or a diagnosis of antisocial personality disorder (Mueser *et al.*, 1999) are linked to higher risks of substance misuse in people with psychotic disorders.

One of the few unique associations between client characteristics and vulnerability to substance use disorders is a relationship between premorbid social functioning and substance misuse. While in the general population there is no established relationship between social competence and vulnerability to addiction, higher premorbid social functioning is often associated with an increased risk of substance misuse among people with serious mental disorders (Salyers and Mueser, 2001). This association may appear counterintuitive at first, because premorbid social functioning is a robust predictor of a more benign course of schizophrenia. A plausible interpretation of the finding is that individuals with better premorbid social functioning are more likely to be exposed to social use of substances and be offered illicit drugs, and to have the skills to develop and maintain a regular supply, than are those who are socially withdrawn or avoidant (Mueser *et al.*, 1998).

In line with an association with better premorbid social functioning, there is also evidence that people with psychosis and co-occurring substance misuse have better average social functioning and less severe negative symptoms than those with schizophrenia alone (Salyers and Mueser, 2001). The direction of this relationship is difficult to disentangle. As in pre-illness phases, it may reflect a greater risk of exposure and regular use of substances in more intact individuals. In the case of nicotine use, there are also beneficial pharmacological effects on cognitive functioning and motivation. Additionally, social functioning may also be enhanced by a tendency for social use of intoxicating drugs to offer tolerant and low-demand social contact. Social facilitation is a frequently reported motive for substance use in persons with serious mental illness (Mueser *et al.*, 1995).

Effects of substance misuse on psychotic disorders

Problems with substance use in the general population are defined in terms of continued use, despite a negative impact on the person's health, social or role functioning (e.g. in work, parenting or school). In substance dependence, indications of impaired control and other signs of physical dependence are seen. Among people with psychotic disorders, even modest levels of substance use can have negative effects, and interact with the course of illness. Substance misuse frequently interferes with medication adherence and contributes to increased symptoms, relapses, and rehospitalization (Drake *et al.*, 1996). Compared with persons with a mental disorder alone, co-occurring substance misuse and mental illness also confers increased risks of housing instability and homelessness, financial problems, family burden, exposure to infectious disease, violence, involvement in the criminal justice system, and demoralization and suicidality.

There is now substantial evidence that substance use not only causes a more severe course of mental disorder, but can also trigger the onset of a psychotic disorder in vulnerable individuals. Drug use is associated with an earlier age of onset of psychosis (Kavanagh *et al.*, 2004; Salyers and Mueser, 2001). This effect is of great importance, given the vocational and social learning and role transitions that occur in late adolescence and early adulthood, and evidence showing that the age at onset of psychosis is strongly predictive of long-term functional outcomes. A history of cannabis use is associated with prodromal symptoms in adolescents, and use of cannabis has been prospectively linked to the development of schizophrenia, with the extent of use showing a dose-dependent relationship to risk of illness (Arseneault *et al.*, 2004). This effect remains after control for potentially confounding variables. Based on these data, some researchers have argued that cannabis may precipitate the onset of schizophrenia in some individuals who would not otherwise have developed the illness (ibid.). Use of cannabis before the age of 14 years seems particularly predictive of later psychosis, suggesting that neurodevelopmental stage may be important to the prediction. It is impossible to know whether a particular individual would have developed psychosis in the absence of cannabis use. However, there is now sufficient evidence to recommend avoidance of substance use, particularly at young ages, and in cases where the familial risk of psychosis is high.

In bipolar disorder, different relationships have been reported between substance misuse and illness onset. People who misuse alcohol before the onset of bipolar disorder have a later age of disorder onset than those whose bipolar disorder came first. Lower rates of bipolar disorder are seen in the families of people whose alcoholism preceded their bipolar disorder, suggesting a lower genetic vulnerability. These people also tend to experience fewer affective episodes and a more rapid recovery than people whose bipolar disorder came first. The findings suggest that alcohol misuse may precipitate first episodes of mania in some people who might not otherwise have developed bipolar disorder, or may have developed it at a later age (Strakowski and DelBello, 2000).

More than "dual diagnosis"?

In describing co-morbidity of substance misuse and mental disorders, the term "dual diagnosis" has typically been used as a shorthand description. However, an important issue is raised if the phrase is taken literally: frequently, there are more than two problems involved. Not only is multiple substance misuse endemic, particularly if nicotine dependence is included (Kavanagh et al., 2004), but so is the co-occurrence of multiple psychiatric disorders or sub-clinical presentations. For example, in addition to psychosis and substance misuse, very commonly we also see co-occurring depression, anxiety, or personality disorder (Mueser et al., 1999). Although some of these problems may often resolve after reduction or cessation of substance use – for example, depressive or anxiety symptoms often improve without specific treatment (Margolese et al., 2006) – others may not. Even transient or secondary symptoms can be important for treatment. For example, dysphoria impairs self-efficacy and negatively skews outcome expectancies (Kavanagh, 1992), undermining engagement in behavior change. Furthermore, people with mental disorders have an increased risk of physical disorders, with cigarette smoking and other substance misuse having an important role (Brown et al., 2000). As already mentioned, multiple skill deficits and practical, social and functional difficulties further compound the picture, and not all of these issues spontaneously resolve after the substance misuse and mental disorders are addressed.

Regardless of the terminology adopted, it may be important to conceptualize this population as a subtype of complex presentation. An advantage of this view may be that practitioners and service planners are encouraged to consider the wide range of interrelated issues that face this group, rather than taking a blinkered perspective on just one or two. A second advantage is that practitioners are typically familiar with the management of complex presentations. Reconceptualizing co-morbid substance misuse and mental disorder in this way may assist them to see the full range of issues as legitimate targets for their involvement.

Models of treatment of co-occurring disorders

Treatment of co-occurring substance misuse in psychotic disorders traditionally relied on either parallel or sequential approaches. In the *parallel approach*, treatments for mental illness and substance misuse were provided separately by different clinicians, usually working for different agencies. In the *sequential approach*, efforts would focus first on treating or stabilizing one disorder, which would then be followed by treatment for the second disorder.

Numerous problems were associated with both of these approaches. Problems with parallel approaches included difficulties accessing both mental health and substance misuse services, lack of assertive follow-up of clients on substance misuse treatment, poor coordination of services, problems with communication about client status and progress, and inconsistencies in goals and treatments (e.g. a focus on abstinence vs harm reduction). The major problem with sequential treatment, particularly with psychosis and substance misuse, was the difficulty of attempting to treat one of the disorders in isolation, given the tendency for each to exacerbate the other (Hides *et al.*, 2006). By the late 1980s, reviews of the treatment research literature on co-morbidity had concluded that these traditional approaches were ineffective, and a consensus emerged that more effective treatment models were needed.

Newer approaches to co-morbidity of serious mental disorders and substance misuse have tended to integrate treatment for these disorders, with the same clinician (or team of clinicians) assuming responsibility for the treatment of both (Minkoff and Drake, 1991). Based on the theme of integration, a number of treatment programs have since been developed for co-morbidity.

Effective application of the concept does not involve the creation of a separate co-morbidity service. Such services may be superficially attractive to programs that seek to refer on everyone with co-morbidity, but as noted above, co-morbidity is the rule rather than the exception in both mental health and substance-use contexts. Furthermore, development of such services would run the risk that many referred people were not 'co-morbid enough', and would constitute yet another way to deny service. Rather, integration entails a fundamental change in existing services, so they develop a capability and willingness to address co-occurring disorders in people who otherwise would fulfill criteria for priority service.

Individual programs differ considerably from one another, but most share a common set of characteristics, including comprehensiveness, motivation enhancement, minimization of treatment-related stress, a harm-reduction philosophy, and assertive outreach.

Comprehensive services

Substance misuse treatment services for clients with serious mental illness are designed to be implemented in the context of comprehensive treatment. Typically, integrated treatments attempt to address a wide range of client needs: not only medical care, pharmacological treatment, illness self-management and substance control, but also needs for housing, vocational rehabilitation, social skills training, and recreation. Attending to these basic treatment and rehabilitation needs is critical to helping clients achieve sobriety and maintain a rewarding, substance-free life (e.g. by developing social networks and activities that do not involve substance misuse).

Motivation enhancement

Traditional substance misuse treatment services are usually initiated when the substance use leads to either significant problems in functioning, or legal problems which force the person into treatment (e.g. driving under the influence of alcohol). In contrast, clients with co-morbidity are usually in treatment for their mental illness and often have established working relationships with treatment providers, but have no clear motivation to work on their substance misuse. Therefore, motivation enhancement (Miller and Rollnick, 2002) is a core feature of integrated co-morbidity treatment programs.

One conceptual framework that assists in tailoring treatment to the motivation and commitment of the person is the idea of *stages of treatment* (Osher and Kofoed, 1989) which was adapted from the *stages of change* descriptive model (Prochaska and DiClemente, 1984). At the *Engagement* stage, the client does not yet have a therapeutic relationship, and therefore the goal is to establish such a relationship before making efforts to persuade the client to work on substance use problems (e.g. outreach to connect with clients in the community, helping resolve a crisis or pressing problem). In the *Persuasion* stage, clients are seeing a clinician on a regular basis and have a working relationship, but are not motivated to develop a sober lifestyle. Therefore, the goal of this stage is to help the client develop motivation before trying to address the substance use (e.g. motivational interviewing, or development of skills in meeting key needs that have been met by substance use, such as socialization or coping with symptoms). When motivation to address substance use has been established, *Active Treatment* focuses on providing additional strategies to help the client to further improve their control (e.g. practising skills for dealing with high-risk situations). *Relapse Prevention* focuses on maintaining awareness that a relapse into substance misuse could occur (e.g. developing a relapse prevention plan), and extending recovery to other areas of functioning, such as work and social relationships. In practice, motivation and commitment to change often wax and wane, particularly in the early stages, and reversion to earlier stages is common. To assist in ensuring that a group is at roughly the same stage, some evidence of initial attempts at change is required before the person shifts to "active treatment".

However, some flexibility is often required in the application of rules associated with stages of treatment. For example, when low self-efficacy is the primary barrier to initiation of change, brief skills training about the key concern (e.g. substance refusal) may be required before the person feels able to start an attempt. Undertaking a behavioural experiment – e.g. testing whether cutting down by one cigarette a day has negative effects – may be needed. An initial goal may sometimes involve stopping substance use for a short period only (e.g. one week), to build self-efficacy and confirm the expected benefits of that action. In all these cases, detailed planning and even focused skills training may be needed in achieving the goal, and if active support were not forthcoming, potential opportunities to foster more ambitious and longer-term goals may be lost. However, that support focuses on the immediate situation, rather than involving extensive skills training that has a goal of sustained and generalized behaviour change. The latter "active treatment" becomes relevant when commitment to change is less ambivalent and tentative. The essence of the concept of stages of treatment is that the nature of the intervention is adjusted to the priorities and attentional focus of the person at that time, so that its immediate relevance is readily appreciated. That principle should be the key driver of session content, rather than a rigid interpretation of the stage model.

For many people with serious mental disorders, motivation to address substance use remains tentative or highly variable over time. There are many potential reasons for this phenomenon – the highly immediate and powerful effects of substances, the lack of alternative goals and sources of pleasure, as well as the depressive mood and amotivation that are endemic in these populations. *Contingency management* (e.g. using monetary contingencies) can be used to increase the rate of drug-free urine screens in people with serious mental disorders (Sigmon and Higgins, 2006). There is a risk that rewarded behaviours return to baseline levels when the contingency is withdrawn, and that the external reward may undermine intrinsic motivation to address substance use. However, if external rewards are small, they are paired with social recognition, and the primary emphasis is on internal motivations and naturalistic rewards, there is some evidence that benefits of contingencies on program attendance and short-term abstinence may be obtained without appreciable risk that its behavioural gains are later extinguished (Bellack *et al.*, 2006).

Minimization of treatment-related stress

People with serious mental illnesses are highly sensitive to the effects of interpersonal stress (Zubin and Spring, 1977), which can worsen the course of both psychiatric illness and substance misuse. In order to avoid such stress, and to optimize the therapeutic relationship, integrated treatment programs eschew stressful, confrontational approaches, and utilize instead supportive techniques that focus on helping clients recognize the benefits of changing their substance use (e.g. use of Socratic questioning to explore effects of substance use).

Harm-reduction philosophy

In the past, services have often focused on abstinence from substances as the only legitimate treatment goal, and some (e.g. many alcohol and other drug programs in the US) continue to have this focus. Most integrated co-morbidity programs, on the other hand, adopt a more pragmatic approach by encouraging abstinence, while also supporting efforts to gradually cut down substance use or reduce the harmful effects of using substances (e.g. encouraging the use of clean needles or water pipes, adoption of safe sexual practices).

While any continued use of substances puts this population at risk of relapse to dysfunctional substance use, initially many clients are unwilling (or feel unable) to adopt abstinence as their goal. A focus on harm reduction does not give the client permission to maintain problematic use – for example, therapists may still express their concerns about negative effects of continued use. Reduction of use and harm reduction involve the person adopting intermediate, functional goals. Assisting with these goals can solidify the therapeutic relationship, build self-efficacy, ameliorate some of the damaging and life-threatening risks of their substance use, and strengthen motivation to make further gains.

Assertive outreach

Many clients with co-occurring disorders are only tenuously engaged in treatment, or have difficulty remembering and keeping appointments, especially during symptom exacerbations. In contrast to many substance misuse treatment services that depend solely on clinic appointments, integrated treatment programs typically provide assertive outreach in the community in order to engage and retain clients in treatment (Drake *et al.*, 1998). Assertive contact can make the difference between a temporary setback and a longer term loss of engagement, or between a minor symptom exacerbation and a full relapse. Such outreach can also be fruitful for engaging significant others in treatment, such as family members (Mueser and Fox, 2002).

Research on integrated treatment

Research on the effects of treatments for co-occurring disorders has grown rapidly over recent years. We conducted a review of all published randomized controlled trials focusing on clients with psychosis and substance misuse, identifying studies by extensive searches of standard databases, checks of reference lists and personal communication with known researchers (Kavanagh and Mueser, 2007). Quasi-experimental and within-subject designs were excluded, as were studies that included some participants without serious mental disorders, or had some without substance-use disorders. Studies were also excluded if they did not report results on substance use outcomes (e.g. solely examining program engagement, housing, employment or forensic measures). Twenty studies were identified. Most had a significant proportion of clients with schizophrenia, but typically they included other diagnoses as well. Study groups varied from young, first-episode participants to people with chronic and disabling disorders. Sample sizes ranged from 25 to 485, with most being substantial (Median = 116). While studies usually had a majority of men (Median = 74 per cent, Range = 48–97 per cent), mean ages (Range = 21–44, Median = 34), diagnoses, chronicity and severity varied widely, and trial durations varied from three months to five years post-baseline (Median = 12 months).

Types of interventions also varied significantly, including residential, individual or group treatment, case management for delivering integrated treatment, and studies of brief, motivational intervention. Intervention contact time ranged from a single 30–45 minute session to assertive community treatment over three years.

Early research on integrated treatment programs was limited by a number of different factors, including the use of insensitive measures of substance misuse in the population of clients with serious mental illness. Over time, the scientific rigor of efficacy trials has steadily improved. Based on data from the published papers, we awarded studies one point for each of ten methodological criteria (> 50 per cent of the eligible sample entering the study, confirmation of diagnosis by standard interview, appropriate randomization procedure, baseline equivalence or statistical control, equivalence of contact time, ≤ 33 per cent loss from attrition, independent checks on protocol adherence, corroboration of substance-use reports, blind ratings, and intention to treat analyses). Total scores rose from 2.0 in 1993, to a median of 7 in 2006 and 5.75 in 2007. The data now permit the drawing of some tentative conclusions:

1   *Limited impact of brief interventions.* In comparison with control conditions, brief interventions tend to have limited effects, especially in the longer term. The primary role of brief interventions for co-occurring disorders, such as motivational interviewing, appears to be engagement in treatment, with further treatment being required before relative improvements in substance use or symptoms are reliably seen across samples.

2   *Little added impact from greater intensity of case management.* Studies comparing integrated treatment delivered on assertive community treatment teams (ACT), with integrated treatment provided by standard case management teams, reported little or no additional benefit on substance use or psychiatric symptoms from the more intensive ACT (e.g. Morse *et al.*, 2006).

3   *Better outcomes from extended cognitive behavioral therapy.* Interventions that extend for substantial periods (e.g. six to nine months) that address substance use disorders and serious mental illness using cognitive behavioral procedures tend to have better outcomes. However, gains may be unstable over time, and differences in substance use between conditions may not be maintained.

4   *Integrated treatment usually appears superior.* Integrated programs tend to have superior outcomes to non-integrated controls, although findings are mixed, and impacts on substance misuse outcomes tend to be modest and inconsistent. Larger reviews of integrated treatment programs for co-morbidity that include a wider range of study methodologies, such as quasi-experimental designs, suggest stronger support for integrated treatment (e.g. Drake *et al.*, 2008).

Sources of variability in findings across controlled studies include their different populations (e.g. first episode vs chronic psychosis, range and severity of co-morbid conditions, degree of housing instability), interventions (e.g. brief motivational enhancement, cognitive behavioral therapy, family intervention, ACT, residential), and treatment durations (one session to three years of intensive case management). In fact, the variability in studies is so great that no single standardized intervention has been examined in more than one published study.

Future directions: Improving treatments

It is possible that some existing treatments are approaching the ceiling on what can be done with psychological interventions for people with substance misuse and serious mental disorders, and that the limited relative power of existing treatments has more to do with the challenging nature of the clients' problems than with deficiencies in the treatments themselves. However, we offer some speculations on aspects that may be important in maximizing treatment effects. These features are already present in many existing approaches; however, our suggestion is that their explicit consideration may offer ideas on further refinement of current practice.

1   *An emphasis on maximizing quality of life.* A significant challenge continues to be maintaining engagement in addressing substance use. If clients stop using substances, they potentially stand to lose a great deal, including immediate and powerful reward or relief effects from the substance, a highly valued recreational activity, and in many cases, a large proportion of their social contacts. Treatments need to ensure that they add more than they take away from the person's quality of life, and have strategies to address periods when net costs may seem to outweigh the benefits. In some situations, this may require focusing on improving housing or other factors affecting quality of life before addressing substance misuse.

2   *Judicious use of contingency management to support initial change, and development of natural reinforcers for maintaining control.* Contingencies may include small monetary incentives and praise for abstinence, together with highlighting of naturally occurring benefits that accrue from changes in substance use. Focusing on aspects that are identified from assessment as being of particular importance to an individual may maximize the benefits of the approach.

3   *Restriction of cognitive and behavioral demands on clients.* More treatment components are not necessarily better, especially if they place excessive concurrent performance demands on clients. Problems with attention and prospective memory that are commonly seen in people with serious mental disorder make this issue especially important in the current context. A corollary is that additional strategies to cue skill utilization in the natural environment or otherwise compensate for symptomatic problems may further increase treatment impact. A second corollary is that treatments may have maximal impact if at each point they focus on incremental changes that are likely to impact on multiple issues faced by that individual (e.g. for a dysphoric client with restricted recreational pursuits, prominent negative symptoms and poor functional skills, a focus on pleasurable, non-drug activity with low performance difficulty may have benefits across the problem domains).

4   *An emphasis on existing strengths and on recovery.* The wide-ranging and often severe deficits that are exhibited by this group may sometimes blind practitioners and clients to individuals' capabilities and achievements. A focus on strengths assists in maintaining the motivation and

self-efficacy of both the client and the practitioner. Given the likelihood of behavioral lapses or symptomatic exacerbations (and the risk that one will trigger the other), it may be particularly important to dwell on transitional achievements. Similarly, an orientation to recovery which encompasses the possibility of chronic or recurring difficulties, but maximizes self-direction and quality of life is needed. Further consideration of the implications of this idea for treatments may be beneficial.

Future directions: Improving the evidence base

Taking the research beyond a test of service integration

As discussed above, integrated treatment from a single therapist or team helps to ensure that people with co-occurring disorders are not excluded from assistance with the full range of their problems, that treatment is coherent and internally consistent and that potential communication blocks between providers are avoided. It is difficult to imagine that a treatment without these features would be more effective. However, those features could (at least in principle) be provided by separate services, working in close liaison. The same is true of the features of motivation enhancement, minimization of treatment-related stress, a harm-reduction philosophy and assertive outreach. Furthermore, while these features are typical of integrated approaches, an integrated service could be imagined that had none of these elements. Integration does not, *in itself*, guarantee effectiveness.

The concept of integration has helped separate services come to terms with the fact that the people they serve often have complex needs that they need to address. However, refinement of treatments may require refinement of the conceptual frameworks as well. With the possible exception of motivational interventions, the hallmark of treatment research in this field has been the use of multi-component interventions. It is time to unpack these interventions and the concept of integration that often underpins them, to isolate components that contribute to positive effects. Maximizing the impact of these effective components may increase the power of interventions. Conversely, showing that some aspects of multi-component interventions do not contribute to effectiveness may allow us to simplify or reduce the cost of treatment.

We argue that the core element of integration as a *feature of the treatment experienced by the person* is not the type of service that delivers the intervention. Rather, it involves a unity of purpose and goals, to encompass the range of issues the person is experiencing. Each aspect of treatment takes into account the presence of the other problems. This more conceptual form of integration has become conflated with the more practical, service delivery aspect.

For example, motivational interviewing is modified in people with psychosis, with shorter sessions, more rehearsal and summaries, a focus on one or two key issues for the person, and greater use of diagrams. Poverty of speech and content of speech mean that more prompts are often required. If depression is present, more effort needs to be invested in recall of success and in eliciting personal attributions for successful performance.

This example illustrates the fact that different people may require these features to differing extents. Indeed, the nature and extent of linkage between co-occurring disorders may also differ from person to person, so that any substance use tends to elicit psychotic symptoms for one person, but another does not usually experience symptomatic exacerbations, and is primarily affected by the more standard, substance-related issues of cost and legal problems. In the former case, management of current psychotic symptoms must encompass substance use, whereas the issue may be less immediate in the latter case (e.g. perhaps arising more in the context of preventing psychotic relapse). This approach to integration suggests that treatment be modified according to a functional analysis incorporating the full set of problems – an idea that is highly compatible with integration and with sound clinical practice, but that has not been explicitly tested in controlled trials.

Use of more sophisticated approaches to detection of treatment effects

Virtually all studies of integrated treatment for co-morbidity indicate significant improvements in substance misuse for both integrated and comparison interventions, especially over the first 6–12 months of treatment. As many studies have limited statistical power, it becomes difficult to demonstrate that integrated treatment is more effective than alternative approaches, when clients in both groups improve over time. One approach to this problem is to provide a relatively brief, standardized treatment program to all study participants, and to then randomize only clients who have persistent substance use problems following the intervention (e.g. six months later) to more extensive treatments. This strategy would reduce the rate of clients who show a rapid remission of their substance misuse early in either integrated or customary treatment, which could serve to highlight the benefits of integrated care for clients with more persistent substance misuse.

An argument can also be made that much of the existing research may be underestimating the true impact of treatment, by focusing primarily on abstinence, days to relapse and similar indices of ultimate success. Given that this population tends to have a variable course, often characterized by patchy improvements across substances, symptoms and functional domains, and by setbacks occurring during symptomatic crises, an emphasis on sustained change in any one area may not fully reflect whether a positive trajectory is in place. More sensitive indices of incomplete or transient improvements may be required in order to detect transitional positive effects from treatments.

Summary and conclusion

Rapid advances in the sophistication of both research and treatment approaches have occurred over recent years, but the evidence that specific treatments provide greater sustained effects than control interventions remains limited. Challenges include a need to both further increase the impact of treatments and take the research to the next level: the replication of effects from specific treatments, identification of effective components and reliable predictors of response, and methods to increase the sensitivity of research methodology in this area.

References

Arseneault, L., Cannon, M., Witton, J. and Murray, R. M. (2004). Causal association between cannabis and psychosis: Examination of the evidence. *British Journal of Psychiatry, 184,* 110–117.

Bellack, A. S., Bennett, M. E., Gearon, J. S., Brown, C. H. and Yang, Y. (2006). A randomized clinical trial of a new behavioral treatment for drug abuse in people with severe and persistent mental illness. *Archives of General Psychiatry, 63,* 426–432.

Brown, S., Inskip, H. and Barraclough, B. (2000). Causes of the excess mortality in schizophrenia. *British Journal of Psychiatry, 177,* 212–217.

Drake, R. E., Mueser, K. T., Clark, R. E. and Wallach, M. A. (1996). The natural history of substance disorder in persons with severe mental illness. *American Journal of Orthopsychiatry, 66,* 42–51.

Drake, R. E., McHugo, G. J., Clark, R. E., Teague, G. B., Xie, H., Miles, K. and Ackerson, T. H. (1998). Assertive community treatment for patients with co-occurring severe mental illness and substance use disorder: A clinical trial. *American Journal of Orthopsychiatry, 68,* 201–215.

Drake, R. E., O'Neal, E. and Wallach, M. A. (2008). A systematic review of research on interventions for people with co-occurring severe mental and substance use disorders. *Journal of Substance Abuse Treatment, 34,* 123–138.

Hides, L., Dawe, S., Kavanagh, D. J. and Young, R. M. (2006). A prospective study of psychotic symptom and cannabis relapse in recent-onset psychosis. *British Journal of Psychiatry, 189,* 137–143.

Kavanagh, D. J. (1992). Self-efficacy and depression. In R. Schwartzer (Ed.), *Self-Efficacy: Thought Control of Action* (pp. 177–193). New York: Hemisphere.

Kavanagh, D. J. and Mueser, K. T. (2007). Current evidence on integrated treatment for serious mental disorder and substance misuse. *Journal of the Norwegian Psychological Association, 44,* 618–637.

Kavanagh, D. J., Waghorn, G., Jenner, L., Chant, D. C., Carr, V., Evans, M., Herrman, H., Jablensky, A. and McGrath, J. J. (2004). Demographic and clinical correlates of co-morbid substance use disorders in psychosis: Multivariate analyses from an epidemiological sample. *Schizophrenia Research, 66*, 115–124.

Margolese, H. C., Carlos Negrete, J., Tempier, R. and Gill, K. (2006). A 12-month prospective follow-up study of patients with schizophrenia-spectrum disorders and substance abuse: Changes in psychiatric symptoms and substance use. *Schizophrenia Research, 83*, 65–75.

Miller, W. R. and Rollnick, S. (Eds.). (2002). *Motivational Interviewing: Preparing People for Change* (2nd ed.). New York: Guilford Press.

Minkoff, K. and Drake, R. E. (Eds.). (1991). *Dual Diagnosis of Major Mental Illness and Substance Disorder* (Vol. 50). San Francisco, CA: Jossey-Bass.

Morse, G. A., Calsyn, R. J., Klinkenberg, D. W., Helminiak, T. W., Wolff, N., Drake, R. E., Yonker, R. D., Lama, G., Lemming, M. R. and McCudden, S. (2006). Treating homeless clients with severe mental illness and substance use disorders: Costs and outcomes. *Community Mental Health Journal, 42*, 377–404.

Mueser, K. T. and Fox, L. (2002). A family intervention program for dual disorders. *Community Mental Health Journal, 38*, 253–270.

Mueser, K. T., Nishith, P., Tracy, J. I., DeGirolamo, J. and Molinaro, M. (1995). Expectations and motives for substance use in schizophrenia. *Schizophrenia Bulletin, 21*, 367–378.

Mueser, K. T., Drake, R. and Wallach, M. (1998). Dual diagnosis: A review of etiological theories. *Addictive Behaviors, 23*, 717–734.

Mueser, K. T., Rosenberg, S. D., Drake, R. E., Miles, K. M., Wolford, G., Vidaver, R. and Carrieri, K. (1999). Conduct disorder, antisocial personality disorder, and substance use disorders in schizophrenia and major affective disorders. *Journal of Studies on Alcohol, 60*, 278–284.

Osher, F. C. and Kofoed, L. L. (1989). Treatment of patients with psychiatric and psychoactive substance use disorders. *Hospital and Community Psychiatry, 40*, 1025–1030.

Prochaska, J. O. and DiClemente, C. C. (1984). *The Transtheoretical Approach: Crossing the Traditional Boundaries of Therapy*. Homewood, IL: Dow-Jones/ Irwin.

Regier, D. A., Farmer, M. E., Rae, D. S., Locke, B. Z., Keith, S. J., Judd, L. L. and Goodwin, F. K. (1990). Co-morbidity of mental disorders with alcohol and other drug abuse: Results from the Epidemiologic Catchment Area (ECA) study. *Journal of the American Medical Association, 264*, 2511–2518.

Salyers, M. P. and Mueser, K. T. (2001). Social functioning, psychopathology, and medication side effects in relation to substance use and abuse in schizophrenia. *Schizophrenia Research, 48*, 109–123.

Sigmon, S. C. and Higgins, S. T. (2006). Voucher-based contingent reinforcement of marijuana abstinence among individuals with serious mental illness. *Journal of Substance Abuse Treatment, 30*, 291–295.

Strakowski, S. M. and DelBello, M. P. (2000). The co-occurrence of bipolar and substance use disorders. *Clinical Psychology Review, 20*, 191–206.

Zubin, J. and Spring, B. (1977). Vulnerability: A new view of schizophrenia. *Journal of Abnormal Psychology, 86*, 103–126.

Chapter 13

Treating trauma in people with first-episode psychosis using cognitive behavioural therapy[1]

Pauline Callcott, Robert Dudley, Sally Standart, Mark Freeston and Douglas Turkington

Introduction

People with psychosis experience high rates of trauma as children and/or as adults (Larkin and Morrison, 2006). This knowledge presents a number of challenges for clinicians. The first is to sensitively enquire about traumatic experiences and to elicit these from people presenting with symptoms that at first may appear unconnected with the earlier events. Second, theoretical models of psychotic symptoms need to incorporate this knowledge about the prevalence of trauma experiences into revised understandings that help the clinician account for the manifestation of distress as psychotic symptoms rather than as post-traumatic stress disorder (PTSD). Third, this understanding has to help inform treatment. These revised models should serve as the basis of a formulation that provides a shared and acceptable understanding of the impact of the trauma on the development and maintenance of the current distressing symptoms. If the models are correct, then targeting these trauma-influenced processes should reduce distress from psychotic symptoms and help keep the person well by preventing or delaying relapse.

This chapter responds to these challenges in three ways. First, we outline how trauma may be related to psychosis. This serves to alert the clinician to the role of trauma in psychosis and enables them to ask sensitively about this potentially crucial factor. Second, we consider how trauma exposure may be understood within existing cognitive models of psychotic symptoms. Third, we provide brief illustrative case studies that show the reader how CBT is adapted to take account of trauma processes. Through meeting these aims it will become clear that there is no simple relationship between trauma and psychotic experiences. However, acknowledging and considering the role of trauma is important in building a therapeutic alliance and tailoring CBT to be optimally effective in alleviating the distress associated with psychotic symptoms.

The role of trauma in psychosis

Childhood trauma

For some, early childhood traumatic experiences seem to be a key vulner-ability for later life difficulties, including the development of psychosis. We know this owing to the work of researchers such as Janssen *et al.* (2004), who prospectively studied a sample of over four thousand people from the general population who were free of psychosis at baseline, and then screened them for the development of psychotic experiences two years later. Those people who went on to develop psychotic symptoms were more likely to have been abused before the age of 16 than people who did not develop psychosis. Moreover, the findings indicated a 'dose response' with those reporting having limited abuse being twice as likely as non-abused participants to develop psychosis. Those unfortunate people who had been severely abused were 48 times more likely to have subsequently developed psychosis in the two-year period.

So the evidence is that early traumatic experiences can increase the risk of the later development of psychosis. More specifically, there may be an association between child abuse and vulnerability to hallucinatory experi-ences. For example, Ensink (1992) reported that 27 per cent of incest survivors experience life long hallucinations. In a study of 200 outpatients, Read *et al.* (2006) noted hallucinations in 19 per cent of non-abused patients, in 47 per cent of those subject to childhood physical abuse, in 55 per cent of those subject to childhood sexual abuse, and in 71 per cent of those subject to both. Therefore, we see evidence of an association between early experiences and vulnerability for both psychotic symptoms generally, and specifically for hallucinations. However, not all people with psychosis report early childhood trauma and hence, the role of adult trauma also needs to be considered.

Adult trauma

Larkin and Morrison (2006) noted high rates of adult trauma and pre-viously unrecognised PTSD symptoms in people with psychosis. There are potentially different routes to the emergence of psychosis in the context of adult trauma, and a brief overview is provided.

Trauma as a precipitant or trigger for psychosis

Traumatic incidents such as violent or sexual assault or rape may act as stressors for some people that exceed the person's capacity to cope and therefore precipitate a psychotic breakdown. Once again, there is a parti-cular association with trauma seeming to act as a trigger for hallucinations.

Romme and Escher (1996) found that 70 per cent of people from their sample had the onset of their hallucinations after a traumatic experience (see also Chapter 2). However, their definition of trauma was broad in that it encompassed a range of events such as accidents, moving home, falling in love, pregnancy and other events that do not necessarily meet the criteria for a PTSD trauma. To address this shortcoming Honig *et al.* (1998) investigated three groups of people who reported hallucinations: non patients, those with dissociative disorder, and those with schizophrenia. They found a large number had been subject to emotional, physical or sexual abuse, and that the majority of individuals in both patient groups could relate the onset of the hallucinations to a particular trauma trigger.

Interaction between adult trauma and pre-existing psychosis vulnerability

Experimental research has indicated that trauma experiences can be interpreted differently according to pre-existing information-processing styles. Interestingly, this reveals a possible interaction between those people who are perhaps more predisposed to psychotic experiences and the impact of traumatic experiences. Steel *et al.* (2008) proposed that people with psychosis proneness have information-processing styles characterised by 'weakened perceptual integration'. In short, this means that current information is not well integrated with past experiences. Supportive of this theory, Holmes and Steel (2004) exposed non-clinical participants to an analogue trauma experience (a video of an accident) and asked people to record the rate of intrusions into consciousness over the coming week. Those people who were higher at baseline in positive symptomatology were more likely to report intrusions into awareness.

Psychosis as a risk factor for trauma

Of course, it is possible that the emergence of psychosis may precede a traumatic event. For example, where a person is in the early stages of the development of psychotic symptoms they may place themselves in situations that increase the chance of being subject to traumatic experiences. This may be as a direct result of the symptoms, perhaps leading a person with emerging psychosis to accuse or threaten other people owing to being scared by a hallucination or delusional belief. The person's actions may in turn lead to other people acting in a hostile manner towards them or even assaulting them. Or it may be that people who are coping with emergent symptoms rely on excessive alcohol or substance misuse and thereby inadvertently increase their risk of being victim to adverse events. Once a person has an established psychosis they may lack the support and structure of work, close family or personal relationships and may find that they are placed in situations where they are more likely to be victimised and exploited. Hence, an emerging or established psychosis may potentially increase the risk of subsequent trauma experience.

Consequently, one of the major challenges facing the clinician is to work with the client to see if together they can make a link between the symptoms and the actual experience in order to determine whether symptoms relate to the stressor.

A further complicating factor is that many professionals may have been trained not to focus on the content of symptoms and their meanings but rather on the presence of symptoms in helping determine a diagnosis and informing a risk assessment. This may be a missed opportunity, as Boevnik (2006), in a moving first-hand account of her experience in the mental health system over a number of years, remarks:

> Nobody ever asked me what had happened to me. Nobody ever asked me: what was it that drove you mad? I was observed, diagnosed, and treated as a disturbed person, but nobody ever looked at the association with my life history.
>
> (Boevnik, 2006, p. 18)

The vital question for these theoretical models to answer is why has this person presented with psychotic symptoms rather than PTSD? This is important theoretically and clinically as at present our ability to help people with PTSD is better than our ability to help people with psychosis in terms of the effectiveness of Cognitive Behavioural Therapy (CBT). Of course, most people with psychosis are not treated using CBT for psychosis (CBTp) but are offered anti-psychotic medication, which is a valuable treatment (Davis et al., 1993). Unfortunately, though, as many as 60 per cent of people continue to experience residual positive and negative symptoms even after an appropriate course of medication (Curson et al., 1988). One possible explanation for the limited impact of CBTp is that it fails to recognise the importance of traumatic experiences in the underpinning model, and hence fails to adapt treatment to directly address these mechanisms.

Models of trauma and psychosis

A number of theoretical models account for the development and maintenance of psychotic symptoms within the field of CBTp (i.e. Garety et al., 2001). While the models differ they also share many common elements. First, they are based on the cognitive model in which the appraisal of experience helps account for the distress. Moment-to-moment appraisals of experience are shaped by more enduring beliefs that are formed as a result of developmental experience. The onset of psychosis is accounted for by precipitating events that either exceed a person's capacity to cope or have a particular resonance or meaning that accesses more negative beliefs about oneself or others. Finally, they share in common the view that the goal of treatment is not so much the removal of the symptoms but a changing of the appraisal of the experience so that the associated distress and impact on behaviour is reduced.

While there is empirical evidence for some of the key mechanisms in the models, evidence for the efficacy of treatment based on such models is limited. Recently, the models have been revised to incorporate features of models of PTSD (i.e. Ehlers and Clark, 2000) in light of the recognition of the role of trauma in psychosis (see Larkin and Morrison, 2006). These models are vital as they serve as the basis of the formulation in which the person's unique experience is matched to the model to help create an understanding of the development and maintenance of the distress and thereby guide treatment choices. A key challenge is how these models account for the impact of trauma and hence help to make links between historical experiences, traumatic events, beliefs about self and others and current symptoms and situations. As has been outlined, people with psychosis have high rates of early adversity and such experiences could contribute to the development of negative beliefs about oneself as vulnerable, worthless or unlovable, and other people as malicious, cruel and rejecting.

Garety *et al.* (2001) highlight the role of early experiences, and particularly early adverse experiences, in the development of enduring cognitive vulnerabilities to psychosis. This developmental route contributes to a multi-factorial maintenance model which is presented in Figure 13.1.

Birchwood *et al.* (2000) similarly describe how interpersonal schema are likely to be important in determining how people with hallucinations appraise their hallucinatory experiences. For example, those who have experienced subordination and marginalisation in other social relationships are more likely to feel the same in relation to their voices. Morrison's (Larkin and Morrison, 2006) work highlights the fact that those who have been exposed to trauma, particularly early in childhood, are likely to have faulty self and other beliefs. It is likely that schemas about mistrust and vulnerability will be prominent in people who have been abused as children.

A number of studies suggest that within people with psychosis, those who are more prone to dissociative symptoms are those who have been abused as children. Ross *et al.* (1994) recruited 84 people diagnosed as suffering with schizophrenia and found that a history of childhood abuse was associated with higher scores on scales of dissociative experiences and also on positive symptoms of schizophrenia scales.

Dissociation may play an important role in the expression of psychotic symptoms by increasing the amount of perceived anomalous experiences, which (Figure 13.1) is a potential route to psychotic symptoms. These anomalous experiences may be intrusive memories or flashback experiences or physiological arousal and fear. What makes them anomalous is that these experiences are not consciously linked to the trauma experience. This

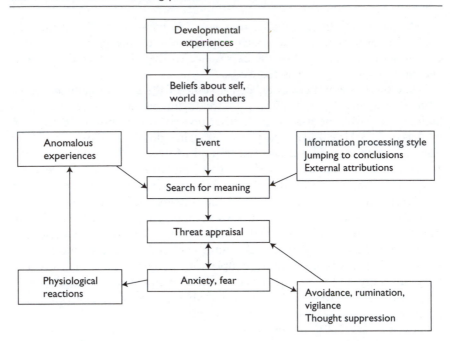

Figure 13.1 A model of maintenance of psychotic symptoms, based on Garety *et al.* (2001)

may be because at the time the trauma happened the person was dissociating, in which case the memory would have few temporal or spatial cues. Hence, any re-experiencing phenomena, such as flashbacks, would more likely be perceived as anomalous or unusual experiences not linked to the trauma event.

Of course, if a person is victim of a trauma incident as an adult while under the influence of drink or substances this will also increase the chance of any subsequent intrusive recollections or flashback experiences being perceived as anomalous experience, as the impairment caused by the substances will impair encoding at the time of the trauma.

If a person experiences a trauma that acts as a precipitant to their psychotic symptoms it may be that the trauma in some way challenged views of the self and others. For instance, if a person regarded other people as generally benign, kind and caring, the experience of a serious assault may be very difficult to accommodate with these views, and may lead the person to developing a delusional explanation to account for this experience. For example, if the view of other people is that they are kind and considerate, one possible explanation of why others have been unkind or cruel is that they are not really people but aliens. In brief, it is evident that trauma experiences can affect the development and maintenance of psychotic symptoms (and particularly delusional beliefs and auditory hallucinations) via the adverse effects on beliefs about the self and other people. There is also likely to be increasing anomalous experiences which are related to the trauma incident but perhaps not linked to the actual trauma because impaired encoding of the experience has occurred owing to dissociation or excessive alcohol or substance use.

Formulation-based CBT for psychosis (CBTp)

The second aim of this chapter is to illustrate how CBT for psychosis is enhanced by trauma-informed models of psychosis.

Ehlers and Clark's (2000) model of PTSD specifically addresses the processing of memory in trauma. The key element of this model is that distressing flashback experiences in PTSD are understood to result from incomplete memory processing. Treatment involves 'reliving' and exposure to this memory via specific verbal reattribution using guided discovery principles. This allows the traumatic memory to be integrated into the broader memory without the associated peak of emotion.

Smucker (Smucker and Dancu, 1999) has developed methods that are particularly helpful in early childhood abuse experiences where there may be less clarity in the memory. The Smucker model involves three stages. The first is exposure, where the client and therapist explore the flashback/ memories and thereby begin the process of memory exposure. The next phase is Empowerment, where the adult self is introduced via guided imagery into the flashback to speak to the abused as adult to adult. The third stage is concerned with self-nurturing, which is developed by the adult self speaking to and forgiving the child.

Smucker also utilised imagery transformation as a method of reducing distress associated with mental images by asking the individual to comment on 'things that don't fit' in the image or by changing frightening and disturbing images to objects of humour, for example. This has been developed as a strategy for dealing with distressing visual hallucinations as well as flashbacks with this case series.

While it is possible to outline how trauma may manifest itself within current models of psychosis, there is to date only modest empirical support for this, and even less knowledge about how best to treat trauma in the context of psychosis apart from case studies (see Larkin and Morrison, 2006). Thus, the final aim of this chapter is to describe the work of a research cognitive therapist working with people in their first episode of psychosis. The purpose of the work was to help improve our understanding of how to adapt and adjust treatments to target the trauma components of psychosis. An overview is offered of the setting in which the work took place and the nature of the work undertaken.

Early Intervention in Psychosis (EIP): Context

A research cognitive therapist worked in an EIP service in which service users are offered a range of approaches including case management, medication, vocational and social support, and family engagement and intervention. The service works with the aim of promoting the optimum functioning for the individual. In this context the CBT was offered as a specific trauma intervention.

Therapist training and skill

The therapist was a trained mental health nurse, with postgraduate training in cognitive therapy and extensive experience in working with depression and anxiety as well as with PTSD.

Participants

Twelve people were identified and approached, ten people engaged in the therapy process (completed more than four sessions) and seven completed a course of treatment from the case series from which these illustrative cases were taken. All 12 of the participants had had a period of admission to hospital. All of the people seen had some form of hallucinatory experience – primarily voices, but also including sensory and visual hallucinations.

Therapy content and format

Appointments usually occurred weekly on an outpatient basis, often in the person's home, for an average of 15 sessions (ranging from two to 30 sessions) over about a five-month period. The CBT was informed by the evidence-based model of psychosis (Garety et al., 2001) and PTSD (Ehlers and Clark, 2000), and drew on treatment manuals for CBTp (Kingdon and Turkington, 2005). CBTp was chosen as the preferred approach to work with trauma in the context of psychosis owing to the evidence base for its value in relation to schizophrenia and PTSD, as well as the purposefully collaborative approach that involves the client in his or her own treatment. This is important when asking people to consider and address potentially very distressing traumatic experiences. Various strategies for engagement included: openly asking about the nature of the trauma experience, understanding presenting issues from the individual's perspective, working on a personally generated problem list, and focusing on shared goals around alleviating distress.

Key goals of the therapy work were to reduce distress, reduce relapse, promote strengths and build resilience. It was not necessarily to stop the symptoms from occurring but rather to reduce the impact on the person.

Psychosis is a potentially multifaceted problem with implications for the individual and his or her family and hence people with psychosis can experience a range of problems, including practical ones such as financial and housing problems, difficulties in work and education, as well as in social and interpersonal relationships. Therefore, joint work in combination with the care coordinator was essential in helping the person address these key difficulties while still allowing the therapist to bring particular value by working on the trauma presentation.

Outcomes

While individual outcomes are reported it is important to note that none of the seven who completed treatment were admitted into hospital while engaged in trauma-oriented CBTp. Given that this approach may well have accessed high levels of distress as trauma issues were addressed, it is important to know that this work can be undertaken without leading to relapse. However, during the period of CBTp, additional support in the way of night sedation and increased visits were offered if needed.

There was also some evidence of improvement in functional outcomes. At the end of treatment one participant ceased using all antipsychotic and antidepressant medication and had started work (after a short placement with a voluntary/back to work scheme). A second participant had established an enduring relationship, and had a child with her partner. Another successfully returned to full-time study. Naturally, we are cautious in interpreting data from a small sample. However, there is reason to be optimistic that the therapy in combination with the other elements of the EIP service helped people achieve personally valued goals. Nevertheless, the main purpose of this research was to consider what was learned about how trauma presented in the context of psychosis and how we adapt our approaches to helping these different presentations. To this end we will draw on a series of disguised case examples to illustrate these features and the related treatments.

Single adult trauma: A clinical vignette

Case A was a 21-year-old man who had been severely physically assaulted (by up to three assailants). The details of the actual assault were somewhat vague as he had very little recall or memory of the experience as he was under the influence of alcohol and illegal substances at the time of the incident. There was no known previous history of psychosis. However, some three months after the incident he presented to services complaining of paranoia and visual and auditory hallucinations and was hospitalised for a period of 12 days, during which antipsychotic medication was initiated.

Some months after his discharge from hospital he began therapy due to the persistence of distressing symptoms. At this time he described particular problems with feeling concerned that other people were going to harm him. He did not relate this only to those people who had attacked him and he was concerned that many people were intent on hurting him. Consequently, he avoided going out. If he was able to go out, he went with a trusted family member and he described feeling extremely anxious, and 'on guard'. Owing to the anxiety he was experiencing he reported smoking cannabis in order to help keep calm. While he was unable to recall much about the assault, he did describe how, when he felt acutely aroused, he would see brief uncontrollable mental images of people attacking him. He said that these were the thoughts and intentions of other people whose minds he could read. He therefore thought he was at risk of being attacked.

Drawing on the conceptual model illustrated in Figure 13.1, the preliminary understanding was that he was experiencing flashback phenomena that led to him experiencing intense arousal in an environment that was in fact safe. Owing to the absence of any memory of the traumatic incident, this current re-experiencing was not linked or anchored to the past, and hence was experienced very much as a present threat. This odd or anomalous experience was explained by information-processing biases that led to hasty and rapid conclusions and external attributions of cause, meaning that this arousal was interpreted as evidence that he was under *current* threat from others. He coped by remaining very vigilant for signs of hostility or malevolence from others, and actually avoided most situations. As he never tested out whether or not he was the victim of persecution, he maintained his views that others were not trustworthy, and the odd experiences continued to provide him with further evidence that something was wrong.

Treatment

In addition to the standard approaches used in CBTp, the key clinical challenge with this case example was that reliving of the trauma memory was virtually impossible owing to the poor encoding of information at the time of the incident as a result of intoxication. This meant that this information was unavailable for reliving and re-exposure. Efforts to do this may have led to the creation of hypothetical 'what if' scenarios that would be potentially very unhelpful. The therapist could not look at the trauma itself and therefore it was necessary to consider the consequences of the assault, which were understood by drawing on the model outlined in Figure 13.1, which served as the basis for the conceptualisation. This formulation acted as a less distressing, and more helpful explanation for his sense of threat. This understanding was enhanced further by drawing on specific features of Ehlers and Clark's (2000) model of PTSD in which arousal is understood to be a response to intrusive memories. A key task was to develop with him an acceptable explanation for why he would experience such intense fear and arousal when he was out. The purpose of the therapy was not to prove that there was no conspiracy against him; rather, it was to provide an alternative and more realistic explanation for his experiences.

His experiences were reframed as flashbacks and were talked about more as PTSD than psychosis. The very brief images he experienced were reframed as being anxiety related and were proposed to have arisen because he was intoxicated at the time of the attack and unable to encode the memory properly. Furthermore, the appraisal that the experience was caused by other people and was uncontrollable was specifically addressed. This was tested by using the camera method as used in PTSD treatments in which an image or memory (in this case the partial memory he experienced) is run in the mind's eye and the participant is able to stop or freeze the image, and run it backwards or forwards. This technique, combined with the process of guided discovery, helped him establish that actually he did have some control over the experience. This fits well with the alternative explanation (the formulation) that it is a flashback memory and is therefore less consistent with it being a sign that others have malevolent intentions towards him.

Having been attacked it was not surprising that he felt reluctant to go out and felt unsafe when he was out. In order to help address this, the value of being 'on guard' when out was tested using behavioural experiments to evaluate whether vigilance drew his attention to more or less potential threat, and what impact it had on his anxiety levels. The value of avoidance was also considered, and in time he agreed to go to places on his own, and then to revisit the area in which he was attacked without relying on his use of being on guard. In addition, there was some work on utilising other forms of stress relief besides cannabis, the use of which reduced mainly to occasions when he was with friends.

Outcome and summary

Case A reported reduced distress associated with the flashback symptoms, reduced conviction in the belief that others were intent on attacking him, and improved mood. This picture of improvement was further supported by his ability to travel to more places independently.

As can be seen, therapeutic efforts to re-experience or relive the trauma lacked the essential retrieval cues and were not possible. Consequently, the main approach was to explain the experience of current threat by normal-ising many of the experiences as resulting from trauma experiences. The formulation served as a less distressing explanation of the experiences. This conceptualisation was then actively tested as a meaningful explanation through the use of behavioural experiments and was used to help promote increased activity and reduce avoidance.

The impact of multiple traumas: A clinical vignette

Here we discuss the case of B, a 22-year-old woman who had come to the UK from a country in the old Soviet Union. She had been in the UK for three years, had presented to services shortly after arriving in the UK and then spent 18 months in hospital. Her presenting issues included flashback experiences, nightmares, suspicious and mistrustful beliefs about others, auditory and visual hallucinations and very low mood. She had made a number of self-harm attempts, had been prescribed various antipsychotic medications during her time in hospital and continued to take medication when discharged.

B reported being exposed to a number of trauma experiences, including witnessing several members of her family being murdered when she was a teenager. Over the course of treatment B revealed that she had experienced earlier adversity and as a child she had been kidnapped and held by another family for many months. She did not know how this had happened or for what reason, but she believed her own family may have had some role in it. It was understood that this would have created mixed feelings for her family, especially for her mother, who she believed should have protected her.

The conceptual understanding developed with B, broadly based on Figure 13.1, was that her early experience had led to her holding negative beliefs about others and being particularly wary, suspicious and mistrusting of others.

This in itself was not sufficient to trigger the onset of psychosis. However, the witnessing of the brutal deaths of many of her family members and the fear for her own life had led to the later development of intrusive memories of her family members. In particular, B said she saw a family member who came to try and speak to her, saying that she was to blame for her family members' deaths. This was experienced as a hallucination rather than a flashback, as the experience had never actually occurred. This experience led B to feel both very anxious that she was at risk and also very sad at the loss of her family members. To cope she would look away from the image and try and distract herself so that the vision would go away. It appeared that at these times B dissociated and could not recall significant periods of time.

Treatment

While clearly there are strong elements of PTSD in the presentation, the extreme nature of this person's experience presents a number of therapeutic challenges. A key treatment approach is the use of normalisation of both the flashback experiences and the psychotic symptoms. This is important but it is crucial that normalisation is not stated in a way that says what happened to the person was in any way normal or that their experiences and symptoms are minor or commonplace. Rather, we use the term normalisation to emphasise that the reaction to the trauma experience is in the range of normal reactions, and that most people will have flashback experiences after a trauma, just as many people will report voice experiences at some point in their lives.

Those with childhood trauma may have schemas relating to their own interpersonal vulnerability, and the dangerousness of others, which could make engagement in therapy difficult. Hence, for this work there was a particular emphasis on relationship building, and purposefully checking out the expectations of others (i.e. the therapist). Questions about the trauma experiences were undertaken in the context of an explicit rationale which was shared with B. Once it was agreed that the trauma experiences may be important to consider in the understanding of her current difficulties, a conceptualisation was developed based on Figure 13.1. Through this process B began to consider that her difficulties may be understood as a form of PTSD. In her view, being a victim of trauma was less distressing than being seen as suffering from madness. This then provided the rationale to introduce symptom management techniques to decrease the level of arousal she experienced. An additional key early target was the understanding of her hallucinatory experiences. In the formulation, her hallucinations of her family member were understood to be intrusive experiences that were understandable given her witnessing of her family member's murder and the important role this person had played in her life. These thoughts and images were understood to be the anomalous experiences that she made sense of as her family member speaking to her. Behavioural experiments for hallucinations were undertaken, including continuing to look at the hallucination and engaging in conversation with it, rather than looking away. She began to see that her family member may have had other reasons for visiting her rather than wanting revenge.

Reducing the distress experienced with the hallucinations then led to specific trauma work that involved cognitive restructuring and reliving of particular periods of trauma. This was complicated by the high levels of dissociation at the time of the trauma, and when she became distressed in the present. Grounding techniques helped bring B back to the present when doing the reliving work. Personal objects such as pictures in the home environment and items such as key fobs with sentimental value that could be carried outside were used in this way.

The reliving work revealed the extent of the horrors that she had witnessed, and a strong sense of guilt that she had survived and a belief that she was to blame for her family members' deaths. This attribution was considered, gently, using the pie chart technique, which draws attention to other important factors that were otherwise being overlooked as contributors to her family members' deaths. The work was slow and difficult owing to the very extensive traumas that had been experienced as well as the recognition that her ability to properly grieve for her losses had been impaired by the need to flee the country of origin and the demands of being an inpatient and seeking asylum.

The early experience of being taken to another family while she was a child was clearly damaging and it led to some ambivalence towards her family. She was naturally suspicious that others would let her down or reject her. As indicated, throughout therapy a key process was the building of trust, while encouraging her to try having her own needs met in an adult manner rather than in a self-fulfilling pattern of rejection. B expressed a view that other people should look after her and if they do not then they do not care. To assist in this and to help overcome her low mood, a behavioural activation approach was used, where the main activities were focused on developing and broadening the nature of her friendships and relationships in order to see if she could have her needs met. Of course this was all in the context of the person being very disadvantaged as an asylum seeker with few financial resource, poor housing, limited social contact, difficulties from language barriers, and an inability to seek work, all of which meant reduced structure and activity in the day and severe financial hardship. Naturally, there was a need to work alongside her consultant psychiatrist and care coordinator who were able to attend to many of the complex factors affecting her (housing needs, asylum application, medication management, etc.). Finally, a relapse prevention plan was put in place with her care coordinator's assistance.

Outcome and summary

B was seen for 32 sessions and post treatment evaluation indicated improvements in mood, and a reduction in the frequency of and distress associated with visual and auditory hallucinations. She remained out of hospital. Following the end of therapy she established a relationship and had her first child. Owing to the themes of being a good, protective parent, particular support and safeguards were put in place around the time of her pregnancy and for the months following.

Conclusions

The more individuals are asked about the nature and origin of their psychotic symptoms, the greater the likelihood that traumatic experiences will be described (Read et al., 2006). Hence, mental health professionals have a duty to find an opportunity to ask about these experiences.

Knowledge of how trauma can contribute to the development of psychosis, and how people with psychosis are more vulnerable to trauma, can facilitate questioning about these experiences. Of course, this then raises the issue of how we help people for whom traumatic experience has contributed to the development or maintenance of psychosis. To this end the role of traumatic life events in the development and maintenance of psychosis is recognised and is being accommodated and integrated into theoretical models of psychotic experiences. Such models are valuable as they help clinicians to sensitively elicit these experiences, develop with the person a joint understanding of the role for trauma processes in psychotic symptoms, and utilise this knowledge to develop and deliver effective treatment that helps alleviate distress.

It is evident that our CBT theoretical knowledge about how trauma, dissociation and psychosis are linked is at an early stage. The work presented in this chapter is based on an existing model of psychotic symptoms. While it is apparently able to account for how trauma may manifest as psychosis it may lack crucial understanding of the links between trauma and psychosis. We may need to rethink how we understand trauma in relation to psychosis. For instance, Kingdon and Turkington (2005) have proposed that there may be five separate groups of psychoses, including a 'traumatic psychosis' group. They conceptualise traumatic psychosis as on a continuum with borderline personality disorder and post traumatic stress disorder, but with the symptoms, particularly voices, being externalised. Auditory hallucinations are seen as particularly characteristic of this group.

Mueser *et al.* (2002) have developed a model which hypothesises that PTSD acts as a mediator for the negative effects of trauma on severe mental illness, both directly through the symptoms of avoidance, over-arousal and re-experiencing, and indirectly through the common correlates of PTSD such as substance abuse, re-traumatisation and interpersonal difficulties. Approaches such as these that foreground the importance of trauma in understanding psychosis may lead to refined treatment methods that address processes that are not articulated in the current models.

From the case illustrations it is clear that the relationship between traumatic life experiences and psychosis is potentially complex. There are different pathways to psychosis, and different ways in which trauma may impact on a person. However, even though the cases were different in many ways, there were some apparent commonalities between them. First, the cases in this chapter had experienced trauma incidents that were at least thematically linked to the content of their psychotic symptoms. In some cases this understanding only emerged later, when the full details of the person's trauma history were understood, but for each person there was a link between the person's own trauma experience and the content of the hallucination or the nature of the paranoid beliefs. Hence, an important challenge for clinicians is to hold in mind that apparently bizarre beliefs and experiences may to some extent have a basis in the reality of the person's experiences. Second, the nature of the trauma experiences were varied (assault, murder) but they shared in common a strong interpersonal focus. These traumas were not random bad luck events but deliberate acts undertaken by other people. Third, while treatment was person-specific and led by the individual's presenting issues and goals, there were certain elements of treatment that were consistent across all the cases in the case series. For instance, in each case there was a strong focus on developing a trusting therapeutic relationship. Next, an understanding of the maintenance and development of the psychotic symptoms was developed that explicitly made reference to the experience of trauma. This was used to create an alternative, potentially less distressing but acceptable explanation of the person's difficulties. This alternative view was supported and developed with normalising information that helped a person recognise that their experiences (voices, visions, unusual beliefs) were common reactions to stressful and traumatic life experiences. This developing alternative conceptualisation was then subject to testing using a series of behavioural experiments. Where necessary, treatment would then focus on more long-standing and deeply held views about the self and others and develop a relapse prevention plan based on this understanding of the person's vulnerabilities.

Therefore, we can see some commonalities between people with different presentations of trauma in the context of psychosis. A particular challenge in working with psychosis is defining the limits of what is a traumatic experience. In this report we have concentrated on people with what we consider to be clearly identifiable traumatic experiences (assault, murder). However, during the course of the work we also came across people for whom emotional abuse or neglect may have had a role in the later development of psychotic symptoms. While these may not strictly be traumatic life events in which the person is in fear for their physical well-being, it can be that severe or sustained emotional abuse can have a profound impact on a person, and may contribute to the later development of psychosis.

For example, a case with whom we worked reported being subject to extensive bullying in his work environment. Even after he left his job he continued to feel he was being watched and monitored by his previous work colleagues and he reported intense mistrust and suspicion of other people to the extent that he held paranoid delusional beliefs that computers were bugged. He was vigilant for signs of threat, and believed cars parked in his street were present in order to watch and follow him and that he was at risk of imminent harm. It appeared that, owing to the bullying and victimisation he experienced, the main impact was on beliefs about self as inadequate and worthless, and beliefs about others as cruel, malicious, and untrustworthy. While his presentation would not fulfil criteria for a trauma it is apparent that, as with the other cases presented, there was a strong interpersonal component to the triggering event. How and where we draw the distinction between adverse life events and those with a particularly traumatic impact is a conceptual challenge.

References

Birchwood, M., Meaden, A., Trower, P., Gilbert, P. and Plaistow, J. (2000). The power and omnipotence of voices: Subordination and entrapment by voices and significant others. *Psychological Medicine*, *30*, 337–344.

Boevnik, W. A. (2006). From being a disorder to dealing with life: An experiential exploration of the association between trauma and psychosis. *Schizophrenia Bulletin*, *32*, 17–19.

Curson, D. A., Patel, M., Liddle, P. F. and Barnes, T. R. E. (1988). Psychiatric morbidity of a long-stay hospital population with chronic schizophrenia and implications for future community care. *British Medical Journal*, *297*, 819–822.

Davis, J. M., Kane, J. M., Marder, S. R., Brauzer, B., Gierl, B., Schooler, N., Casey, D. E. and Hassan, M. (1993). Dose response of prophylactic antipsychotics. *The Journal of Clinical Psychiatry*, *54*, 24–30.

Ehlers, A. and Clark, D. M. (2000). A cognitive model of post traumatic stress disorder. *Behaviour Research Therapy*, *38*, 319–345.

Ensink, B. (1992). *Confusing Realities. A Study of Child Sexual Abuse and Psychiatric Symptoms*. Amsterdam: Vu University Press.

Garety, P. A., Kuipers, E., Fowler, D., Freeman, D. and Bebbington, P. E. (2001). A cognitive model of the positive symptoms of psychosis. *Psychological Medicine*, *31*, 189–195.

Holmes, E. A. and Steel, C. (2004). Schizotypy: A vulnerability factor for traumatic intrusions. *Journal of Nervous and Mental Disease*, *192*(1), 28–34.

Honig, A., Romme, M., Ensink, B., Escher, S., Pennings, M. and Devries, M. (1998). Auditory Hallucinations: A comparison between patients and non-patients. *The Journal of Nervous and Mental Disease*, *186*, 646–651.

Janssen, I., Krabbendam, L., Bak, M., Hanssen, M., Vollebergh, W., Graaf, R. and van Os, J. (2004). Childhood abuse as a risk factor for psychotic experiences. *Acta Psychiatrica Scandinavica*, *109*, 38–45.

Kingdon, D. and Turkington, D. (2005). *Cognitive Therapy of Schizophrenia*. New York: Guilford Press.

Larkin, W. and Morrison, A. (2006). Relationships between trauma and psychosis: From theory to therapy. In W. Larkin and A. P. Morrison (Eds.), *Trauma and Psychosis: New Directions for Theory and Therapy*. London: Routledge.

Mueser, K. T., Rosenberg, S. D., Goodman, L. A. and Trumbetta, S. L. (2002). Trauma, PTSD and the course of severe mental illness: An interactive model. *Schizophrenia Research*, *53*, 123–143.

Read, J., Agar, K., Argyle, N. and Aderhold, V. (2006). Sexual and physical assault during childhood and adulthood as predictors of hallucinations, delusions and thought disorder. *Psychology and Psychotherapy*, *76*, 1–22.

Romme, M. and Escher, S. (Eds.). (1996) Hearing voices in patients and non-patients. In *Understanding Voices: Coping with Auditory Hallucinations and Confusing Realities*. Maastricht: Rijksuniversitiet.

Ross, C. A., Anderson, G. and Clark, P. (1994). Childhood abuse and the positive symptoms of schizophrenia. *Hospital and Community Psychiatry*, *45*, 489–491.

Smucker, M. R. and Dancu, C. V. (1999). *Cognitive Behavioral Treatment for Adult Survivors of Childhood Trauma: Imagery Rescripting and Reprocessing*. Oxford: Rowman & Littlefield Publishers.

Steel, C., Mahmood, M. and Holmes, E. (2008). Positive Schizotypy and trait dissociation as vulnerability factors for post traumatic stress distress. *British Journal of Clinical Psychology*, *47*, 245–249.

Note

1 We would like to thank the participants in this work. We would also like to extend our thanks to Hannah Osborne, who assisted with the data collection, as well as Brian Martindale and other colleagues from the Early Intervention in Psychosis service, who worked to help recruit participants and supported the research.

Richters (1995) found that criticism and hostility rates rose rapidly in the first few years of the course of illness: in 14 per cent of families with less than one year of illness, 35 per cent within 1–3 years of onset and peaking at 50 per cent of the sample after five years. A study by the author compared components of EE (rejection, warmth, protectiveness and fusion) across three samples. In two of the samples the subjects had an established schizophrenic or mood disorder and in the third the subjects were at high risk for an initial psychosis. Parental scores for rejecting attitudes and emotional over-involvement were all but identical in the two established-disorder samples but were markedly higher than scores in the prodromal sample (McFarlane and Cook, 2007). These studies strongly suggest that expressed emotion is largely reactive to deterioration manifested by the young person developing a psychotic disorder.

Attribution – the relatives' beliefs about the causes of illness-related behavior – has also been associated with expressed emotion. Relatives described as critical or hostile misperceive the patient as somehow responsible for unpleasant, symptomatic behavior, whereas more accepting relatives saw identical behaviors as characteristic of the illness itself. This is an especially acute risk in the prodromal phase and in the first episode, during which symptoms and deficits often develop slowly, appearing to reflect personality or behavioral faults. An individual who is cognitively impaired, denying illness, paranoid, angry, hostile, affectively labile, socially withdrawn or anhedonic will be much less available to receive the support needed to function at an optimal level. If family members confronted by such symptoms in a loved one have little formal knowledge of the illness, they are likely to respond with increased involvement, emotional intensity or criticism.

Stigma

Stigma is often associated with a withdrawal of social support, demoralization, and loss of self-esteem, and can have far-reaching effects on daily functioning, particularly in the workplace or school. With the availability of new medications and concomitant emphases on improved functioning and rehabilitation, this arena becomes an ever more important focal point for intervention. As Link et al. (1991) observed, stigma had a strong continuing negative impact on well-being, even though proper diagnoses and treatment improved symptoms and levels of functioning over time. Stigma affects the family as well. Effects include withdrawal and isolation on the part of family members, which in turn are associated with a decrease in social network size and emotional support, increased burden, diminished quality of life and exacerbations of medical disorders. Self-imposed stigma tends to reduce the likelihood that early signs will be addressed and treatment sought and accepted, especially during the first episode.

Communication deviance

Communication deviance, a measure of distracted or vague conversational style, has been consistently associated with schizophrenia (see Chapter 9). It was the other factor in the prospective long-term outcome study that predicted the onset of schizophrenic psychosis in families of disturbed, but non-psychotic, adolescents (Goldstein, 1985). More recent studies have demonstrated that it is correlated with cognitive dysfunction in the relatives which is of the same type, but of lower severity, as is seen in patients with schizophrenia. This suggests that some family members have difficulty holding a focus of attention, with important implications for treatment design. The result is that a child with subtle cognitive impairments may learn to converse in a communication milieu that is less able or inclined to compensate for and correct thinking disorder.

Social isolation

The available evidence across several severe and chronic illnesses indicates that ongoing access to social contact and support prevents the deterioration of such conditions and improves their course (Penninx et al., 1996). Family members of the most severely ill patients seemed to be isolated, preoccupied with, and burdened by, the patient. Brown et al. (Brown et al., 1972) showed that 90 per cent of the families with high expressed emotion were small in size and socially isolated. In addition, social support buffers the impact of adverse life events and is one of the key factors predicting medication compliance, behavior toward treatment in general, schizo-phrenic relapse, quality of life and subjective burden experienced by relatives. Social network size decreases with number of episodes, is lower than normal prior to onset and decreases during the first episode.

Effects of psychosis on the family

Because there is so much evidence that some family members of patients with established psychotic disorders share sub-clinical forms of similar deficits and abnormalities, treatment for early stages of psychosis must be designed to compensate for some of those difficulties. Those deficits lead to diminished coping ability, which is required in abundance in order to provide a therapeutic influence on the affected family member. Further, the psychotic disorders exact an enormous toll on family members, in terms of anxiety, anger, confusion, stigma, rejection and exacerbation of medical disorders. The organization of most families undergoes a variety of changes, including alienation of siblings, exacerbation or even initiation of marital conflict, severe disagreement regarding support versus behavior control, even divorce. Almost every family undergoes a degree of demoralization and self-blame, which may be inadvertently reinforced by some clinicians. During the prodromal phase, family members are mystified by the often dramatic emotional, cognitive and behavior changes that they are seeing, and react in a wide variety a ways, from anger to denial to profound anxiety and worry.

Prospective studies of family interaction prior to onset

Tienari *et al.* (2004) have shown in a prospective study that family expressed emotion and communication deviance, especially negativity directed toward the at-risk young person, predict onset of psychosis, interacting with genetic (having a biological mother with schizophrenia) or psychiatric (already having non-psychotic symptoms and behavioral difficulties) risk. In support of the stress (or environmental risk) part of the stress-diathesis model, the Finnish Adoption Study rigorously combined and tested both psychosocial and genetic risk factors, and their interaction, in a developmentally sensitive design. This study provided the first compelling evidence for a gene–environment interaction for schizophrenia-spectrum disorders. The results indicated that risk for development of schizophrenia-spectrum disorders was much higher among genetically at-risk adoptees reared in families in which there were higher levels of negativity (expressed emotion), family constrictedness (flat affect, lack of humor), and family boundary problems (e.g. generational enmeshment, chaotic family structure, unusual communication). There was no increase whatsoever in the incidence of schizophrenia-spectrum disorders among genetically at-risk adoptees reared in less distressed families. Thus, not only were certain types of common family dynamics implicated in triggering the onset of schizophrenia in vulnerable children, but healthier family dynamics also played a *protective* role (i.e. *preventing* an illness in genetically predisposed individuals).

A model of reciprocal causation

These critical factors lead to psychosis via (a) a general sensitivity to external stimulation and (b) a discrepancy between current stimulus complexity and cognitive or information-processing capacity. Sub-clinical cognitive deficits, effects of the psychosis on the family and characteristic coping styles combine to contribute to external illness-generated stresses that induce a spiraling and deteriorating process that ends in a major psychosis. These factors are potential targets for family psychoeducation and multifamily groups (see Figure 14.1).

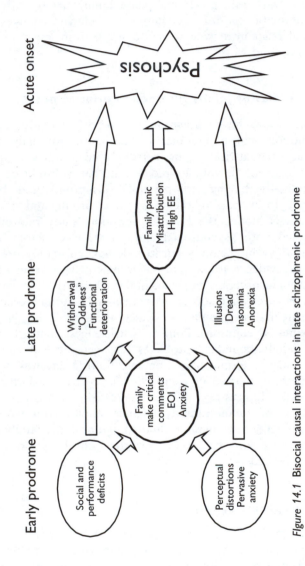

Early prodrome   Late prodrome   Acute onset

Psychosis

Social and performance deficits

Withdrawal "Oddness" Functional deterioration

Family make critical comments EOI Anxiety

Family panic Misattribution High EE

Perceptual distortions Pervasive anxiety

Illusions Dread Insomnia Anorexia

Figure 14.1 Bisocial causal interactions in late schizophrenic prodrome

Family psychoeducation: Outcomes in schizophrenia and other psychiatric disorders

Family intervention alters critical environmental influences by reducing ambient social and psychological stresses, by building barriers to excess stimulation and by buffering the effects of negative life events. The family psychoeducational model defines schizophrenia and other psychotic and mood disorders as brain disorders which are sensitive to the social environment. Thus, this form of treatment is seen as bimodal, influencing both the disease, through medication, and the social environment, through techniques which deliberately reduce to tolerable levels stimulation, negativity in interpersonal interaction, rate of change and complexity. The approach achieves that goal by providing relevant education, training and support to family members and others, who in turn provide support, protection and guidance to the patient.

The cumulative record of efficacy for family intervention, variously termed family psychoeducation, family behavioral management or family work (but not family therapy) is remarkable. Over 20 controlled clinical trials have demonstrated markedly decreased relapse and rehospitalization rates among patients whose families received psychoeducation compared with those who received standard individual services – 20–50 per cent over two years. At least eight literature reviews have been published in the past decade, all finding a large and significant effect for this model of intervention. Since 1978, there has been a steady stream of rigorous validations of the positive effects of this approach on relapse in schizophrenic disorders. Overall, the relapse rate for patients provided with family psychoeducation has hovered around 15 per cent per year, compared with a consistent 30–40 per cent for individual therapy and medication or medication alone. This effect size equals the reduction in relapse in medicated vs unmedicated patients in most drug maintenance studies.

McFarlane *et al.* have consistently shown that when a very similar version of family psychoeducation is incorporated, multi-family groups lead to lower relapse rates and higher employment than single-family sessions (McFarlane, Link *et al.*, 1995; McFarlane, Lukens *et al.*, 1995). The simplest explanation is that enhanced social support, inherent only in the multi-family format, reduces vulnerability to relapse, probably by reducing anxiety and general distress and increasing options for coping skills (Dyck *et al.*, 2002). In two studies – across seven sites with simultaneous replication – of differential effects in schizophrenia of single-family therapy (SFT) and multi-family group (MFG) forms of the same psychoeducational treatment method, better outcomes were observed for multi-family groups among those having their first hospitalization, including very low relapse rates over four years (12.5 per cent per year). Both of these randomized clinical trials strongly suggest a multi-dimensional effect as the explanation for improved clinical outcomes. This argument is strengthened further by recent studies showing dramatic improvements in employment among people with schizophrenia, especially when combined with other interventions, such as supported employment, that are designed to achieve functional goals (McFarlane *et al.*, 1996; McFarlane *et al.*, 2000).

Recent reports have added to the strong validation of the effects on relapse, particularly because these later studies have been conducted in a variety of international and cultural contexts. Reductions in relapse for family intervention, compared with the control conditions, have been demonstrated in several studies around the world. The universality of this approach seems to have been demonstrated in contexts that are different enough to suggest that further generalization in other cultures and countries appears likely to succeed, especially if the necessary adaptations are made.

These and other studies have demonstrated significant effects on other areas of functioning, going beyond relapse as the main dimension of outcome. Many patients and their family members are more concerned about the functional aspects of the illness, especially housing, employment, social relationships, dating and marriage, as well as general morale, than about remission, which tends to be somewhat abstract as a goal. Several of the previously mentioned models, particularly the American versions – those of Falloon, Anderson and McFarlane – have used remission (the absence of relapse) as both a primary target of intervention but also a necessary first step toward rehabilitative goals and recovery. In addition, these models all include major components designed to achieve functional recovery, and the studies have documented progress in those same domains. Several investigators, including our research team, have shifted focus to targeting these more human aspects of illness and life. Other effects have been shown for:

- Improved family-member well-being (Cuijpers, 1999)
- Increased patient participation in vocational rehabilitation (Falloon *et al.*, 1985)
- Substantially increased employment rates (McFarlane *et al.*, 2000)
- Decreased psychiatric symptoms, including negative symptoms (Dyck, *et al.*, 2000)
- Improved social functioning (Montero *et al.*, 2001)
- Decreased family distress (Dyck *et al.*, 2002)
- Reduced costs of care (Rund *et al.*, 1994).

As a result of the compelling evidence, the Schizophrenia Patient Outcomes Research Team (PORT) project included family psychoeducation in its set of treatment recommendations. The PORT recommended that all families in contact with their relative who has mental illness be offered a family psychosocial intervention spanning at least nine months and including education about mental illness, family support, crisis intervention, and problem-solving skills training (Lehman *et al.*, 1998). Other best practice standards (APA, 1997) have also recommended that families receive education and support programs. In addition, an expert panel that included clinicians from various disciplines, families, patients and researchers emphasized the importance of engaging families in the treatment and rehabilitation process (Coursey *et al.*, 2000).

It is important to note that most studies evaluated family psychoeducation for schizophrenia or schizoaffective disorder only. However, several controlled studies do support the effects of family interventions for other psychiatric disorders, including:

- Dual diagnosis of schizophrenia and substance abuse (McFarlane, Lukens *et al.*, 1995)
- Bipolar disorder (Miklowitz *et al.*, 2000)
- Major depression (Leff *et al.*, 2000)
- Mood disorders in children (Fristad *et al.*, 2009)
- Obsessive-compulsive disorder (Van Noppen, 1999)
- Anorexia nervosa (Geist *et al.*, 2000)
- Borderline personality disorder (Gunderson *et al.*, 1997), including single- and multi-family approaches.

Psychoeducational multi-family group treatment of prodromal and early first-episode psychosis

The psychoeducation multi-family group treatment model described here is designed to assist families directly in coping with the major burdens and stresses during the prodromal and psychotic phases of these disorders. This approach (a) Allays anxiety and exasperation; (b) Replaces confusion with knowledge, direct guidance, problem-solving and coping-skills training; (c) Reverses social withdrawal and rejection by participation in a multi-family group that counteracts stigma and demoralization; and (d) Reduces anger by providing a more scientific and socially acceptable explanation for symptoms and functional disability. In short, it relieves the burdens of coping while more fully engaging the family in the treatment and rehabilitation process, and compensating – non-pejoratively – for the expected sub-clinical symptoms that many relatives can be expected to manifest. The goal of intervention is to provide optimal treatment as early as possible for those who are experiencing a first episode of psychosis. The multi-family group intervention, which incorporates elements of family psychoeducation and family behavioral management, is described briefly here and in detail elsewhere (McFarlane, 2002). The intervention model consists of four treatment stages that roughly correspond to the phases of an episode of schizophrenia, from the acute phase through the recuperative and rehabilitation phases. These stages are: (1) Engagement; (2) Education; (3) Re-entry; and (4) Social/Vocational Rehabilitation (Anderson *et al.*, 1986).

Engagement

Contact with the families and with the newly admitted individuals is initiated within 48 hours after a hospital admission or onset of psychosis. Initial contact with the patient is deliberately brief and non-stressful. The young person is included in at least one of the joining sessions, and is excluded from at least one. If the patient is actively psychotic, they are not included in these sessions, but engaged only in a patient-clinician format. The aim is to establish rapport and to gain consent to include the family in the ongoing treatment process. The clinician emphasizes that the goal is to collaborate with the family in helping their relative recover and avoid further deterioration or relapse. The family is asked to join with the clinician in establishing a working alliance or partnership, the purpose of which is to provide the best post-hospital environment for the patient to recover. In particular, these sessions are devoted to elucidating early warning signs and specific precipitants for an individual patient, outlining the family's social support network and empathically understanding each member's experience of the onset and course of the illness. In most families there is also a part of the session spent on the members' sense of loss and the degree to which they mourn that loss. Especially in the prodromal and first-episode phases, education and guidance specific to that family are provided as needed during the engagement process. This phase includes typically three to seven single-family sessions for the multiple-family group format, but more may be required until a sufficient number of families is engaged.

Education

Once the family is engaged, and while the patient is still being stabilized, the family is invited to a workshop conducted by the clinicians who will lead the group. These six-hour sessions are conducted in a formal, classroom-like atmosphere, involving five or six cases. Biological, psychological and social information about psychotic disorders and their management are presented through a variety of formats, such as videotapes, slide presentations, lectures, discussion, and question and answer periods. Information about the way in which the clinicians, patient and family will continue to work together is presented. The families are also introduced to guidelines for management of the disorder and the underlying vulnerability to stress and information overload (see Table 1). Patients attend these workshops if clinically stable, willing, interested and seemingly able to tolerate the social and informational stress.

Guidelines for families: Ways to hasten recovery and to prevent a recurrence

Believe in your power to affect the outcome: You can

Make forward steps cautiously, one at a time. Go slow. Allow time for recovery. Recovery takes time. Rest is important. Things will get better in their own time. Build yourself up for the next life steps. Anticipate life stresses.

Consider using medication to protect your future

A little goes a long way. The medication is working and is necessary even if you feel fine. Work with your doctor to find the right medication and the right dose. Have patience, it takes time. Take medications as they are prescribed. Take only medications that are prescribed.

Try to reduce your responsibilities and stresses, at least for the next six months or so

Take it easy. Use a personal yardstick. Compare this month to last month rather than last year or next year.

Use the symptoms as indicators

If they re-appear, slow down, simplify and look for support and help, quickly. Learn and use your early warning signs and changes in symptoms. Consult with your family clinician or psychiatrist.

Create a Protective Environment

Keep it cool. Enthusiasm is normal. Tone it down. Disagreement is normal. Tone that down too.

Give each other space

Time out is important for everyone. It's okay to reach out. It's okay to say "no".

Set limits

Everyone needs to know what the rules are. A few good rules keep things clear.

Ignore what you can't change

Let some things slide. Don't ignore violence or concerns about suicide.

> **Keep it simple**
>
> Say what you have to say clearly, calmly, and positively.
>
> **Carry on business as usual**
>
> Reestablish family routines as quickly as possible. Stay in touch with family and friends. Solve problems step by step.

In the early intervention version, the clinicians build education and information-sharing on each patient and family's unique and evolving experience, as assessed during the engagement process. Psychosis is defined as a reversible, treatable condition, like diabetes. The core problem is presented as an unusual sensitivity to sensory stimulation, prolonged stress and strenuous demands, rapid change, complexity, social disruption, illicit drugs and alcohol, or negative emotional experience. As for blame and assigning fault, the clinicians take an important position: neither the patient nor the family caused that sensitivity. Whatever the underlying biological cause might be, whether of genetic or neurodevelopmental origin, it is part of the person's physical personhood, with both advantages and disadvantages. Families are explicitly urged not to blame themselves for this vulnerability.

The re-entry phase

Following the workshop the clinicians begin meeting twice monthly with the families and patients in the multiple-family group format. The goal of this stage of the treatment is to plan and implement strategies to cope with the vicissitudes of a person recovering from an acute episode of psychosis or to facilitate recovery from the prodromal state. Major content areas include treatment compliance, stress reduction, buffering and avoiding life events, avoiding street drugs and/or alcohol, lowering of expectations during the period of negative symptoms and a temporary increase in tolerance for these symptoms. Two special techniques are introduced to participating members as supports to the efforts to follow family guidelines: formal problem solving and communications skills training (Falloon *et al.*, 1984).

Social and vocational rehabilitation

Approximately one year following initiation of treatment or an acute episode, most patients begin to evidence signs of a return to spontaneity and active engagement with those around them. This is usually a sign that the negative symptoms are diminishing and the patient can now be challenged more intensively. The focus of this phase deals more specifically with his/her rehabilitative needs, addressing the three areas of functioning in which there are the most common deficits: social skills, academic challenges and the ability to get and maintain employment.

Multi-family groups

These groups address elements of expressed emotion, social isolation, stigmatization and burden directly by education, training and modeling. Some of this effort focuses on modulating emotional expression and clarifying and simplifying communication. However, much of the effectiveness of the approach results from increasing the size and density of the social network, reducing the experience of being stigmatized, providing a forum for mutual aid, and providing an opportunity to hear similar experiences and find workable solutions from others in the group.

A stable membership of from five to seven families meets with two clinicians on a bi-weekly basis, usually for one to three years, following the onset of an initial episode of psychosis; all family members would have participated in an educational workshop. Unless psychotic, the patients also attend the group, although the decision to do so is based upon the patient's mental status and susceptibility to the amount of stimulation such a group occasionally engenders. Each session lasts for an hour and a half.

A case example

The multi-family group approach often provides opportunities for patients to break through seemingly intractable problems that are limiting their options in living. Although the initial stage of work in the psychoeducational framework is focused on preventing relapse and overcoming symptoms, the second phase is explicitly focused on achieving the life goals of the patient, with the family's and the group's assistance. The case presented here illustrates how the psychoeducational multi-family group approach promotes functional recovery, almost always by proceeding in small steps, carefully thought through in the problem-solving process with input from many – and often all – members of the group.

R is a woman in her mid 20s with a serious mental illness that is presently stable. She tries to take good care of herself and to stay on her medication regimen. Although she lives alone, her mother attends the MFG with her regularly. She has recently started working 20 hours a week as a caretaker for severely mentally retarded adults in a group home. So far, she likes the training and the work, but feels she cannot remember all of the information that she is receiving. This experience is starting to make her feel stressed and inadequate. Although she is working closely with an employment specialist, she does not want on-site supervision or to disclose her illness to her employer. She is wondering what she can do to feel less stressed and more in control of the situation while learning a new skill. The group process addressing this conflict was as follows.

Step 1: What is the problem?

How can R receive support with her training and best approach her job in order to be successful?

Step 2: List all possible solutions

The group generated the following suggestions for R:

- Review the written literature that the group home offers about specific tasks during the training period
- Ask for a written job description
- Speak to co-workers about what to expect on the job while training and shadowing
- Don't be afraid to ask questions
- Ask for extra training if you feel you need it, and tell the employer what helps you learn the best
- Know who to call for support
- Make notes of questions to ask your supervisor and write down the answers
- Make notes of tasks while being trained
- Don't be afraid to go to your supervisor.

Step 3: Discuss each possible solution

R decided she liked all of the suggestions and did not eliminate any during this section of the problem-solving process.

Step 4: Choose the best solution or combination of solutions

R thought the following suggestions would be worth trying, and her mother agreed:

- Make notes of questions to ask your supervisor and write down the answers
- Make notes of tasks while being trained
- Speak to co-workers about what to expect on the job while training and shadowing.

Step 5: Plan how to carry out the best solution

- Bring a notebook and pen to work the first day and from then on keep it with you.
- Try to approach a co-worker who seems friendly and has worked there for a while; ask that person about what you can do to make the learning process less stressful. They might share their own learning experiences and offer helpful tips!

R tried these suggestions and found that they were actually important for improving her performance at work and making her feel more comfortable and less isolated.

Conclusion

Family psychoeducation and multi-family groups have shown remarkable outcomes in more than a score of studies, and multi-family groups appear to have a specific efficacy in earlier phases. Our experience suggests strongly that family-oriented, supportive, psychoeducational treatment is acceptable to families and in clinical trials appears to meet many of their needs. There is theoretical support for the efficacy of these methods, with their strategy of stress-avoidance, -protection and -buffering, while the multi-family group format adds an inherent element of social support and network expansion.

References

Anderson, C., Hogarty, G. and Reiss, D. (1986). *Schizophrenia and the Family*. New York, NY: Guilford Press.

American Psychiatric Association (1997). *Practice Guidelines for the Treatment of Schizophrenia*. Washington, DC: American Psychiatric Association.

Bebbington, P. and Kuipers, L. (1994). The predictive utility of expressed emotion in schizophrenia: An aggregate analysis. *Psychological Medicine, 24*, 707–718.

Brown, G. W., Birley, J. L. T. and Wing, J. K. (1972). Influence of family life on the course of schizophrenic disorders: A replication. *British Journal of Psychiatry, 121*, 241–258.

Cook, W. L., Strachan, A. M., Goldstein, M. J. and Miklowitz, D. J. (1989). Expressed emotion and reciprocal affective relationships in families of disturbed adolescents. *Family Process, 28*, 337–348.

Coursey, R., Curtis, L. and Marsh, D. (2000). Competencies for direct service staff members who work with adults with severe mental illness in outpatient public mental health managed care systems. *Psychiatric Rehabilitation Journal, 23*(4), 370–377.

Cuijpers, P. (1999). The effects of family interventions on relatives' burden: A meta-analysis. *Journal of Mental Health, 8*, 275–285.

Dyck, D. G., Short, R. A., Hendryx, M. S., Norell, D., Myers, M., Patterson, T. *et al.* (2000). Management of negative symptoms among patients with schizophrenia attending multiple-family groups. *Psychiatric Services, 51*(4), 513–519.

Dyck, D. G., Hendryx, M. S., Short, R. A., Voss, W. D. and McFarlane, W. R. (2002). Service use among patients with schizophrenia in psychoeducational multiple-family group treatment. *Psychiatric Services, 53*(6), 749–754.

Falloon, I., Boyd, J. and McGill, C. (1984). *Family Care of Schizophrenia.* New York, NY: Guilford.

Falloon, I., Boyd, J., McGill, C., Williamson, M., Razani, J., Moss, H. *et al.* (1985). Family management in the prevention of morbidity of schizophrenia. *Archives of General Psychiatry, 42*, 887–896.

Fristad, M., Goldberg-Arnold, J. and Gavazzi, S. (2009). Multi-family psychoeducation groups in the treatment of children with mood disorders. *Journal of Marital and Family Therapy, 29*(4), 491–504.

Geist, R., Heinmaa, M., Stephens, D., Davis, R. and Katzman, D. (2000). Comparison of family therapy and family group psychoeducation in adolescents with anorexia nervosa. *Canadian Journal of Psychiatry-Revue Canadienne De Psychiatrie, 45*, 173–178.

Goldstein, M. (1985). Family factors that antedate the onset of schizophrenia and related disorders: The results of a fifteen-year prospective longitudinal study. *Acta Psychiatrica Scandinavica, 71*(Suppl. 319), 7–18.

Gunderson, J., Berkowitz, C. and Ruiz Sancho, A. (1997). Families of borderline patients: A psychoeducational approach. *Bulletin of the Menninger Clinic, 61*(4), 446–457.

Hooley, J. and Richters, J. E. (1995). Expressed emotion: A developmental perspective. In D. Cicchetti and S. L. Toth (Eds.), *Emotion, Cognition and Representation* (Vol. 66, pp. 133–166). Rochester: University of Rochester Press.

Leff, J., Vearnals, S., Brewin, C., Wolff, G., Alexander, B., Asen, E. *et al.* (2000). The London Depression Intervention Trial: Randomised controlled trial of antidepressants v couple therapy in the treatment and maintenance of people with depression living with a partner: Clinical outcome and costs. *British Journal of Psychiatry, 177*(2), 95–100.

Lehman, A. F., Steinwachs, D. M., Buchanan, R., Carpenter, W. T., Dixon, L. B., Fahey, M. *et al.* (1998). Translating research into practice: The Schizophrenia Patient Outcomes Research Team (PORT) treatment recommendations. *Schizophrenia Bulletin, 24*(1), 1–10.

Link, B. G., Mirotznik, J. and Cullen, F. T. (1991). The effectiveness of stigma coping orientations: Can negative consequences of mental illness labeling be avoided? *Journal of Health and Social Behavior, 32*, 302–320.

McFarlane, W. R. (2002). *Multifamily groups in the treatment of severe psychiatric disorders.* New York, NY: Guilford Press.

McFarlane, W. R. and Cook, W. L. (2007). Family expressed emotion prior to onet of psychosis. *Family Process, 46*(2), 185–198.

McFarlane, W. R., Link, B., Dushay, R., Marchal, J. and Crilly, J. (1995). Psychoeducational multiple family groups: Four-year relapse outcome in schizophrenia. *Family Process, 34*(2), 127–144.

McFarlane, W. R., Lukens, E., Link, B., Dushay, R., Deakins, S. A., Newmark, M. *et al.* (1995). Multiple-family groups and psychoeducation in the treatment of schizophrenia. *Archives of General Psychiatry, 52*(8), 679–687.

McFarlane, W. R., Dushay, R. A., Stastny, P., Deakins, S. M. and Link, B. (1996). A comparison of two levels of Family-aided Assertive Community Treatment. *Psychiatric Services*, *47*(7), 744–750.

McFarlane, W. R., Dushay, R. A., Deakins, S. M., Stastny, P., Lukens, E. P., Toran, J., Link, B. (2000). Employment outcomes in Family-aided Assertive Community Treatment. *American Journal of Orthopsychiatry*, *70*(2), 203–214.

Miklowitz, D., Simoneau, T., George, E., Richards, J., Kalbag, A., Sachs-Ericsson, N. and Suddath, R. (2000). Family-focused treatment of bipolar disorder: One-year effects of a psychoeducational program in conjunction with pharmacotherapy. *Biological Psychiatry*, *48*, 582–592.

Montero, I., Asencio, A., Hernandez, I., Masanet, M. S. J., Lacruz, M., Bellver, F. *et al.* (2001). Two strategies for family intervention in schizophrenia: A randomized trial in a Mediterranean environment. *Schizophrenia Bulletin*, *27*(4), 661–670.

Penninx, B. W. J. H., Kriegsman, D. M. W., van Eijk, J. T. M., Boeke, A. J. P. and Deeg, F. J. H. (1996). Differential effect of social support on the course of chronic disease: A criterion-based literature review. *Families, Systems and Health*, *14*(2), 223–244.

Rund, B. R., Moe, L., Sollien, T., Fjell, A., Borchgrevink, T., Hallert, M. *et al.* (1994). The Psychosis Project: Outcome and cost-effectiveness of a psychoeducational treatment programme for schizophrenic adolescents. *Acta Psychiatrica Scandinavica*, *89*(3), 211–218.

Tienari, P. A., Wynne, L. C., Sorri, A., Lahti, I., Läksy, K., Moring, J. *et al.* (2004). Genotype–environment interaction in schizophrenia-spectrum disorder. *British Journal of Psychiatry*, *184*, 216–222.

Van Noppen, B. (1999). Multi-family behavioral treatment (MFBT) for OCD. *Crisis Intervention and Time-Limited Treatment*, *5*, 3–24.

Chapter 15

Psychological interventions to improve work outcomes for people with psychiatric disabilities[1]

Morris D. Bell, Jimmy Choi and Paul Lysaker

Introduction

Inactivity and loss of productive function commonly accompany severe psychiatric disorders (e.g. schizophrenia, other psychotic disorders, mood disorders, PTSD). Yet, surveys (Becker, 2002) indicate that more than 75 per cent of people with these disorders wish to return to productive activity of some kind. When they attempt to return to work, however, they often have no access to appropriate work activity. They become discouraged when they fail to find a job or fail to keep a job once they get one. As research has shown (ibid.), unemployment itself can lead to deterioration in mental and physical health among previously healthy individuals, and these consequences are all the more serious for those with severe mental disorders.

Vocational services such as supported employment (SE) have helped people with severe and persistent mental illness to obtain community-based competitive jobs by finding them appropriate opportunities, often with accommodations and supportive services. SE is now regarded as an evidence-based practice (Bond *et al.*, 2002). As pointed out in the Patient Outcomes Research Team USA study, individuals with severe mental disorders have up to now been unlikely to receive vocational rehabilitation services in mental health settings, and the study strongly recommends that such services should be provided. A manualized version of SE for severe mental illness (SMI) populations called Individual Placement and Support (IPS), has advanced the implementation of SE. A toolkit is available comprised of training procedures for clinical staff, administrators and consumers, a fidelity scale, and consultants to assist in implementation (Becker, 2002).

While SE appears superior to other types of vocational services for SMI, employment outcomes remain modest. Only about half of those who receive SE services achieve competitive employment and those who do have difficulty maintaining it. Only about a third are working at any one time, and the job complexity is generally low. Moreover, rates of employment are significantly worse for those with a schizophrenia diagnosis, which suggests that this large subsample of people with SMI may need interventions that target illness-specific features related to their work impairments.

Therefore, SE only partially addresses the problem. It may provide appropriate support and work opportunities, but patients' work disability remains apparent. People with severe mental illness in SE continue to have difficulty performing their job tasks and often their interpersonal problems disrupt their work, which leads as many as 50 per cent to have unsatisfactory job terminations, defined as being fired, or quitting without having other job plans. In this report, we present psychological interventions to enhance work services, each of which addresses illness-related deficits that cannot be sufficiently overcome through on-the-job supports.

Work behavior feedback groups with goal setting

Participants receiving work services meet in a weekly group (usually four to eight workers with a facilitator) for approximately one hour to review on-site evaluations of members' work performance and to problem-solve and set performance goals for the following week. We have developed these groups in a number of different settings that include transitional and supported employment programs.

To provide systematic feedback, we created the Work Behavior Inventory (WBI) as a standardized work performance assessment instrument (Bryson et al., 1997). Detailed information regarding its development, administration and psychometric properties is available elsewhere (Bryson et al., 1997). The WBI is rated by a trained vocational counselor who observes workers on the job and interviews their supervisors. The WBI scales include Work Habits, Work Quality, Social Skills, Cooperativeness and Personal Presentation. These scales were derived through factor analysis, and represent dimensions similar to those from other instruments (e.g. The Work Personality Profile). The WBI demonstrated good inter-rater reliability, concurrent validity, factorial validity and discriminant validity. Evidence for predictive validity was also found (Bryson et al., 1999). WBI scores from the third week of work predicted the number of hours worked over a six-month paid work program, with Social Skills, Personal Presentation and Cooperativeness as the best predictors. A composite of WBI scores from their last six weeks of work predicted the number of hours worked and money earned during a six-month follow-up period. These findings indicated that work performance measured by the WBI has a significant relationship to subsequent work outcomes.

In the workers' meetings, half the members receive feedback each week, but all participate in problem solving and goal setting. The facilitator (usually a vocational specialist or clinician) encourages a process of accurate empathy in which true achievement is acknowledged and praised and problems are realistically confronted. A good deal of social learning occurs as members help each other and learn from each other's experiences. Each week, members report on their progress toward their individual goals and set new goals, often based on the WBI feedback they have received. Goals might include on-the-job behaviors such as increasing hours of work, being more punctual, being tidier in appearance, taking fewer breaks, or approaching a co-worker about having lunch together. In programs that begin with transitional employment with an expectation of moving on to competitive employment, goals might also include preparing a resume, networking for another job or going on a job interview. There are currently experimental studies under way to determine whether rewards for goal attainment increase vocational outcomes, but results are not yet available.

Rationale

There are several important reasons for believing that regular work performance feedback and goal setting are especially important for psychiatrically impaired veterans. First, severe psychiatric disorders often impair people's ability to perceive themselves and others accurately. Related cognitive impairments in emotion recognition, theory of mind, attention, memory and executive function can make it even more difficult for workers with a psychiatric disorder to understand accurately what is going on between themselves and their social environment at work. Feedback not only provides information to workers about their work habits and work quality, but also, importantly, evaluates their social skills, personal presentation, and cooperativeness on the job. These interpersonal behaviors are crucial for vocational success, yet they are not usually addressed directly by supervisors or co-workers in helpful ways. Work supervisors are expected to confront workers who show up late for work repeatedly or who make a lot of mistakes on the job, and they may have good ideas about how to help workers improve in those areas. However, they usually feel reluctant to talk with workers about social withdrawal, odd appearance, or difficulty taking criticism. Supervisors may be uncomfortable with such matters or, out of misguided kindness, they may believe that they are doing the person a favor by not saying anything. They may also have no clear idea about how such problems can be remediated. Yet, left alone, these problems can build up until there is a critical incident leading to job loss. Regular and systematic feedback can provide many people with psychiatric disorders a social prosthesis for their impairments in reading cues from their social environment about their interpersonal behaviors, while goal setting and problem solving can often successfully address these issues.

Second, motivation, sense of purpose, and self-confidence can be profoundly affected by psychiatric disorders. Regular feedback provides workers with a psychiatric disorder continual reassurance about what they are doing right as well as what they need to improve on. Since feelings of worthlessness often lead these workers to believe that others are seeing them as inadequate, getting accurate feedback about how they are viewed by their supervisors can reduce mistrust and provide greater confidence in dealing with people at work. By displaying charts showing progress over time, workers are encouraged with concrete evidence of their successes. As goals are set and attained, workers develop greater feelings of self-efficacy and become more willing to attempt new challenges.

Finally, research literature from industrial and organizational psychology strongly supports the effectiveness of work feedback and goal setting for improving individual and organizational productivity. In *Building a Practically Useful Theory of Goal Setting and Task Motivation: a 35-Year Odyssey*, Locke and Latham (2002) review the literature on motivation and their experiments in work feedback and goal setting. They conclude with a discussion of the generalization of their theory:

> With goal-setting theory, specific difficult goals have been shown to increase performance on well over 100 different tasks involving more than 40,000 participants in at least eight countries, working in laboratory, simulation and field settings. The dependent variables have included quantity, quality, time spent, costs, job behavior measures, and more. The time spans have ranged from 1 minute to 25 years . . . In short, goal-setting theory is among the most valid and practical theories of employee motivation in organizational psychology.

Research support

Studies published in industrial and organizational psychology and management journals strongly endorse work performance evaluations and feedback to improve productivity. They also show that combining feedback with goal setting leads to better performance outcomes than when they are not combined. Other studies demonstrate that frequent and specific feedback, encouragement of self-appraisal, and goal setting are factors that improve goal attainment.

There is only a small literature on the use of evaluation and feedback in rehabilitation settings. In one controlled study (Kravetz *et al.*, 1990), 49 males in a correctional vocational training program were randomized to receive feedback on worker trait ratings or to meet in a group to discuss the importance of worker traits. Feedback included ratings and the behaviors they were based on. Independent ratings of work performance revealed significant improvement for those receiving feedback. In a second controlled study (Hartlage and Johnsen, 1975), 75 people described as "hard-core unemployed" were randomized to receive daily video playback of work behavior or 15 minutes of daily counseling. After 15 days those receiving feedback showed greater improvement in their production, time working and social behaviors on the job. Follow-up job placement was also better. A third controlled study (Fishwick *et al.*, 1972) of 60 schizophrenia patients in a rehabilitation training program compared specific feedback on speed and accuracy with non-specific feedback and found that specific feedback facilitated the acquisition of performance accuracy.

Finally, our own study (Bell, Lysaker and Bryson, 2003) involved 74 patients with schizophrenia in a transitional work program who were randomized to receive work performance feedback and goal-setting or usual services. Those receiving feedback showed greater overall improvement in work performance. Results showed that those randomized to the work feedback and goal setting condition had significantly greater improvement on the WBI, with Social Skills, Cooperativeness, Personal Presentation and WBI total score being significantly greater. They also worked significantly more hours and weeks during the six-month transitional work period. Additionally, they showed greater improvements on the intrapsychic dimension of the Quality of Life scale, which reflects increased motivation, sense of purpose, and enjoyment in life. These results indicated that specific feedback and goal setting could increase work performance, particularly for interpersonal behaviors that are less likely to be addressed by work supervisors; may increase overall productive activity; and may increase feelings of motivation, sense of purpose and enjoyment in life.

These studies vary in population, type of intervention, and work activity, but combined with the larger literature with normal workers, the research points toward the benefits of feedback and goal setting to improve work performance. In subsequent studies that employed CBT or cognitive remediation (to be described below), we have included the work feedback and goal setting groups as part of the rehabilitation services. We did so because we feel that other psychological interventions combine easily with these groups and that these feedback and goal-setting groups may be necessary to generalize the effects of these other interventions.

The Indianapolis Vocational Intervention Program: A cognitive behavioral approach

The Indianapolis Vocational Intervention Program (IVIP) offers participants engaged in work activity both a weekly group and individual intervention. Together these interventions jointly target beliefs and behaviors which might interfere in their ability to sustain work. Examples of beliefs and behaviors that might lead to poor work outcomes include expectations that co-workers or supervisors will reject the participant no matter how hard they try to succeed or a tendency to be verbally aggressive when criticized. In the IVIP model, groups are generally used to teach participants didactic material. Individual sessions are used to apply these to weekly work experience.

Overall both group and individual sessions of the IVIP are based on the principles of cognitive behavior therapy (CBT). Groups are led by two co-therapists and follow a manual with a standard agenda composed of three sections: check-in, intervention and wrap-up. The primary objectives of the 10-15 minute check-in are: (1) to assist participants to identify potential problems at work; (2) to give them positive social reinforcement for accomplishments; (3) to provide a bridge from the last session; and (4) to assess how well participants understand the didactic material while reinforcing major concepts. Although the IVIP employs standard agenda items typical of CBT, the group leader collaborates with participants to finalize the session agenda.

The intervention section of the group is generally 30-40 minutes and involves three activities: (1) teaching the week's didactic material; (2) assisting participants to put the didactic material into practice with some type of application exercise; and (3) giving work feedback to participants. As adapted from other sources, the IVIP didactic curriculum is organized into four two-week modules (a total of eight sessions). These are presented in order and repeated at least three times during participants' six-month program. The content of each of these modules is summarized in Table 15.1.

During the didactic presentation, the scheduled material is presented both abstractly and applied to participants' actual work experiences using a wide variety of exercises. These include scripted, videotaped, and spontaneous role play, practicing progressive muscle relaxation, and generating in-session thought records.

Work feedback, the last aspect of the intervention section, is derived from the Work Behavior Inventory (Bryson et al., 1997) and WBI feedback is given to participants every other week for the first eight weeks and then monthly. The final section of the group session is the 10–15-minute wrap-up during which the group leader asks participants to summarize what they have learned and/or identify what made the most impact on them. The group leader may also provide feedback to group members about their participation in addition to bridging to the didactic topic for the next week.

The individual counseling component of the IVIP is designed to be an opportunity for participants to review and apply didactic materials from groups and to learn to identify and conceptualize concerns using the cognitive behavioral model. Sessions generally begin the week before work with the first two sessions conceived as introductory sessions. These introductory sessions have at least four objectives: (1) begin to establish a therapeutic alliance; (2) orient participants to program routines and schedules; (3) assess participants' current expectations of work; and (4) address immediate and/or potential barriers to success at work. During this phase therapists

Table 15.1 Description of IVIP Group Didactic Modules

Module Title	Session Number and Title	Session Objectives (examples of concepts and skills to be addressed)
Thinking and Work	1. Thinking Errors and Work	Recognize impact of negative thinking
		Identify automatic thoughts that impact work
	2. Modifying Self-Defeating Thinking	Modify dysfunctional cognitions using 4 A model[1]
		Apply 4 A model to participants' work experiences
Barriers To Work	3. Problem Solving Barriers to Work	Identify existing or potential barriers to work
		Employ steps of problem solving to work barriers
	4. Coping with Emotions	Define emotional states that threaten work
		Learn CBT skills to manage difficult emotions
Workplace Relationships	5. Accepting and Learning from Feedback	Differentiate constructive and destructive criticism
		Apply steps for responding to feedback at work
	6. Effective Self-Expression	Learn assertive communication principles
		Practice giving feedback in work settings effectively
Realistic Self-Appraisal	7. Thinking about Capabilities and Limitations	Identify thinking errors compromising self-appraisal
		Identify strengths, limitations and necessary accommodations
	8. Managing Success	Define failure and success via the cognitive model
		Modify dysfunctional cognitions regarding work failures

Note
1 The 4 A model emphasizes the connections between being "aware," "answering," "acting" and "accepting".

employ primarily behavioral methods to help participants identify and overcome any initial barriers to working.

Individual sessions are comprised of the same three sections as the group session: check-in, intervention and wrap-up. Before the therapy session begins, participants rate the strength of their conviction and the extent of its impact for up to four beliefs that participants and therapists have collaboratively identified. Next, during the "check-in" section, participants report the extent to which they worked on and accomplished a mutually agreed upon between-session assignment and give a brief update of the past work week including any mental health concerns. The therapist also reviews the written practice assignment from the last group session. Generally 15 minutes is needed to complete written practice assignments, with more cognitively impaired participants needing more time. As an incentive to complete the written practice assignment participants are paid for an hour of work for each completed assignment.

Rationale

As the result of several factors, including the stigma of mental illness and the losses associated with the illness, many with schizophrenia view themselves as having limited competence, relatively low value in the eyes of others in their community and little chance of success at work, even with help. They may believe they have little ability to influence their lives and have developed a personal narrative in which failure in social and vocational contexts is expected (Lysaker and Buck, 2006).

Consistent with these observations, negative beliefs about self in schizophrenia have been found to predict poorer employment outcome. Indeed it seems likely that with such negative beliefs about themselves and work, many with schizophrenia enter work anticipating that difficulties will occur, see little to be gained from persevering during trying times, and therefore lose opportunities when challenges arise. The IVIP was created to help persons with schizophrenia-spectrum disorder learn to identify and monitor their own thoughts and behaviors regarding work and to give themselves an optimal chance for success. The groups assist persons to learn to understand the links between their thoughts, feelings and behaviors, and the individual sessions provide them a place to explore and change how they see themselves and work.

Research support

To date one randomized controlled study has examined the impact of the IVIP on work outcomes (Lysaker et al., 2005a). In this study, 50 participants with schizophrenia or schizoaffective disorder were recruited from a Midwestern Veterans Administration (VA) medical center, offered a six-month job placement and randomized to receive IVIP (n = 25) or support services (n = 25). Support services in this study were modeled after standard VA vocational support services and included a weekly group in which participants were invited to share their concerns and receive assistance with problem solving.

All participants were male and were receiving medication management by an assigned clinician. On average, participants were 48.1 years old (SD = 5.7), and had 12.5 years of education (SD = 1.2) and 10.5 lifetime psychiatric hospitalizations (SD = 9.52) with the first occurring at age 24.7 (SD = 6.2). All participants were in a post-acute phase of illness as defined by having no hospitalizations or changes in psychotropic medication or housing in the month before entering the study. Participants were excluded who had a diagnosis of mental retardation or another neurological disorder.

Following randomization, hours worked were measured weekly and job performance was assessed every two weeks using the Work Behavior Inventory (WBI). Hope and self-esteem were assessed at baseline and five months using the Beck Hopelessness Scale and the Rosenberg Self Esteem Scale. Analysis of Variance (ANOVA) revealed that participants in the IVIP group worked significantly (p < .05) more weeks than those in the support group (20.39 weeks, SD = 8.00 vs 13.71 weeks, SD = 10.44) and had better average work performance on the WBI (WBI total 118.34, SD = 20.30 vs WBI total 107.55, SD = 8.49). Repeated Measures ANOVA of baseline and follow-up scores indicated the IVIP group sustained initial levels of hope and self-esteem through follow-up while the support group experienced declines. Results thus provide initial evidence that the IVIP can assist persons to persist at work and to sustain their hope and enthusiasm over time. This has also been illustrated by one case report to date (Davis *et al.*, 2005). A further randomized controlled trial, of 100 persons with schizophrenia spectrum disorders, was under way at the time of going to press.

Workplace fundamentals: A social skills approach

The University of California, Los Angeles (UCLA) Social and Independent Living Skills Program is a manualized social skills training intervention for persons with SMI designed to be easily disseminated into various psychiatric rehabilitation programs (Wallace and Tauber, 2004). The overall training curriculum includes modules that teach important problem-solving skills in domains associated with independent daily living, such as medication management and interpersonal communication. Tauber and Wallace developed a self-contained module for this training program which focuses on learning and practicing fundamental problem-solving skills in the workplace as a supplement to supported employment services.

Similar to other modules in the package, the Workplace Fundamental Skills Module includes step-by-step instructions for the clinician, a videotape demonstration of skills to be acquired, and participant handouts including workbooks with checklists and homework assignments. Instruction is provided utilizing the same behavioral teaching techniques as the other modules with the same basic "learning activities": introduction to skill sets; videotape demonstration; role playing with clinician and peers; step by step problem solving to resolve lack of resources to implement skills (e.g. money, time); problem solving to resolve disparity between learned skills and unexpected outcomes; in-vivo assignments to practice skills outside the group under the trainer's supervision; and homework assignments designed to generalize skills to the workplace. These activities are intended to explain information about problematic situations which can occur in the work environment, and then teach and repeatedly practice skills to use in the actual situation. Skills are generally taught in weekly group sessions lasting about 90 minutes with participants finishing the module in 12 to 24 sessions. There is no special training or specific educational background required to teach this program as the trainer's manual specifies exactly what the trainer is to say and do during each session.

The overall goal of the module is to teach nine specific skills grouped into three skill sets on how to sustain employment by achieving goals that the participant and employer find equally satisfying. Skills Set One identifies key procedures in the workplace (e.g. break times, pay days). This skill set teaches how to identify and obtain information about investments made by the participant at work, called "Gives" (time, tools, relationships, etc.), and rewards they receive when they work, called "Gets" (pay, satisfaction, etc.). In Skill Set Two, participants are taught to "be on the alert for problems" so they can examine their work environment and develop a profile of potential problem areas, called "Sweats" (getting along with co-workers, difficult job task, etc.). Skill Set Three is about preventing and solving problems identified in the previous set. Participants are taught how to use a general problem-solving method to prevent and solve work related problems in areas of mental and physical health, substance abuse, interactions with supervisors and co-workers, work performance, and motivation.

The core focus of the Workplace Fundamentals Module is to learn general problem-solving methods that help participants with SMI to recognize and solve common workplace problems, and then implement these solutions to specific work environments. The authors note in the trainer's manual that the module "is not focused on helping participants find a job. It does not teach skills such as obtaining job leads, producing a resume, and participating in job interviews". The module is designed to assist people who are or will be employed and receiving supported employment or other vocational services (Wallace and Tauber, 2004).

Given the difficulties that people with schizophrenia and other persistent mental illness may have in taking what they learn in the modules and applying this to everyday life, Liberman *et al.* (2002) developed the In Vivo

Amplified Skills Training (IVAST) to enhance generalization of the modules to everyday functioning, including the workplace. IVAST uses a specialist case manager who provides tailored, community-based instruction to promote independence in the community and workplace by reducing participant reliance on case managers and therapists. A more detailed explanation of IVAST is found elsewhere (ibid.).

Rationale

Although there is strong empirical evidence to show that supported employment is a worthwhile vocational approach for improving work outcome in people with persistent mental illness, the prevalence of social skills deficits may limit the capacity of persons to maximize the benefits from supported employment. Studies have shown that people with schizophrenia demonstrate a wide range of interpersonal deficits compared with healthy controls and these deficits impede the ability to function independently in the community, whether it be developing meaningful relationships, finding and keeping employment, or managing symptoms. Deficits in social skills and poor social adjustment have been recognized as major contributors to premature job termination among persons in supported employment. Tenures in various work positions are comparatively short-lived for persons in supported employment, and methods to sustain long-term employment have become increasingly important to the efficacy of the supported employment model (Wallace and Tauber, 2004).

Research support

The empirical literature behind the UCLA Social and Independent Living Skills Program is substantial, with the programs translated into over 15 foreign languages by separate independent investigators, adapted to numerous ethnic cultures on every continent, and disseminated all over the world to hospitals, inpatient and outpatient programs, community centers, and day treatment programs. The Workplace Fundamentals Module developed by Tauber and Wallace is, however, relatively new and investigations are only now emerging regarding its validation and efficacy. To date, only two empirical studies have reported findings on the module in relation to supported employment and both provide only weak support of its efficacy.

Wallace and Tauber (2004) conducted a randomized controlled trial to determine whether the module helped workers with severe mental illness to maintain their jobs in the community compared with those receiving only supported employment. Thirty-four participants in a community mental health agency (54 per cent schizophrenia, 43 per cent bipolar) who had a history of unsuccessful job experiences ending in premature termination (fired, quit job without prospects) were randomly assigned to receive either supported employment only (n = 17) or supported employment plus the workplace skills module (n = 17). After 18 months, preliminary analyses showed no differences in total wages earned, total hours worked, or social functioning. However, the supported employment only group had a higher rate of job turnover and were less satisfied with their jobs compared with those who received workplace skills training in addition to supported employment. Preliminary findings suggest the Workplace Fundamental Skills Module may be a useful adjunct to supported employment services for persons with a history of unsuccessful employments.

Mueser *et al.* (2005) evaluated whether supplementary social skills training using the Workplace Fundamental Skills Module would improve work outcome for those recently employed through a free-standing supported employment community agency (total average days in competitive employment before entry into study was 56 ± 37). The participants were 35 persons meeting the state criteria of "severe and persistent mental illness" who had been referred by their mental health center to the supported employment agency. Similar to the study by Wallace and Tauber (2004), participants were randomly assigned to supported employment only (n = 18) or supported employment plus the workplace fundamentals program (n = 17). Follow-up after 18 months showed no significant difference between groups on cumulative hours worked, wages earned, or days worked for first job obtained during 18 months, or all jobs obtained in 18 months. In addition, there was no difference between groups in how successfully the first job ended. The study notes the sample population was more educated, possibly more motivated for employment, and had longer tenures on the first job compared with previous studies in supported employment, thus suggesting the sample was in less need of social skills training. The authors suggest that "reserving the workplace fundamentals program for clients who have recently experienced work-related difficulties may avoid the problem of providing the intervention to clients who do not need it" (Mueser *et al.*, 2005). Nevertheless, both studies report that employment rates were high for the workplace skills group and that job turnover was relatively low. The effect of supplementing supported employment services with skills training is currently under investigation with various skill programs also showing promise, including job-specific skills training and a cognitive social skills training milieu to enhance residential, vocational and recreational functioning.

Neurocognitive Enhancement Therapy: A cognitive remediation approach

Neurocognitive Enhancement Therapy (NET) was developed by Bell *et al.* (2001) to directly address impairments in elemental cognitive processes that may interfere with new learning, such as occurs in vocational rehabilitation. NET is primarily comprised of computer-based training tasks with graduated levels of difficulty that require cognitive abilities that are often compromised in mental illness (e.g. attention, memory and executive function). We have used several sources for the cognitive training exercises, and several other software packages are either available or in development. We have primarily used the CogReHab software developed by Psychological Software Services, which was originally developed for people with compromised brain function and modified by us for use with people with schizophrenia. The second set of exercises was developed by us in conjunction with Scientific Learning Corporation, now PositScience (www.positscience.com). Cognitive training tasks include those targeting simple attention, complex attention and response inhibition, verbal and visual memory, language-mediated cognition, category formation, and planning and strategy.

The approach is to have some exercises that narrowly target specific cognitive processes (e.g. visual reaction time), which may have associations to specific brain areas, and to have other types of exercises that use many integrated brain processes. The curriculum of exercises begins with simpler tasks and builds to more complex ones. Thus, simpler and more complex processes are exercised and integrated as training progresses. Subjects will graduate to a more difficult level when they achieve and sustain a prescribed level (e.g. 90 per cent correct). If performance plateaus below graduation criteria, participants will be moved on to other exercises.

Cognitive training occurs in the "Cog Lab", an attractive learning center with multiple computer work stations. Efforts are made to create an upbeat, reinforcing environment with postings of individual accomplishments and sometimes small prizes for achieving various levels of success. The Cog Lab is supervised by trained facilitators who provide one-to-one orientation and monitoring. Even participants who have never used a computer quickly learn the procedures. After a short time, most participants are able to work through the exercises with minimal assistance. While little is known about how much training is needed, we encourage participants to practice these exercises every day for an hour and believe that at least 40 sessions is probably the minimum necessary to achieve clinical benefit, although it takes more than 100 hours to complete the entire curriculum of exercises.

One advantage of computer-based exercises is that each participant receives the same procedure within each exercise, and the curriculum is set so that everyone proceeds systematically through the same progression of exercises. Individualization naturally results as the participant progresses quickly through a task that taps a cognitive strength and then must spend relatively more time on another that confronts a cognitive weakness.

We have incorporated these cognitive training sessions into a comprehensive rehabilitation program that includes the work performance feedback and goal setting group described previously, with the addition of specific feedback about cognitive functioning on the job. This feedback is based upon the Vocational Cognitive Rating Scale (VCRS; Greig *et al.*, 2004), which is rated along with the WBI. Participants may set goals which relate to attention, memory or problem-solving issues that they are having on the job. The vocational specialist working with the participant may use WBI and VCRS ratings in developing supports and strategies to help the person perform better on the job. This type of follow-through is similar to the approach taken in McGurk *et al.*'s (2005) "Thinking Skills for Work" program. Because social information processing is difficult to simulate and train on a computer, we have also incorporated a group that provides exercises for that purpose. Fuller descriptions of these interventions are available elsewhere (Bell *et al.*, 2005; Wexler and Bell, 2005).

Rationale

Cognitive impairments are common in schizophrenia and other psychotic disorders and have been identified as "rate-limiting" factors in social and occupational domains. Over the past few years, a number of studies have found that specific cognitive deficits predicted work performance and outcomes. McGurk and Meltzer (2000) found that better performance on executive function, working memory and vigilance distinguished full-time from part-time and unemployed work status, and found poor premorbid function, negative symptoms, and cognitive dysfunction to be significantly associated with unemployment. Bell and Bryson (2001) found that up to 79 per cent of the variance in improvement in work performance could be predicted from baseline cognitive performance. Others have reported that baseline measures of verbal learning and memory, and symptoms of cognitive disorganization were modestly related to work performance. Finally, Lysaker *et al.* (2005b) found that schizophrenic participants in vocational rehabilitation who did not have impairments in processing speed and executive function showed superior work performance over time compared with participants with impairments in one or both domains. A major implication of the association between vocational disability and cognitive impairment is that remediation of cognitive deficits might improve vocational outcomes.

Evidence of brain plasticity offers a scientific foundation for cognitive remediation. The exciting possibility of restoring lost elemental brain function through cognitive retraining has gained strong support from studies of brain plasticity in non-human primates and in humans. A review of advances in brain plasticity research by Mark Hallett, Chief of the Medical Neurology Branch of the National Institute of Neurological Disease at the US National Institutes of Health, indicates compelling evidence for the brain as a self-organizing, experience-based organ that responds rapidly at cellular and molecular levels to environmental change. Hallet abstracts several basic principles from the literature. The first is that there is competition between body parts for representation in the central nervous system and changes can occur rapidly. A second principle is that use of a body part increases representation and disuse decreases representation, as seen, for example, in a study of a group of people with broken ankles after a ski accident who lost representation of the body part because of its immobility. A third basic principle is that there is multimodal plasticity. For example, Braille readers whose blindness occurred before age 13 activated the visual cortex when reading, and with transcranial magnetic stimulation inhibition of the occipital lobe, they could no longer read Braille. Recovery in stroke patients is due to brain plasticity. In a study of stroke patients with hemiparesis who had a full recovery, neuroimaging revealed that this had occurred through a reorganization of the cortex.

There are several examples of clinical applications of these principles outside of psychiatry. Constraint-induced movement therapy (CIMT) has been shown to produce better post-stroke hemiparesis rehabilitation by retraining the unaffected limb and performing six hours/day of intensive task practice aimed at the impaired upper extremity. In a review paper Taub et al. (2003) attribute the improvement to two separate but linked mechanisms: overcoming learned non-use and facilitating use-dependent cortical reorganization. Auditory discrimination training for people with hearing aids boosted their ability to process sound from noise because hearing loss had decreased cortical representation of those sounds and hearing aids alone, while providing a clearer input, did not increase perception. Eight weeks of computer-based training significantly increased auditory discrimination over amplification alone. Perceptual learning through computer-based training can drive neuronal reorganization in visual and auditory modalities, and it has been effectively applied to central auditory processing disorder and dyslexia. As these examples illustrate, neuroplasticity research is spawning new approaches to rehabilitation. In schizophrenia and other mental illnesses, the basic mechanisms of overcoming learned non-use and facilitating use-dependent cortical reorganization may have application. Regarding learned non-use, it is very likely that "disuse atrophy" of associated neural resources occurs because patients avoid situations that tax cognitive weaknesses so these cognitive functions go unexercised and unrewarded. By using simple computer-based cognitive exercises and building up to more complicated problem solving, cognitive remediation forces patients to employ cognitive processes that they would otherwise avoid, thus reversing learned non-use. This vigorous exercising of cognitive functions may thus facilitate use-dependent cortical reorganization.

Research support

Several literature reviews of cognitive remediation have been published. They have found weighted mean effect sizes (Cohen's d) for improvements in neuropsychological performance = .32, for reductions in symptom severity = .26 and for improvements in everyday function = .51.

We have conducted two randomized clinical trials that combine our NET training with work services. The first was performed at the Department of Veterans Affairs (VA) Connecticut Healthcare System and involved six months of NET plus work therapy (NET+WT) compared with WT alone (n = 145). The second was at the Connecticut Mental Health Center and involved a year of active intervention that included NET plus supported employment (NET+SE) compared with SE alone (n = 76). Participants in both studies were diagnosed with schizophrenia or schizoaffective disorder and were in outpatient treatment. Details of method are available elsewhere (Bell *et al.*, 2001; Wexler and Bell, 2005).

In these studies we reasoned that if NET is effective, there should be a chain of effects from the most proximal to the cognitive training (i.e. improvement on the trained tasks) to more distal ones, including work outcomes. In a series of published reports we found that participants receiving NET improved on training tasks and that almost half of those with significant clinical deficits on working memory tasks reached normal levels of performance by the conclusion of training (Bell *et al.*, 2003). We tested the generalization of the training to similar but untrained tasks on neuropsychological testing and found significantly greater improvement for those receiving NET at the conclusion of training (Bell *et al.*, 2001). We subsequently found that these improvements endured for six months after the end of the active training (Fiszdon *et al.*, 2004). We also have unpublished evidence that those receiving NET showed greater improvement in work performance (WBI scores) and cognitive performance on the job (VCRS scores) during the active interventions. Most importantly, work outcomes were better for those receiving NET with their work services. In the VA study, those in NET+WT worked significantly more hours (p < .05) and earned more money during the six months following the intervention (see Figure 15.1).

In the CMHC study, we found that NET combined with supported employment led to significantly more hours (p < .05) worked during the 12 months after the intervention (transitional and competitive employment combined hours, see Figure 15.2) and significantly higher rates (p < .05) of obtaining competitive employment, which is shown in Figure 15.3 (Wexler and Bell, 2005).

Taken together these findings suggest that cognitive retraining can have significant functional benefits when included in a comprehensive rehabilitation program that affords opportunity to acquire practical new learning. We believe that cognitive training improves cognitive processing and thereby makes it possible for participants to gain more from other forms of rehabilitation.

Over the past several years we have been gratified to see our work adopted and extended by our colleagues. McGurk *et al.* (2005) have recently published the first small (n = 44) effectiveness study combining

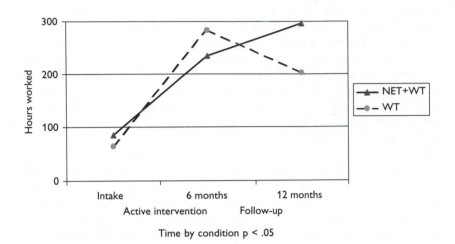

Time by condition p < .05

Figure 15.1 Hours worked by intervention for the six months prior to intake, six months of active intervention and six months of follow-up

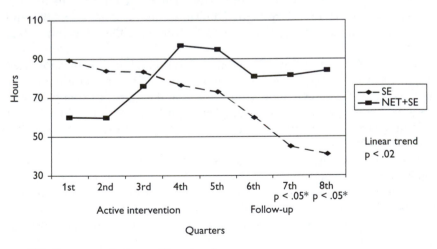

* Significant group-by-time and linear trend

Figure 15.2 Hours worked by intervention over two years

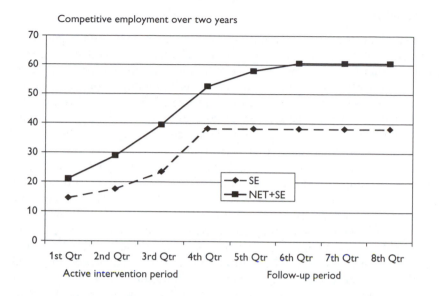

Figure 15.3 Cumulative rates of competitive employment

supported employment with cognitive training. Their intervention was based at two vocational agencies servicing mental health clients. They used supported employment augmented with COGPACK cognitive training (www.cogpack.com) and a follow-through method of having the cognitive training specialist consult regularly with the employment specialist to discuss "job supports to address cognitive challenges on the job". This is a useful variation of our approach of providing feedback to the patient and job specialist about cognitive performance on the job and setting goals to address such problems. McGurk *et al.* (ibid.) call their program "Thinking Skills for Work". Clients with severe mental illness who had had a previous job failure were randomized to receive supported employment or supported employment augmented with their program. Cognitive and psychopathology assessments were conducted at three months (the conclusion of their cognitive intervention) and employment data were collected for one year. Results were remarkable. Those receiving the cognitive augmentation showed significantly greater improvement on cognitive functioning and on depression and autistic preoccupation scores on the Positive and Negative Syndrome Scale (PANSS). Clients receiving cognitive augmentation worked more hours and earned more wages. Most importantly, 69.6 per cent achieved competitive employment as compared with only 4.8 per cent of those receiving supported employment alone (p = .000). They attributed the very low rate for their control condition to their selection criteria, which consisted of patients with prior vocational failures.

Discussion

Those looking for ways to improve the lives of people recovering from persistent and severe mental illness may find excitement and hope in the programs that have been presented here. Supported employment and other work services offer opportunities for community reintegration through the constructive social roles that working provides. For some, working may lead to reduced symptoms, greater self-esteem and a higher quality of life.

The four interventions we have described address overlapping but distinct areas of impairment that accompany mental illness and may be barriers to achieving work success. Work feedback with goal setting compensates for impairments in self monitoring and social perception and enhances motivation and problem solving. The IVIP focuses on negative cognitions and improves coping. Workplace Fundamentals attempts to teach social skills in common areas of weakness that may be particularly challenged in work life, and Neurocognitive Enhancement Therapy attempts to restore elemental cognitive functions that have been impaired by illness so that new learning through rehabilitation may occur. Each of these approaches has a sound rationale and at least some evidence of efficacy. Most programs have a manual or a systematic description that make it possible to replicate the methods in other settings.

There is every reason to believe that a comprehensive approach to vocational rehabilitation could combine these interventions to the benefit of the patient. We are not yet at the point where we can be prescriptive about exactly what methods to apply to which patients, and some of these interventions may be better suited to some settings than others. Yet there is sufficient evidence to warrant clinicians and vocational specialists, using their own judgment, to enhance their existing work services with these psychological approaches. It is the hope that these interventions will allow people with mental illness to more speedily and effectively reintegrate into their community so that they may lead more satisfying lives.

References

Becker, D. (2002). *Supported Employment Toolkit*. Lebanon, NH: Psychiatric Research Center.

Bell, M. D. and Bryson, G. (2001). Work rehabilitation in schizophrenia: Does cognitive impairment limit improvement? *Schizophrenia Bulletin*, 27(2), 269–279.

Bell, M., Bryson, G., Greig, T., Corcoran, C. and Wexler, B. W. (2001). Neurocognitive enhancement therapy with work therapy: Effects on neuropsychological test performance. *Archives of General Psychiatry*, 58(8), 763–768.

Bell, M., Bryson, G. and Wexler, B. E. (2003). Cognitive remediation of working memory deficits: Durability of training effects in severely impaired and less severely impaired schizophrenia. *Acta Psychiatrica Scandinavica*, 108(2), 101–109.

Bell, M. D., Bryson, G. J., Greig, T. C., Fiszdon, J. M. and Wexler, B. E. (2005).

Neurocognitive enhancement therapy with work therapy: Productivity outcomes at 6- and 12-month follow-ups. *Journal of Rehabilitation Research and Development*, *42*(6), 829–838.

Bond, G. R., Becker, D. R., Drake, R. E., Rapp, C. A., Meisler, N. and Lehman, A. F. (2002). Implementing supported employment as an evidence-based practice. *Psychiatric Services*, *52*(3), 313–322.

Bryson, G., Bell, M. D., Lysaker, P. and Zito, W. (1997). The Work Behavior Inventory: A scale for the assessment of work behavior for people with severe mental illness. *Psychiatric Rehabilitation Journal*, *20*(4), 47–55.

Bryson, G., Bell, M. D., Greig, T. C. and Kaplan, E. (1999). The Work Behavior Inventory: Prediction of future work success of people with schizophrenia. *Psychiatric Rehabilitation Journal*, *23*(2), 113–117.

Davis, L. W., Lysaker, P. H., Lancaster, R. S., Bryson, G. J. and Bell, M. D. (2005). The Indianapolis Vocational Intervention Program: A cognitive behavioral approach to addressing rehabilitation issues in schizophrenia. *Journal of Rehabilitation Research and Development*, *42*(1), 35–45.

Fishwick, L. V., Ayer, M. J. and Butler, A. J. (1972). The effects of specific and general feedback information on the speed and accuracy of schizophrenic work performance. *Journal of Clinical Psychology*, *28*(4), 581–583.

Fiszdon, J. M., Bryson, G. J., Wexler, B. E. and Bell, M. D. (2004). Durability of cognitive remediation training in schizophrenia: Performance on two memory tasks at 6-month and 12-month follow-up. *Psychiatry Research*, *125*(1), 1–7.

Greig, T., Bryson, G. J. and Bell, M. D. (2004). Development of a scale for the assessment of cognitive impairments in vocational rehabilitation: Reliability and predictive validity. *Journal of Vocational Rehabilitation*, *21*, 71–81.

Hartlage, L. and Johnsen, R. (1975). Video playback as a rehabilitation tool with the hard-core unemployed. *Rehabilitation Psychology*, *20*, 116–120.

Kravetz, S., Florian, V. and Nofer, E. (1990). The differential effects of feedback of trait ratings on worker traits in vocational rehabilitation workshops in a correctional institution. *Vocational Evaluation and Work Adjustment Bulletin*, *23*(2), 47–54.

Liberman, R. P., Glynn, S., Blair, K. E., Ross, D. and Marder, S. R. *et al.* (2002). In-vivo amplified skills training: Promoting generalization of independent living skills for clients with schizophrenia. *Psychiatry*, *65*(2), 137–155.

Locke, E. A. and Latham, G. P. (2002). Building a practically useful theory of goal setting and task motivation. A 35-year odyssey. *American Psychologist*, *57*(9), 705–717.

Lysaker, P. H. and Buck, K. D. (2006). Narrative enrichment in the psychotherapy for persons with schizophrenia: A single case study. *Issues in Mental Health Nursing*, *27*(3), 233–247.

Lysaker, P. H., Bond, G., Davis, L. W., Bryson, G. J. and Bell, M. D. (2005a). Enhanced Cognitive Behavioral Therapy for vocational rehabilitation in schizophrenia: Effects on hope and work. *Journal of Rehabilitation Research and Development*, *42*, 673–682.

Lysaker, P. H., Bryson, G. J., Davis, L W. and Bell, M. D. (2005b). Relationship of impaired processing speed and flexibility of abstract thought to improvements in work performance over time in schizophrenia. *Schizophrenia Research*, *75*(2–3), 211–218.

McGurk, S. R. and Meltzer, H. Y. (2000). The role of cognition in vocational functioning in schizophrenia. *Schizophrenia Research*, *45*(3), 175–184.

McGurk, S. R., Mueser, K. T. and Pascaris, A. (2005). Cognitive training and supported employment for persons with severe mental illness: One-year results from a randomized controlled trial. *Schizophrenia Bulletin*, *31*(4), 898–909.

Mueser, K. T., Aalto, S., Becker, D. R., Ogden, J. S., Wolfe, R. S. and Schiavo, D. (2005). The effectiveness of skills training for improving outcomes in supported employment. *Psychiatric Services*, *56*(10), 1254–1260.

Taub, E., Uswatte, G. and Morris, D. M. (2003). Improved motor recovery after stroke and massive cortical reorganization following constraint-induced movement therapy. *Physical Medicine and Rehabilitation Clinics of North America*, *14*(1 Suppl), S77–S91.

Wallace, C. J. and Tauber, R. (2004). Supplementing supported employment with workplace skills training. *Psychiatric Services*, *55*(5), 513–515.

Wexler, B. E. and Bell, M. D. (2005). Cognitive remediation and vocational rehabilitation for schizophrenia. *Schizophrenia Bulletin*, *31*(4), 931–941.

Note

1 Funded by grants to Morris D. Bell and Paul Lysaker from the Rehabilitation and Development Service, US Department of Veterans Affairs.

Part IV

CBT and bipolar disorders

Chapter 16

The psychology of bipolar disorders

Sara Tai

Introduction

Nearly everything written on bipolar disorder has begun by stating how it has long been a neglected area of research within psychopathology, largely conceptualised in biological terms with little understanding of psychological mechanisms. The last ten years have witnessed an increased interest in the disorder so that the picture has slowly been changing and, following a surge of research activity within the last five years, this is certainly no longer the case. The limited efficacy of pharmacological interventions, a need to understand the mechanisms underlying the disorder more, and the success of psychological approaches within the field have facilitated recognition of the importance of understanding bipolar disorder in psychological terms. Subsequently, an abundance of psychological research has begun to emerge, radically impacting on the way we think about the development and maintenance of the disorder.

This chapter begins by providing an overview of the phenomenology of bipolar disorder, followed by an examination of the concept of a broader spectrum of bipolar disorders. The primary objective is to summarise some of the main advances in psychological understanding of bipolar disorders. Such developments have increased awareness of how the most meaningful way in which to understand this complex disorder could be through a more integrated biopsychosocial perspective of the mechanisms involved. Finally, consideration is given to how current understanding within this field might be shaped in the future by utilising an integrative perspective of current models of the disorder.

Bipolar disorder

Bipolar disorder involves periods of extreme disruptions to mood, behaviour and cognitive functioning. People with the disorder typically experience periods of severe depression, mania or hypomania, in addition to periods of relatively stable mood. However, even during periods of so-called 'remission' sufferers experience functional impairment and can still display mood swings and subclinical symptoms (Judd *et al.*, 2003). The majority of sufferers tend to spend significantly more time depressed as opposed to manic (Post *et al.*, 2003). Bipolar II (depression with hypomanic episodes) is the most common expression of bipolar disorder (Judd *et al.*, 2003).

Bipolar disorder is a serious public health problem constituting the sixth leading cause of disability-adjusted life years in the world among people aged 15–44 years. Mood disorders are likely to remain highly prevalent with depression being one of the most common causes of disability.

Approximately 1–1.5 per cent of the general population in the US and UK meet the DSM-IV criteria for this mental disorder. It is estimated that many more people, around 5–10 per cent of the population, experience significant symptoms which impact on their daily functioning, although the duration, intensity and frequency of these symptoms are not such that they meet full diagnostic criteria (Paykel *et al.*, 2006). Diagnosis of the disorder is often delayed, and there is evidence that the age of onset could be much earlier than first thought, with childhood onset in many cases (Jones *et al.*, 2006). Bipolar disorder is a lifelong mental health problem with less than 1 per cent of sufferers experiencing an episode as a one-off. Sufferers endure a recurring and relapsing course with approximately half of people relapsing within one year of recovery from an initial episode. Post *et al.* (2003) examined the prevalence and persistence of mood episodes in 258 bipolar patients as assessed by clinicians over a twelve-month period. Individuals spent 44 per cent of the year either depressed or manic and 63 per cent of the sample experienced four or more episodes per year, despite being in receipt of appropriate psychotropic medication. Similar findings were obtained in a British sample of 204 people with bipolar disorder interviewed weekly for 18 months (Paykel *et al.*, 2006).

Many people with mood disorders experience significant psychotic symptoms during mood episodes. In a review of 26 studies, Goodwin and Jamison (1990) reported that 58 per cent of people with bipolar disorder had a lifetime history of at least one of a whole range of psychotic symptoms – such as hallucinations and delusions – previously thought to exist only in schizophrenia.

Rates of substance abuse are high, with studies in community settings reporting rates of 60–70 per cent. There is also evidence of increased substance abuse in people identified as having an increased risk of developing the disorder both through genetic risk and trait markers of hypomania (Jones *et al.*, 2006). It is therefore possible that the mechanisms underlying substance dependency and mood disorders are similar to those involved in bipolar disorders, so that having bipolar disorder could increase the chances of substance abuse.

Unsurprisingly, there is an elevated risk of attempting or completing suicide in people with bipolar disorder, mainly during phases associated with depression and particularly for individuals with early onset. Bipolar disorder is the most common psychiatric disorder associated with suicide, with rates of completed suicide being twenty times higher compared with the general population. Because of the persistent, recurrent and severe course of bipolar disorder, it has significant impact on family relationships and the physical and psychological well-being of caregivers. It is understandable therefore that people with bipolar disorder experience a higher rate of divorce and relationship breakdown, greater levels of social dysfunction even during periods of 'remission' and a lower quality of life. Occupational functioning is also disrupted, costing the UK billions per annum. Individuals struggle to find employment. Despite many being educated to college level, the majority of people with bipolar disorder in the UK are unemployed.

Bipolar spectrum disorders

Most phenomenological research includes only those people who meet formal diagnostic criteria. Such approaches are founded upon the assumption that bipolar disorder is a discrete disorder that is distinguishable from other forms of affective disorder. However, there is an ever growing body of evidence that this is not the case and that the formal DSM-IV diagnostic criteria only account for a small proportion of wide-ranging symptoms that form the basis of a much more variable and broader spectrum of related disorders. It has been argued that all major depressions involve some degree of hypomania and that these are related to premorbid cyclothymic or hyperthymic temperamental characteristics. The concept of a bipolar temperament or personality is not a new idea. From this perspective, the number of those affected with spectrum disorders is likely to be much greater and often with severe consequences (Akiskal et al., 2000).

Evidence making the case for a spectrum of bipolar disorders is plentiful. Akiskal et al. (2000) estimate that up to 6.4 per cent of the general population experience 'soft symptoms' of the condition. Also, there is a growing body of evidence that bipolar spectrum disorders overlap with other syndromes not previously considered to be affective disorders. People diagnosed with borderline personality disorder (BPD) often show bipolarity when criteria are used for full mania to soft signs, which could suggest that borderline states are part of a spectrum in which the same underlying mechanisms could be shared. Evidence for the bipolar spectrum comes from Nardi et al. (2005), who reported considerable overlap between symptoms of schizophrenia and bipolar disorder, coining the term 'schizo-bipolar disorder'. They claimed differences between this new 'group' and conventionally understood schizophrenia in terms of prescribed drugs, but similarities for age of onset, suicide attempts and family history of suicide attempts. Similar findings have also been reported in respect to anxiety disorders. Anxiety-co-morbid mood disorder has been reported as the most prevalent co-morbid disorder, more so than pure mood disorder, making a case for these being incorporated within a bipolar spectrum (Valenca *et al.*, 2005). Akiskal *et al.* (2006) interviewed 107 people with bipolar II and found that 46.7 per cent met DSM criteria for panic disorder and agoraphobia. Valenca *et al.* (2005) found that people with social anxiety, compared with those with bipolar II, had a similar number of previous depressive episodes, alcohol abuse, suicide attempts and family history for mood disorder. Interestingly, they describe a subgroup of patients with social anxiety who, when treated with antidepressants, showed improvement that consisted of a presentation identical to a mild to moderate hypomanic state. Withdrawal of the antidepressants led to the return of the social anxiety symptoms. In adolescents, co-morbid anxiety is common but can often be misdiagnosed as pharmacologic (hypo)mania.

Co-morbidity is a common feature of bipolar disorder, but is often the reason for misdiagnosis resulting in expensive and ineffective treatments. People with mood-related problems but also presenting with co-morbid patterns of personality disorder, alcohol abuse, psychotic disorder, generalised anxiety disorder and panic could benefit from being screened for bipolar disorder.

Whether bipolar disorder is conceptualised as a specific category of symptoms or as a wider range of related syndromes that make up a spectrum of bipolar disorders, what we are describing is something where the common component would appear to be depression. 90 per cent of people who experience mania also have depressive episodes (Goodwin and Jamison, 1990). Cassidy *et al.* (1998) found depression was the second most reported symptom in 72 per cent of their sample of people with bipolar disorder, irritability being the first.

It would appear that only a small minority of people experience unipolar mania and even in these cases there is evidence that if full histories are obtained, depressive episodes are apparent. Many studies documenting unipolar mania have severe methodological limitations, with some including people who have had no more than one or two episodes of mania, or for whom the follow-up time period has not been reported, making it unclear whether sufficient time has lapsed in which further depressive episodes might have occurred. What with uncertainty about whether mixed episodes, secondary mania or antidepressant-induced mania are included in the criteria, small samples and the recruitment from multiple sites, the reliability of these studies is problematic.

Depression in bipolar disorder appears to resemble unipolar depression and numerous studies have examined the possible differences between the two. In comparison with unipolar depression, bipolar depression is associated with poorer quality of life in terms of social, physical and emotional domains; more behavioural symptoms such as hypersomnia, lethargy and apathy; more suicide attempts; and greater reporting of the co-occurrence of symptoms such as sleep disturbance, loss of energy and anhedonia (Jones *et al.*, 2006). However, these findings have not been reliably replicated and most studies report contradictory findings. For such distinctions to be made, subtypes of bipolar disorder (I and II) would need to be considered separately with bipolar II depression as having more hypomanic or mixed symptoms than unipolar depression. This would add support to the case for there being no real difference between the actual depressive component of bipolar and unipolar presentations, an idea that is supported by a wealth of evidence.

Bipolar disorder is perhaps best conceptualised as depression with (hypo)mania in addition. However, mania and hypomania are complicated and dynamic phenomena, composed of a multitude of dimensions susceptible to change and fluctuation over time (Cassidy *et al.*, 1998). The underlying mechanisms are difficult to explain. The common denominator is the affective components, which the main theories of bipolar disorder focus on and attempt to explain.

Behavioural inhibition and activation systems (BIS/BAS)

The Behavioural Activation hypothesis of (hypo)mania is based on a model that was independently formulated by Depue *et al.* (1981) and Gray (1994). The hypothesis stated the existence of two neural motivational systems – Behavioural Activation Systems (BAS) and Behavioural Inhibition Systems (BIS) – that regulate approach and withdrawal behaviour.

BAS controls appetitive motivation and moderates approach behaviour in response to environmental cues of reward through dopaminergic activity within the mesolimbic system (Gray, 1994). Meyer and Hautzinger (2003) described how BAS generates approach-related affect in the presence of an incentive stimulus, triggering positive affect such as hope and excitement when a person is confronted with an incentive stimulus. They conceptualised BAS as an essential mechanism for enhancing the chances of actualising incentive acquisition. However, if BAS activation is excessive, it causes increased motor activity, heightened reward responsiveness and related heightened emotions.

BIS is hypothesised as an opposing system that governs the withdrawal of behaviours related to goal attainment and motivation of activity that could result in punishment or adverse consequences. It is sensitive to cues of threat and punishment and activates corresponding threat and avoidance through noradrenergic and serotonergic activity within the septohippocampal system (Gray, 1994). This system is responsible for generating behavioural inhibition and associated negative affect, including emotions such as anxiety, fear, disgust and embarrassment.

Of the two systems, it is BAS which is considered to be the essential mechanism for developing bipolar disorders. From this perspective, mania and depression are assumed to be opposites of only one dimension – behavioural activation. A behavioural facilitation system could exist of which 'regulatory strength' acts to control BAS reactivity. Carver and White (1994) proposed that BAS strength is a stable characteristic which can be measured, for which purpose they devised the BIS/BAS scales. Analogue studies have demonstrated that BAS strength correlates with mania and depression (Meyer and Hautzinger, 2003).

Considerable evidence for the theory of behavioural activation has come from studies examining the effect of goal-attainment life events on people with bipolar disorder. As predicted, the events believed to trigger the BAS do indeed seem to cause increases in manic symptoms (Johnson *et al.*, 2005). Similarly, it is negative life events which seem to play a greater role in depressive symptomatology as opposed to (hypo)manic symptoms (Alloy *et al.*, 2006). Work examining the role of dysfunctional beliefs relating to extreme goal attainment, perfectionism and need for approval may have suggested a possible interaction with these life events, increasing risk of an episode (Johnson *et al.*, 2005).

The relevance of goal attainment life events in bipolar disorder is fairly well established within the literature and forms the main evidence base upon which the application of the BAS theory is founded. However, it does not provide substantive support for whether an actual biological system exists. Some of the earliest evidence of a behavioural activation system was provided by Rosenthal *et al.* (1984), whose study of 29 people with seasonal bipolar affective disorder demonstrated that behavioural engagement appears to correspond to levels of light. BIS/BAS is largely hypothetical, and there are a number of difficulties in applying this as a causal explanation of bipolar disorder. BAS alone could be considered an over-simplistic explanation for a complex set of phenomena and individual differences on BAS reactivity do not adequately explain the inter-individual differences observed for vulnerability to bipolar disorders. In addition, BAS reactivity does not fully account for the mechanisms involved in the transition from a manic to a depressive phase and vice versa; if a depressed individual has low BAS, how does that explain a sudden change to mania?

Depression avoidance and self-esteem

Bentall *et al.* (2006) examined (hypo)mania as a form of depression avoidance. The main premise is that opposed depression and mania are both essentially forms of depression but manifest themselves as behaviourally different response styles. People become manic as a response to trying to avoid depression. Evidence that depression forms a core part of mania is used to support this hypothesis. In a longitudinal study of 20 people with bipolar disorder, Kotin and Goodwin (1972) reported how depression ratings were sometimes higher during manic than during depressive episodes and Lyon *et al.* (1999) demonstrated how manic participants showed depressive-type responding on some psychological tests. Furthermore, Winters and Neale (1985) demonstrated how people suffering from bipolar disorder have a pessimistic attributional style even during remission. Lyon *et al.* (1999) also presented supporting data demonstrating differences between implicit and explicit attributional style in manic people.

Central to the depression avoidance theory is the compelling evidence that self-esteem has a role within bipolar disorders in the form of abnormal beliefs about the self and instability of beliefs about the self and affect (Knowles *et al.*, 2007). Bentall *et al.* (2006) suggested that self-esteem instability is key and this could be due to latent negative self schemas, or dysfunctional attempts to regulate self-esteem.

There is also evidence of abnormal coping styles where people with unipolar depression and bipolar disorders have a similar ruminative style of coping with depression. However, people with bipolar disorders tend to employ the additional strategy of behavioural risk taking, which contributes to the specific symptoms of mania (Bentall *et al.*, 2006).

The main difficulty with this line of thinking is that although it provides strong evidence for self-esteem and coping mechanisms playing a significant role in maintaining the disorder, it does not outline specific mechanisms through which individuals make the transition from one phase to another. There is also mixed evidence for mania functioning as a form of depression avoidance.

Cognitive vulnerability: Appraisal of affect

One of the other main areas of psychological research within bipolar disorder has been the examination of cognitive vulnerability utilising the traditional cognitive behavioural style of formulation of depression. Originally, mania was formulated as the opposite cognitive style to depression, consistent with the view of mania being the polar opposite of depression. Mania was seen to constitute a positive cognitive triad as opposed to a negative one. Unfortunately, this early formulation does not fully account for dysphoria and irritability, which are core features of mania; neither does it translate well in light of mixed episodes. Despite the limitations of this model and the absence of sufficient clinical data to support it, there have been few attempts to develop alternatives. There are a number of studies that investigate the role of cognitive vulnerability in relation to bipolar disorder, many indicating that cognitive style has negative characteristics that are similar to those found in unipolar depression. Numerous studies have found that perfectionism and need for approval from others, as well as poor social problem-solving skills, were more specific to bipolar disorders. Lam *et al.*

(2004) argued that cognitions around goal attainment and achievement are pertinent and are features considered to be consistent with high BAS sensitivity. They found that perfectionism, autonomy and self-criticism, as well as performance and high self-standards, were central themes in cognitive style. However, Alloy *et al.* (2006) highlighted the need for further research clarifying the role of cognitive styles, summarising that to date findings have yielded mixed results depending on which phase of bipolar disorder an individual is in. Research outlining the role of cognitions in manic and mixed phases is less clear.

Jones (2001) developed a cognitive framework that emphasises the role of circadian rhythms as a primary causal mechanism in mania. Although Jones's theory is an elaborate model integrating biological and cognitive systems, in essence it postulates that mania and depression are consequences of the way in which individuals interpret altered internal states or activity levels that come about in relation to disruption of social rhythms. In the development of mania, neuropsychological symptoms may be appraised in ways that are positive and self-dispositional as opposed to situational. For example, if a person experiences their thinking as faster than usual, this could be interpreted as a sign of increased intelligence or as evidence of special powers. Subsequently, changes to social rhythms that bring about altered internal states (i.e. changes related to affect or cognition) might lead to behaviours that disrupt rhythms even more. In addition, cognitive distortions about physical state can disrupt social routines necessary for recovery, feeding a vicious cycle of escalating symptoms.

As causal models, cognitive theories have not yet sufficiently accounted for the wide-ranging symptoms observed within bipolar disorder. Although they illuminate the importance of stress diathesis approaches with a potential for more integrative biopsychosocial perspectives to bipolar disorder, in doing so there is a heavy emphasis on behavioural components – social coping mechanisms such as rumination and risk taking, disrupted daily rhythms and behavioural activation. Unfortunately there is insufficient specification on the exact nature in which cognitive mechanisms are implicated. Such accounts might justify a plausible pathway into mania, but again there is a lack of clarification on the way in which transition from one phase to another occurs, or on mixed phases.

In recognition of many of these limitations Mansell *et al.* (2007) developed a cognitive model and a cognitive therapy manual aimed at understanding mood swings and bipolar disorders. The model hypothesised that an individual has multiple conflicting interpretations of the changes and fluctuations they experience in their internal state. They have a tendency to appraise these changes by attaching extreme personal meaning to them, a process influenced by specific sets of beliefs about affect and its regulation and about the self and relations with others. The appraisals of internal state are the central explanatory factor in this model; it is this process, in which conflict is a central theme, which explains how attempts at affect regulation are disturbed through the exaggerated efforts to enhance or exert control over internal states, subsequently causing further internal-state changes. Subsequently, counterproductive attempts at control occur, classified as either ascent behaviours (increasing activation) or descent behaviours (decreasing activation); these can lead to experiences that confirm dysfunctional beliefs. This vicious cycle becomes self-perpetuating as the process can maintain or exacerbate symptoms, producing an interaction that increases vulnerability to relapse. The model can account for why individuals make the transition from (hypo)manic to depressed states and can experience mixed episodes. It also incorporates important metacognitive processes, providing the interactive perspective that affective disturbances are multi-faceted, dynamic and variable over time. The model is subject to ongoing investigation in order to further establish empirically its utility.

Conclusions

It would appear that the very nature of bipolar disorders presents a confusing picture with some pertinent factors to be considered when interpreting the findings to date. First, there are severe limitations in any attempts to map linear causal mechanisms to relapse. Second, fluctuation is likely to be of central importance. Factors such as self-esteem, behavioural activation and social coping mechanisms are unlikely to be low or high, or functional versus dysfunctional; rather, they are naturally fluctuating. Fluctuation is an essential process within normal emotional regulation, but its intensity and extremity is the key to understanding bipolar disorders. Finally, assumption of bipolarity could simply be incorrect. The evidence available could well indicate that rather than depression and mania existing as polar opposites of the same dimension, they are two separate dimensions that are interrelated and, on occasion, co-dependent. Johnson *et al.* (in press) have recently completed a study investigating the way in which depression and mania co-vary over time. They argue that if a unidimensional model were plausible, mania and depression would be negatively correlated. However, their longitudinal study of symptom ratings from 236 people with bipolar I over 40 weeks showed this not to be the case. They found that depression and mania vary in an independent manner; some individual symptoms of mania might correlate with depression and vice versa, whereas other symptoms might function as opposites.

One possible direction for future research of bipolar disorder is to consider the variety of theories to date not as contradictory or competing, but as consistent within a multi-factorial problem. As singular causative models each has limitations, but in conjunction they represent the variety of processes and mechanisms that operate within bipolar disorder. This model of conceptualising psychological processes is also applicable to other mental disorders.

It is plausible that numerous factors contribute to psychopathology not only in an additive way, but also through an interactive process. Therefore, at any one point in an individual's life, they must experience the right combination, amount and interaction of various factors in order to experience an episode. It is possible, for example, that certain life events might have less or no bearing to an individual on one occasion, while, with the presence and interaction of key factors such as low self-esteem and poor coping mechanisms, specific thinking styles are likely to occur which would heighten the probability of disturbed sleep, and activated BAS, so that mania could ensue. The iterative effects of feedback processes may further exacerbate and increase vulnerability to relapse.

References

Akiskal, H. S., Bourgeois, M. L., Angst, J., Post, R., Moller, H.-J. and Hirschfeld, R. (2000). Re-evaluating the prevalence of and diagnostic composition within the broad clinical spectrum of bipolar disorders. *Journal of Affective Disorders*, *59*, S5–S30.

Akiskal, H. S., Akiskal, K. K., Perugi, G., Toni, C., Ruffolo, G. and Tusini, G. (2006). Bipolar II and anxious reactive "co-morbidity": Toward better phenotypic characterization suitable for genotyping. *Journal of Affective Disorders*, *96*, 239–247.

Alloy, L. B., Abramson, L. Y., Neeren, A. M., Walshaw, P. D., Urosevic, S. and Nusslock, R. (2006). Psychosocial risk factors for bipolar disorder: Current and early environment and cognitive styles. In S. H. Jones and R. Bentall (Eds.), *The Psychology of Bipolar Disorder: New Developments and Research Strategies* (pp. 11–39). Oxford: Oxford University Press.

Bentall, R. P., Tai, S. J. and Knowles, R. (2006). Psychological processes and the pathways to mania: exploring the manic defence hypothesis. In S. Jones and R. P. Bentall (Eds.), *The Psychology of Bipolar Disorder*. Oxford: Oxford University Press.

Carver, C. S. and White, T. L. (1994). Behavioral inhibition, behavioral activation, and affective responses to impending reward or punishment: The BIS/BAS Scales. *Journal of Personality and Social Psychology*, *67*, 319–333.

Cassidy, F., Forest, K., Murry, M. and Carroll, B. J. (1998). A factor analysis of the signs and symptoms of mania. *Archives of General Psychiatry*, *55*, 27–32.

Depue, R. A., Slater, J. F., Wolfstetter-Kausch, H., Klein, D., Goplerud, E. and Farr, D. (1981). A behavioral paradigm for identifying persons at risk for bipolar depressive disorder: A conceptual framework and five validation studies. *Journal of Abnormal Psychology*, *90*, 381–437.

Goodwin, F. K. and Jamison, K. R. (1990). *Manic-Depressive Illness*. Oxford: Oxford University Press.

Gray, J. (1994). Three fundamental emotion systems. In P. Ekman and R. J.

Davidson (Eds.), *The Nature of Emotion: Fundamental Questions* (pp. 243–247). Oxford: Oxford University Press.

Johnson, S., Ruggero, C. and Carver, C. (2005). Cognitive, behavioral, and affective responses to reward: Links with hypomanic symptoms. *Journal of Social and Clinical Psychology, 24*, 894–906.

Johnson, S. L., Morriss, M., Scott, S., Kinderman, P., Paykel, E. and Bentall, R. E. (in press). Testing whether depression and mania function as two poles within bipolar disorder. *Acta Psychiatrica Scandinavica.*

Jones, S. H. (2001). Circadian rhythms, multilevel models of emotion and bipolar disorder – an initial step towards integration? *Clinical Psychology Review, 21*, 1193–1209.

Jones, S. H., Tai, S., Evershed, K., Knowles, R. and Bentall, R. (2006). Early detection of bipolar disorder: A pilot familial high-risk study of parents with bipolar disorder and their adolescent children. *Bipolar Disorders, 8*, 362–372.

Judd, L., Schettler, P. J., Akiskal, H. S., Maser, J., Coryell, W., Solomon, D., Endicott, J. and Keller, M. (2003). Long-term symptomatic status of bipolar I vs bipolar II disorders. *International Journal of Neuropsychopharmacology, 6*, 127–137.

Knowles, R., Tai, S., Morriss, R., Jones, S. and Bentall, R. P. (2007). Stability of self-esteem in bipolar disorder: Comparison of remitted bipolar patients, remitted unipolar patients and healthy controls. *Bipolar Disorders, 9*, 490–495.

Kotin, J. and Goodwin, F. K. (1972). Depression during mania: Clinical observations and theoretical implications. *American Journal of Psychiatry, 129*, 679–686.

Lam, D., Wright, K. and Smith, N. (2004). Dysfunctional assumptions in bipolar disorder. *Journal of Affective Disorders* 79, 193–199.

Lyon, H., Startup, M. and Bentall, R. P. (1999). Social cognition and the manic defense. *Journal of Abnormal Psychology, 108*, 273–282.

Mansell, W., Morrison, A. P., Reid, G., Lowens, I. and Tai, S. (2007). The interpretation of and responses to changes in internal states in bipolar disorder: An integrative cognitive model. *Behaviour and Research Therapy, 35*, 515–539.

Meyer, T. D. and Hautzinger, M. (2003). Screening for bipolar disorders using the Hypomanic Personality Scale. *Journal of Affective Disorders, 75*, 149–154.

Nardi, A. E., Nascimento, I., Freire, R. C., de-Melo-Neto, Valfrido L., Valenca, M. A., Dib, M., Soares-Filho, G. L., Veras, A. B., Mezzasalma, M. A., Lopes, F. L., de Menezes, G. B., Grivet, L. O. and Versiani, M. (2005). Demographic and clinical features of schizoaffective (schizobipolar) disorder – A 5-year retrospective study. Support for a bipolar spectrum disorder. *Journal of Affective Disorders, 86*, 11–18.

Paykel, E. S., Abbott, R., Morriss, R., Hayhurst, H. and Scott, J. (2006). Subsyndromal and syndromal symptoms in the longitudinal course of bipolar disorder. *British Journal of Psychiatry, 189*, 118–123.

Post, R. M., Denicoff, K. D., Leverich, G. S., Altshuler, L. L., Frye, M. A., Suppes, T. M., Rush, A. J., Keck, P. E., Jr., McElroy, S. L., Luckenbaugh, D. A., Pollio, C., Kupka, R. and Nolen, W. A. (2003). Morbidity in 258 bipolar outpatients followed for 1 year with daily prospective ratings on the NIMH life chart method. *Journal of Clinical Psychiatry, 64*, 680–690; quiz 738–739.

Rosenthal, N. E., Sack, D. A., Gillin, J. C., Lewy, A. J., Goodwin, F. K., Davenport, Y., Mueller, P. S., Newsome, D. A. and Wehr, T. A. (1984). Seasonal affective disorder. A description of the syndrome and preliminary findings with light therapy. *Archives of General Psychiatry, 41*, 72–80.

Valenca, A. M., Nardi, A. E., Nascimento, I., Lopes, F. L., Freire, R. C., Mezzasalma, M. A., Veras, A. B. and Versiani, M. (2005). Do social anxiety disorder patients belong to a bipolar spectrum subgroup? *Journal of Affective Disorders, 86*, 11–18.

Winters, K. C. and Neale, J. M. (1985). Mania and low self-esteem. *Journal of Abnormal Psychology, 94*, 282–290.

Chapter 17

Cognitive theory and therapy of bipolar disorders

Jan Scott

Introduction

Until recently, bipolar disorders were widely regarded as biological disorders best treated with medications (Scott and Colom, 2005). This view is gradually changing for two reasons. First, recent decades have seen a greater emphasis on stress-diathesis models which have led to the development of new etiological theories of severe mental disorders that emphasize psychological and social aspects of vulnerability and risk. Second, there is a significant efficacy–effectiveness gap for pharmacological treatments for bipolar disorder (Tacchi and Scott, 2005). Mood stabilizer prophylaxis protects about 60 per cent of individuals against relapse in research settings, but protects only 25–40 per cent of individuals against further episodes in clinical settings. The introduction of newer medications has not improved prognosis (ibid.). This chapter explores key aspects of cognitive models of bipolar disorder, especially research on dysfunctional attitudes and beliefs. It then comments on the clinical applicability of cognitive therapy for bipolar disorder and reviews some of the outcome studies available.

Cognitive models of bipolar disorder

Early descriptions

Beck's (1976) original cognitive theory suggests that depressed mood states are accentuated by patterns of thinking that amplify mood shifts. Cognitive vulnerability to depression is thought to arise as a consequence of dysfunctional underlying beliefs (e.g. "I'm unlovable") that develop from early learning experiences, and drive thinking and behaviour. It is hypothesized that these beliefs may be activated by life events that have specific meaning for that individual. For example, an individual who holds the belief that "I'm unlovable" may experience depression in the face of rejection by a significant other.

Beck's original description (ibid.) suggested that mania was a mirror image of depression and was characterized by a positive cognitive triad regarding the self, world, and future, and positive cognitive distortions. The self was seen as extremely lovable and powerful with unlimited potential and attractiveness. The world was filled with wonderful possibilities; experiences were viewed as overly positive and the future was one of unlimited opportunity. Hyper-positive thinking (stream of consciousness) was typified by cognitive distortions, as in depression, but in the opposite direction. Positive experiences were selectively attended to, and it was hypothesized that in this way underlying beliefs and self-schema (such as "I am special" or "I am different") that guide behaviours, thoughts and feelings were maintained and strengthened.

In contrast to Beck's model of depression, there have been few attempts to confirm or refute his ideas about mania through research. Beck's original model of mania was largely derivative, based on the careful observation of individuals in a manic state. It took a traditional stance, viewing mania as the polar opposite of depression. Neither mixed states nor dysphoric mania were considered and there are some obvious gaps in this early model. For example, there is no discussion about any similarities or differences in the specific dysfunctional beliefs held by individuals with bipolar disorders as compared with unipolar disorders and the role of personality styles (sociotropy and autonomy) was not incorporated. However, it was a useful step forward from psychoanalytic models, and has recently provided an important starting point for the research that is reviewed below.

Empirical evidence

This section reviews studies of cognitive models of bipolar disorder. It is organized into two sub-groups: those exploring cognitive style and those exploring dysfunctional beliefs and the role of "matching" life events in symptom exacerbation in clinical and non-clinical samples.

Descriptive studies

Most studies of cognitive models in bipolar disorder have used the model of unipolar disorder as a template. As such, the early research comprised cross-sectional studies comparing subjects with bipolar disorder with other client populations on measures such as dysfunctional beliefs, self-esteem and cognitive processing. Apart from in one early study, data on dysfunctional attitudes in individuals with bipolar disorder who were not currently manic demonstrate a similar pattern to that seen in individuals in the euthymic and depressive phases of unipolar disorder (Hammen *et al.*,

1992). Unfortunately, there is limited data on changes during the manic phase, but Alloy *et al.* (1999) found that attributional style and dysfunctional attitudes were similar in individuals with related disorders – namely cyclothymia and dysthymia – and were more negative than normal controls.

Only two studies have explored mood-congruent or mood-dependent memory in individuals with bipolar disorder. Weingartner, Miller and Murphy (1977) showed that bipolar subjects were more able to retrieve memories when their mood at testing matched their mood at encoding, while Eich *et al.* (1997) noted that individuals with rapid cycling bipolar disorder, like healthy controls, showed mood-dependent changes in autobiographical memory recall. However, their subjects also demonstrated mood-dependant recognition, an effect that healthy controls rarely show. Eich *et al.* propose that this effect may arise because bipolar subjects experience stronger, more intense moods.

Scott *et al.* (2000) explored several aspects of the cognitive model simultaneously, including dysfunctional attitudes, positive and negative self-esteem, autobiographical memory and problem-solving skills. In comparison with healthy controls, clients with bipolar disorder had more fragile, unstable levels of self-esteem, and higher levels of dysfunctional attitudes (particularly related to need for social approval and perfectionism). These statistically significant differences persisted when current depression ratings were taken into account. Within the bipolar disorder group, those individuals who had multiple previous affective episodes and/or earlier age of onset of bipolar disorder showed the greatest level of cognitive dysfunction. Scott *et al.* (ibid.) argue that, although it was not possible to determine whether these cognitive abnormalities were a cause or a consequence of bipolar relapses, it was noteworthy that these differences persisted in clients who were medication adherent. This suggests that long-term medication alone may not extinguish cognitive and affective symptoms nor fully protect against relapse.

To explore further whether dysfunctional beliefs in individuals with bipolar disorder are similar to those observed in unipolar disorder, Scott and Pope (2003) identified a further group of unipolar and bipolar patients. When current symptoms and other demographic and clinical characteristics were controlled for, unipolar and bipolar subjects showed more similarities than differences in cognitive style. Overall scores on the self-esteem rating and the dysfunctional attitudes scale did not show any significant differences. On sub-scale scores, subjects differed on only two measures. Individuals with unipolar disorder had higher mean levels of negative but not positive self-esteem and subjects with bipolar disorder showed higher levels of preference for affiliation. When subjects with bipolar disorder were classified as depressed (n = 38), hypomanic (n = 13) or remitted (n = 26), some interesting sub-group differences emerged. There was a fairly consistent pattern of remitted subjects with bipolar disorder having the highest mean score for self-esteem, and the lowest for dysfunctional attitudes. This pattern was reversed for depressed subjects with bipolar disorder. The mean scores for hypomanic subjects with bipolar disorder lay between those of the other sub-groups. It was noteworthy that while total Rosenberg Self-Esteem Questionnaire scores followed the same pattern (scores for hypomania falling between remission and depression), hypomanic subjects with bipolar disorder recorded the highest mean scores on both the negative and the positive self-esteem sub-scales.

Winters and Neale (1985) wrote a highly influential article in which they hypothesized that although subjects with remitted bipolar disorder do not usually report impaired self-esteem, these subjects possess a cognitive schema of low self-esteem. This idea evolved from data suggesting that, although subjects with bipolar disorder and healthy controls showed higher levels of self-esteem than individuals prone to unipolar depression, the bipolar disorder group scored higher than either the unipolar or the healthy control group on measures of social desirability and self-deception. In another study, Lyon et al. (1999) used explicit and implicit measures of attributional style and a recall measure of self-schema in subjects with bipolar disorder who were currently manic or currently depressed and compared their results with a group of healthy controls. Manic subjects showed a normal self-serving bias on the explicit attributional style questionnaire, attributing positive events more than negative events to self. As predicted, depressed subjects attributed negative events rather than positive events to self. However, on implicit measures, manic and depressed subjects with bipolar disorder both attributed negative events more than positive events to self. On the self-referent encoding memory task, manic subjects were more likely than depressed subjects to endorse positive words as true of themselves. However, in a surprise recall test, both manic and depressed subjects recalled more negative than positive trait words.

One of the main difficulties with all the above studies was the problem of sample selectivity. Therefore Scott, in collaboration with genetics researchers (Jones et al., 2005), explored dysfunctional beliefs and self-esteem in carefully defined samples of individuals with bipolar disorder (n = 116) and unipolar disorder (n = 265), and compared their ratings with matched controls (n = 264) who did not have a history of mood disorders. There were statistically significant differences between groups on all measures. The patient groups differed significantly from the controls but there were few differences in the pattern of results in the unipolar and bipolar probands. The unipolar group showed the lowest levels of self-esteem (low positive and high negative self-esteem), and the bipolar group scored significantly lower on the self-esteem ratings than the controls but higher than the unipolar group. The unipolar patients also showed the highest level of dysfunctional attitudes, followed by the bipolar group, followed by the controls. This pattern was true for each of the sub-scales of the dysfunctional attitudes scale. When current levels of depression were taken into account no differences emerged between the two patient groups on any of the measures. However, both patient groups still exhibited lower levels of self-esteem and more dysfunctional attitudes than the control subjects. As such they did not show a pattern of dysfunctional beliefs that is unique to individuals with bipolar disorder.

The above studies identify that unipolar disorder and bipolar disorder are indistinguishable in the depressed phase, sharing a similar cognitive profile that includes abnormalities in information processing, dysfunctional attitudes and attributional style. Remitted subjects with bipolar disorder show similar cognitive style to remitted unipolar subjects on explicit measures, but this is not always as clear on implicit measures. Data on levels of self-esteem is equivocal as variations may be a function of lability or of differences between implicit and explicit ratings. Alternatively, the discrepancy between explicit and implicit measures of self-esteem or self-representations in remitted unipolar subjects and subjects with bipolar disorder might be explained if we assume that social desirability schemata are activated even in subjects with bipolar disorder even in the euthymic state. There is minimal evidence that the abnormalities in individuals with bipolar disorder are trait vulnerabilities that specifically predispose to the onset of bipolar disorder. It is possible that trait aspects of cognitive style may increase the likelihood of early age of first episode or influence the frequency of recurrence.

Interactions between life events and dysfunctional beliefs

In their excellent review, Johnson and Miller (1995) confirm the association between adverse life events and either an exacerbation of affective symptoms or relapse into an episode of bipolar disorder. However, few studies have explored the interaction between aspects of cognitive style and life events. A study by Hammen et al. (1992) reported that individuals with bipolar disorder who had high levels of sociotropy experienced an exacerbation of affective symptoms in response to interpersonal life events. Alloy et al. (1999) reported that an internal, stable, global, attributional style interacted with life stress to predict increases in affective symptoms in individuals with sub-syndromal bipolar disorder and unipolar disorder. In a further study, Reilly-Harrington et al. (1999) identified probable cases of bipolar and unipolar disorders in a non-clinical sample and assessed them at baseline and at one-month follow-up. In individuals with bipolar disorder, negative cognitive style at initial assessment interacted significantly with a high number of negative life events to predict an increase in manic or depressive symptoms. A study by Johnson et al. (2000) is of particular interest as it fits with much of the current thinking on cognitive and neurotransmitter theories of bipolar disorder and reward systems. Johnson *et al.* showed that goal-attainment life events might specifically precede manic as opposed to depressive relapse. This finding supports information provided by clients in clinical settings and the hypothesis that individuals with bipolar disorder may have abnormalities in the Behavioural Activation System (BAS). This system is thought to control psychomotor activation, incentive motivation and positive mood. Individuals with bipolar disorder show a greater increase in BAS activity, a slower return to normal baseline levels and consequently an increase in manic symptoms in the two months after a goal-attainment life event. It is hypothesized that the symptoms occur in vulnerable individuals because of a failure to regulate motivation and affect after the trigger.

Summary

It is increasingly recognized that the cognitive behavioural processes that may maintain psychological disorders are common to several disorders, and can be regarded as "transdiagnostic". However, the cognitive content appears to vary substantially across different disorders and is important in distinguishing between disorders. Given the very different clinical presentations seen in manic as compared with depressive episodes, it is perhaps surprising that there are more similarities than differences in the dysfunctional beliefs of individuals with unipolar disorder and bipolar disorder. Alternative views and more modern reformulations of the manic defence hypothesis (e.g. Bentall, 2003) do not propose that mania necessarily masks depression but that the drive into mania is an active process that prevents or suppresses feelings of failure or negative mood states. In some ways this explanation bypasses the question of why certain individuals, i.e. those with bipolar disorder, find themselves becoming manic as a way of avoiding negative experience at certain times in their lives but not at others, whereas those with unipolar disorder never become manic as a method to avoid negative experiences. The lack of current evidence should not be taken as proof of a lack of specificity in the nature of the beliefs held by individuals with bipolar disorder as compared with unipolar disorder. At risk of stating the obvious, researchers can only find what they look for. As patients with bipolar disorder are also at high risk for depression, they are likely to share similar cognitive styles.

The study of dysfunctional beliefs in bipolar disorder is beginning to provide important insights into the evolution of episodes. It appears that bipolar disorder is similar to other psychological disorders in being associated with elevated levels of dysfunctional beliefs, which is encouraging with respect to the potential of psychological interventions. However, to develop specific therapeutic interventions for bipolar disorder we require a considerable amount of further research to fully establish the shared and unique assumptions and beliefs, and most importantly we need a comprehensive account of their implications for the development of mania.

Cognitive therapies of bipolar disorders

Brief overview of cognitive therapy

An optimal course of cognitive therapy begins with a cognitive formulation of the individual's unique problems related to bipolar disorder, particularly emphasizing the role of core maladaptive beliefs (such as excessive perfectionism or unrealistic expectations for social approval) that underpin and dictate the content of dysfunctional automatic thoughts and drive patterns of behaviour. This formulation dictates which interventions are employed with a particular individual and at what stage of therapy that approach is used. Although each individual will define a specific set of problems, there are several common themes that arise in cognitive therapy for patients with bipolar disorder. Cognitive therapy may be used to:

1 Facilitate adjustment to the disorder and its treatment
2 Enhance medication adherence
3 Improve self-esteem and self-image
4 Reduce maladaptive or high-risk behaviours
5 Recognise and modify psychobiosocial factors that destabilize day-to-day functioning and mood state
6 Help the individual recognise and manage psychosocial stressors and interpersonal problems
7 Teach strategies to cope with the symptoms of depression, hypomania, and any cognitive and behavioural problems
8 Teach early recognition of relapse symptoms and develop effective coping techniques
9 Identify and modify dysfunctional automatic thoughts (negative or positive) and underlying maladaptive beliefs
10 Improve self-management through homework assignments.

At the first cognitive therapy session, the individual is encouraged to tell their story and to identify problem areas through the use of a life chart. Current difficulties are then classified under three broad headings: intrapersonal problems (e.g. low self-esteem, cognitive processing biases), interpersonal problems (e.g. lack of social network) and basic problems (e.g. symptom severity, difficulties coping with work). These issues are explored in about 20–25 sessions of cognitive therapy that are held weekly until about week 15 and then with gradually reducing frequency. A few "booster sessions" are used to review the skills and techniques learned. The overall cognitive therapy programme comprises four stages:

Socialization into the cognitive therapy model and development of an individualized formulation and treatment goals

Therapy begins with an exploration of the patient's understanding of bipolar disorder and a detailed discussion of previous episodes. The focus is on identification of prodromal signs, events or stressors associated with onset of previous episodes; typical cognitive and behavioural concomitants of both manic and depressive episodes; and an exploration of interpersonal functioning (e.g. family interactions). A diagram illustrating the cycle of change in bipolar disorder is used to allow the individual to explore how changes in all aspects of functioning may arise. Early sessions include development of an understanding of key issues identified in the life chart, education about bipolar disorder, facilitation of adjustment to the disorder by identifying and challenging negative automatic thoughts, and developing behavioural experiments particularly focused on ideas about stigmatization and fragile self-esteem. Other sessions further develop an individualized formulation of the patient's problems, which takes into account underlying maladaptive beliefs.

Cognitive and behavioural approaches to symptom management and dysfunctional automatic thoughts

These sessions help people to learn self-monitoring and self-regulation techniques, which enhance self-management of depressive and hypomanic symptoms, and to explore skills for coping with depression and mania. For example, this involves establishing regular activity patterns, daily routines, and regular sleep patterns; developing coping skills, time management, and use of support; and recognizing and tackling dysfunctional automatic thoughts about self, world and future using automatic thought diaries.

Dealing with cognitive and behavioural barriers to treatment adherence and modifying maladaptive beliefs

Problems with adherence to medication and other aspects of treatment are tackled, e.g. through exploration of barriers (challenging automatic thoughts about drugs, beliefs about bipolar disorder, and excessive self-reliance; or exploring attitudes to authority and control) and using behavioural and cognitive techniques to enhance treatment adherence. This and data from previous sessions are used to help the patient identify their maladaptive assumptions and underlying core beliefs, and to commence work on modifying these beliefs.

Anti-relapse techniques and belief modification

Further work is undertaken on recognition of early signs of relapse and coping techniques (fortnightly sessions). For example, identifying possible prodromal features (the "relapse signature") and developing a list of "at risk situations" (e.g. exposure to situations that activate specific personal beliefs) and high risk behaviours (e.g. increased alcohol intake). This is combined with a hierarchy of coping strategies for each and planning how to cope and self-manage problems after discharge from cognitive therapy. Sessions also include typical cognitive therapy approaches to the modification of maladaptive beliefs, which may otherwise increase vulnerability to relapse.

Does cognitive therapy improve outcome?

Despite the lack of a coherent cognitive stress-vulnerability theory of bipolar disorder, encouraging anecdotal and single case reports on the use of cognitive therapy in clients with bipolar disorder have been followed by large-scale randomized controlled trials (RCTs) that support the benefits of adjunctive therapy.

Studies of individual cognitive therapy

Following a successful small scale (n = 25) pilot study (Lam *et al.*, 2000), Lam *et al.* (2003) undertook a larger scale single-centre RCT of over 100 participants with euthymic bipolar disorder. Participants were randomly allocated to cognitive therapy as an adjunct to mood stabilizing medication or to usual treatment alone (mood stabilizers plus outpatient support). The cognitive therapy model particularly utilizes cognitive therapy techniques to cope with the prodromal symptoms of an affective episode and subjects were offered up to 20 sessions of therapy over about six months. Although the approach has some similarities to Perry *et al.*'s (1999) model, Lam *et al.* also targeted longer-term vulnerabilities and difficulties arising as a consequence of the disorder. Independent assessments demonstrated that, after controlling for gender and illness history, the intervention group had significantly fewer bipolar disorder relapses (cognitive therapy group = 43 per cent; control group = 75 per cent), psychiatric admissions (15 per cent versus 33 per cent) or total days in episode (about 27 days versus 88 days) over 12 months than the control group. The reduction in total number of episodes comprised significant reductions in major depressive (21 per cent versus 52 per cent) and manic episodes (17 per cent versus 31 per cent) but not mixed episodes. Furthermore, the benefits of cognitive therapy extended for about two years after entering the RCT, although most of the benefit was in reduction in risk of depressive relapse (Lam *et al.*, 2005).

A pilot study by Scott *et al.* (2001) examined the effect of 20 sessions of cognitive therapy on 42 clients with bipolar disorder. Clients were initially randomly allocated to the intervention group or to a "waiting list" control group. This randomized phase (six months) allowed assessment of the effects of cognitive therapy plus usual treatment as compared with usual treatment alone. At initial assessment, 30 per cent of participants met criteria for an affective episode, 35 per cent for substance misuse, and 45 per cent for co-morbid disorder. The results demonstrated that, compared with subjects receiving treatment as usual, those who received additional cognitive therapy experienced statistically significant reductions in symptoms, and improvements in global functioning and work and social adjustment, with reduced relapses in the 18 months post-therapy compared with the 18 months prior to therapy.

The above study was the forerunner of the Medical Research Council pragmatic effectiveness trial, which recruited over 250 subjects with bipolar disorder from five centers across Britain (Scott *et al.*, 2006) and randomly assigned subjects to usual treatment or usual treatment plus 22 sessions of cognitive therapy. Patients were assessed every eight weeks for 18 months. Over 50 per cent of the sample had a recurrence by 18 months, with no evidence of significant differences between groups. However, there was a highly significant interaction between randomized treatment and number of episodes recorded at baseline assessment, such that adjunctive cognitive therapy was significantly more effective than treatment as usual in subjects with fewer than 12 previous episodes, but less effective in those with more episodes. The authors suggest that cognitive therapy may benefit individuals with bipolar disorder who have comparatively fewer previous mood episodes. However, this study recruited a sample that was more heterogeneous than previous RCTs in bipolar disorder patients, including individuals with (a) current substance abuse or dependence, (b) very recurrent bipolar disorder (often reporting 20–30+ previous episodes) who had relapsed in the previous six months, (c) other co-morbid axis 1 disorders, or (d) a major bipolar disorder episode at randomization (30 per cent had significant depressive symptoms). As such, it may be that the most important finding is that cognitive therapy is highly efficacious in preventing relapses in those with fewer co-morbidities or additional consequences of bipolar disorder who are euthymic when therapy commences (as in Lam *et al.*, 2003), but less effective for those who have complicated or extensive histories of illness. A secondary analysis of other studies of 22 sessions of evidence-based psychological therapies in bipolar disorder has supported the notion that those with a prior history of multiple episodes do not do any better than those offered usual treatment (Scott *et al.*, 2007).

Conclusions

The empirical data reviewed indicate that research into cognitive theory and therapy for bipolar disorder is still evolving. There is no robust evidence that underlying schemata play a unique causal role in the first onset of mania, nor are there consistent differences in the underlying beliefs of those at risk of bipolar disorder as compared with unipolar disorder. However, there is evidence that cognitive factors may influence vulnerability to bipolar disorder relapse. The potential interaction between life events and cognitive style is easier to understand for depressive than for manic relapse as the events associated with the onset of bipolar disorder depression have many similarities to those linked with unipolar depression (Mansell *et al.*, 2005). Mania may arise in association with negative life events such as bereavement, but also following events that disrupt an individual's day-to-day social rhythms, such as following long-haul flights, the sudden cessation of mood-stabilizing medication, or the onset of significant physical disorder, etc. A number of researchers suggest that a common link between these events is that they can all significantly disrupt circadian rhythms. In turn, circadian dysrhythmia may lead to sleep disturbance and affective shifts. The work of researchers such as Johnson and Lam on goal-attainment life events and hyper-positive sense of self (see Mansell and Scott, 2006, for a review) is an exciting area of development that makes intuitive sense in thinking about the specific factors that may lead to the development of manic episodes or prevent recovery from bipolar disorder episodes.

Even if we have not yet established a robust specific cognitive therapy model of bipolar disorder, it is clear that psychosocial problems may be causes or consequences of bipolar disorder relapses and adding cognitive therapy to usual treatment approaches may improve the prognosis of those at risk of persistent symptoms or frequent episodes. The different types of approaches are technique-driven interventions, group cognitive therapy and individual cognitive therapy. The fundamental difference between the technique-driven interventions and formal cognitive therapy is that the former are briefer than the specific therapies (about 6–9 sessions compared with about 20–22 sessions) and usually do not use individualized formulations, but offer a generic, fixed treatment package targeted at a circumscribed issue such as medication adherence or managing early symptoms of relapse. These brief interventions can be delivered by a less skilled or experienced professional than the specific models and appear to be potentially very useful in day-to-day clinical practice in general adult psychiatry settings. However, the main benefit is in preventing the cascade of early symptoms of mania into a hypomanic or manic episode, with little effect on preventing depression. The reasons for this are not entirely clear, but they are possibly related to the evolution of symptoms into episodes and the nature and speed of action of available treatments (Scott and Colom, 2005). To clarify this, larger scale randomized trials should be encouraged. The results of the multi-center RCT in the USA with group cognitive therapy as a treatment option is awaited with interest as the group format has the additional advantage of allowing individuals to share their views of bipolar disorder with others and to learn adaptive coping strategies from observing other group members as well as having regular contact with an expert therapist. There is also a potential cost saving from one or two therapists simultaneously leading a group that may include 8–12 individuals with bipolar disorder.

Is there a problem with individual cognitive therapy? The results of Lam *et al.*'s study (2003) and Scott *et al.*'s study (2006) are not really that difficult to integrate – together these RCTs demonstrate which populations are likely to do well with adjunctive cognitive therapy and which are not likely to benefit or will struggle to make gains unless offered an extended course of cognitive therapy of more than 22 sessions. Given that in both the large RCTs there were reductions in relapse rates and hospitalizations associated with the use of cognitive therapy as an adjunct to medication in euthymic subjects with bipolar disorder who did not currently have multiple complications, these studies indicate that the targeted use of cognitive therapy is likely to prove to be both clinically and cost effective as well as contributing to a significant improvement in the quality of life of a significant proportion of individuals with bipolar disorder (and indirectly to that of their significant others). As such, cognitive therapy and other evidence-based brief therapies represent an important component of good clinical practice in the management of bipolar disorder. The only real argument is about which individuals with bipolar disorder will benefit most from cognitive therapy and when is the best moment in time to introduce therapy (Scott *et al.*, 2006).

References

Alloy, L., Reilly-Harrington, N., Fresco, D., Whitehouse, W. and Zeichmeister, J. (1999). Cognitive styles and life events in subsyndromal unipolar and bipolar mood disorders: Stability and prospective prediction of depressive and hypomanic mood swings. *Journal of Cognitive Psychotherapy*, *13*, 21–40.

Beck, A. T. (1976). *Cognitive Therapy and the Emotional Disorders*. London: Penguin Psychology.

Bentall, R. (2003). *Madness Explained: Psychosis and Human Nature*. London: Penguin.

Eich, E., MacAulay, D. and Lam, R. W. (1997). Mania, depression and mood dependent memory. *Cognition and Emotion*, *11*, 607–618.

Hammen, C., Ellicott, A. and Gitlin, M. (1992). Stressors and sociotropy/autonomy: A longitudinal study of their relationship to the course of bipolar disorder. *Cognitive Therapy and Research*, *16*, 409–418.

Johnson, S., Meyer, B., Winett, C. and Small, J. (2000). Social support and self-esteem predict changes in bipolar depression but not mania. *Journal of Affective Disorders*, *58*, 79–86.

Johnson, S. and Miller, I. (1995). Negative life events and time to recovery from episodes of bipolar disorder. *Journal of Abnormal Psychology*, *106*, 449–457.

Jones, L., Scott, J., Jones, I., Haque, S., Gordon-Smith, K., Heron, J. *et al.* (2005). Cognitive and personality style in bipolar disorders. *British Journal of Psychiatry, 187,* 431–437.

Lam, D. H., Bright, J., Jones, S., Hayward, P., Schuck, N., Chisolm, D. and Sham, P. (2000). Cognitive therapy for bipolar illness: A pilot study of relapse prevention. *Cognitive Therapy and Research, 24,* 503–520.

Lam, D., Bright, J., Jones, S., Hayward, P., Schuck, N., Chisolm, D. and Sham, P. (2003). A randomized controlled trial of cognitive therapy for relapse prevention in bipolar disorders. *Archives of General Psychiatry, 60,* 145–152.

Lam, D. H., Hayward, P., Watkins, E. R., Wright, K. and Sham, P. (2005). Relapse prevention in patients with bipolar disorder: Cognitive therapy outcome after 2 years. *American Journal of Psychiatry, 162,* 324–329.

Lyon, H., Startup, M. and Bentall, R. P. (1999). Social cognition and the manic defense: Attributions, selective attention, and self-schema in bipolar affective disorder. *Journal of Abnormal Psychology, 108,* 273–282.

Mansell, W. and Scott, J. (2006). Dysfunctional beliefs in bipolar disorders. In S. Jones and R. P. Bentall (Eds.), *The Psychology of Bipolar Disorders.* Oxford: Oxford University Press.

Mansell, W., Colom, F. and Scott, J. (2005).The nature and treatment of depression in bipolar disorder: A review and implications for future psychological investigation. *Current Psychology Reviews, 25,* 1076–1100.

Perry, A., Tarrier, N., Morriss, R., McCarthy, E. and Limb, K. (1999). Randomized controlled trial of efficacy of teaching patients with bipolar disorder to identify early symptoms of relapse and obtain treatment. *British Medical Journal, 318,* 149–153.

Reilly-Harrington, N., Alloy, L., Fresco, D. and Whitehouse, W. (1999). Cognitive style and life events interact to predict unipolar and bipolar symptomatology. *Journal of Abnormal Psychology, 108,* 567–578.

Scott, J. (1995b). Cognitive therapy for clients with bipolar disorder: A case example. *Cognitive and Behavioural Practice, 3,* 1–23.

Scott, J., Stanton, B., Garland, A. and Ferrier, I. (2000). Cognitive vulnerability in bipolar disorders. *Psychological Medicine, 30,* 467–472.

Scott, J. and Pope, M. (2003). Cognitive styles in individuals with bipolar disorders. *Psychological Medicine, 33,* 1081–1088.

Scott, J. and Colom, F. (2005). Psychological therapies for bipolar disorders. *Psychiatric Clinics of North America, 28,* 371–374.

Scott, J., Garland, A. and Moorhead, S. (2001). A pilot study of cognitive therapy in bipolar disorder. *Psychological Medicine, 31,* 459–467.

Scott, J., Paykel, E., Morriss, R., Bentall, R., Kinderman, P., Johnston, T., Hayhurst, H. and Abbott, R. (2006). A randomised controlled trial of CBT versus usual treatment in severe and recurrent bipolar disorders. *British Journal of Psychiatry, 188,* 313–320.

Scott, J., Colom, F. and Vieta, E. (2007). A meta-analysis of relapse rates with adjunctive psychological therapies compared to usual psychiatric treatment for bipolar. *International Journal of Neuropsychopharmacology, 10,* 123–129.

Tacchi, M. J. and Scott, J. (2005). *Improving Medication Adherence in Schizophrenia and Bipolar Disorders.* Chichester: John Wiley & Sons.

Weingartner, H., Miller, H. and Murphy, D. L. (1977). Mood-state-dependent retrieval of verbal associations. *Journal of Abnormal Psychology*, *86*, 276–284.

Winters, K. C. and Neale, J. M. (1985). Mania and low self-esteem. *Journal of Abnormal Psychology*, *94*, 282–290.

Name index

Subject index